DATE DUE

Second language acquisition research

Issues and implications

PERSPECTIVES IN
NEUROLINGUISTICS, NEUROPSYCHOLOGY, AND PSYCHO-LINGUISTICS: A Series of Monographs and Treatises

Harry A. Whitaker, Series Editor
DEPARTMENT OF PSYCHOLOGY
THE UNIVERSITY OF ROCHESTER
ROCHESTER, NEW YORK

HAIGANOOSH WHITAKER and HARRY A. WHITAKER (Eds.).
Studies in Neurolinguistics, Volumes 1, 2, 3 and 4

NORMAN J. LASS (Ed.). Contemporary Issues in Experimental Phonetics

JASON W. BROWN. Mind, Brain, and Consciousness: The Neuropsychology of Cognition

SIDNEY J. SEGALOWITZ and FREDERIC A. GRUBER (Eds.). Language Development and Neurological Theory

SUSAN CURTISS. Genie: A Psycholinguistic Study of a Modern-Day "Wild Child"

JOHN MACNAMARA (Ed.). Language Learning and Thought

I. M. SCHLESINGER and LILA NAMIR (Eds.). Sign Language of the Deaf: Psychological, Linguistic, and Sociological Perspectives

WILLIAM C. RITCHIE (Ed.). Second Language Acquisition Research: Issues and Implications

PATRICIA SIPLE (Ed.). Understanding Language through Sign Language Research

MARTIN L. ALBERT and LORAINE K. OBLER. The Bilingual Brain: Neuropsychiological and Neurolinguistic Aspects of Bilingualism

TALMY GIVÓN. On Understanding Grammar

CHARLES J. FILLMORE, DANIEL KEMPLER and WILLIAM S-Y. WANG (Eds.). Individual Differences in Language Ability and Language Behavior

JEANNINE HERRON (Ed.). Neuropsychology of Left-Handedness

FRANÇOIS BOLLER and MAUREEN DENNIS (Eds.). Auditory Comprehension: Clinical and Experimental Studies with the Token Test

R. W. RIEBER (Ed.). Language Development and Aphasia in Children: New Essays and a Translation of "Kindersprache und Aphasie" by Emil Fröschels

GRACE H. YENI-KOMSHIAN and CHARLES A. FERGUSON. Child Phonology, Volume I: Production

In preparation

GRACE H. YENI-KOMSHIAN and CHARLES A. FERGUSON. Child Phonology, Volume II: Perception

FRANCIS J. PIROZZOLO and MERLIN C. WITTROCK (Eds.). Neuropsychological and Cognitive Processes in Reading

JASON W. BROWN (Ed.). Jargonaphasia

Second language acquisition research

Issues and implications

Edited by

William C. Ritchie

Faculty of Foreign Languages and Literatures
Syracuse University
Syracuse, New York

ACADEMIC PRESS   New York   San Francisco   London   1978

A Subsidiary of Harcourt Brace Jovanovich, Publishers

ACADEMIC PRESS, INC.
111 Fifth Avenue, New York, New York 10003

United Kingdom Edition published by
ACADEMIC PRESS, INC. (LONDON) LTD.
24/28 Oval Road, London NW1   7DX

Library of Congress Cataloging in Publication Data

Main entry under title:

Second language acquisition research.

    (Perspectives in neurolinguistics & psycholinguistics)
    Includes bibliographies.
    1. Language and languages--Study and teaching--
Psychological aspects--Addresses, essays, lectures.
2. Psycholinguistics--Addresses, essays, lectures.
3. Children--Language--Addresses, essays, lectures.
I. Ritchie, William C.
P53.S38   401'.9   78-6884
ISBN 0-12-589550-X

PRINTED IN THE UNITED STATES OF AMERICA
80 81 82   9 8 7 6 5 4 3

Contents

List of contributors

Janet I. Anderson (91), American University of Cairo, Cairo, Egypt

Lloyd Anderson (109), Linguistics Research Laboratory, Gallaudet College, Washington, D. C.

Nathalie Bailey (109), Linguistics Department, Queens College of the City University of New York, Flushing, New York

Marina Burt (65), Educational Linguistics and Assessment, Bloomsbury West, San Francisco, California

Heidi Dulay (65), Child Development and Education, Bloomsbury West, San Francisco, California

Miriam Eisenstein (109), Adult Resource Center, Jersey City State College, Jersey City, New Jersey

Judith Olmsted Gary (185), Department of English, University of California, Los Angeles, Los Angeles, California

Evelyn Hatch (137), Department of English, University of California, Los Angeles, Los Angeles, California

Howard H. Kleinmann* (157), Department of Linguistics, University of Pittsburgh, Pittsburgh, Pennsylvania

Stephen D. Krashen (175), Linguistics Department, University of Southern California, Los Angeles, California

Diane E. Larsen-Freeman (127), Department of English, University of California, Los Angeles, Los Angeles, California

Carolyn Madden (109), Department of Linguistics, Queens College of the City University of New York, Flushing, New York

William C. Ritchie (1, 33), Faculty of Foreign Languages and Literatures, Syracuse University, Syracuse, New York

Wilga M. Rivers (201), Department of Romance Languages and Literatures, Harvard University, Cambridge, Massachusetts

Herbert W. Seliger (11), Department of Linguistics, Queens College of the City University of New York, Flushing, New York

Harry A. Whitaker (21), Department of Psychology, Department of Neurology, University of Rochester, Rochester, New York

*Present address: Allegheny Intermediate Unit, Pittsburgh, Pennsylvania 15212.

Preface

Until quite recently, virtually all research on the acquisition and use of second languages was related directly to the practical problems of foreign and second language instruction and, more specifically, to attempts to relate general work in the basic disciplines of psychology and linguistics to these practical problems. Since the late 1960s, however, a number of lines of basic research have taken shape which are devoted specifically to the development of a theory of second language acquisition and use. Such a theory, properly formulated and substantiated empirically, will not only provide a rational basis for the conduct of foreign and second language instruction but will also make available theoretical conclusions—based on data gathered both within the foreign and second language classroom and outside of it—which bear on a number of important questions in neurolinguistics and psycholinguistics. For example, research on second language acquisition provides the most plentiful source of empirical results bearing on the question of critical periods for language acquisition.

The purpose of the present volume is to bring together, for the use of researchers and students in these and related fields, a broad sample of the kinds of work that are to be found in foreign and second language research. There are four discernible subdivisions within the book. After an Introduction, Chapters 2–4 are discussions of the neurological and cognitive character of the "initial state" of the language acquirer beyond the normal age for first language acquisition. Chapters 5–9 are concerned with the process of second language acquisition in general (Chapters 5 and 8), in the child (Chapter 9), and in the adult (Chapters 6 and 7). Chapters 5, 7, and 8 include extensive discussion of methodological problems in second language research. Chapters 10 and 11 are concerned with adult second language performance. Chapters 2, 3, 6, 10, 11, and especially 12 and 13 include implications of basic research for the conduct of language instruction.

Second language researchers will find not only new interpretations of previous work (Chapters 1–3, 5, 7–9, and 11–13) but also empirical studies that have not appeared previously (Chapters 4, 6, and 10).

Acknowledgments

This volume grew out of a conference on second language learning and teaching which took place on the campus of the State University of New York, at Oswego, Oswego, New York, July 16–18, 1976. As the organizer of that conference, I wish to thank the Office of Research and Graduate Affairs of Syracuse University, sponsors of the conference, and, in particular, the Vice-President of Research and Graduate Affairs, Donald E. Kibbey, for his generous and expeditious support.

The conference was held in conjunction with the Linguistic Society of America's 1976 Linguistic Institute at Oswego. I acknowledge with gratitude the Director of that Institute, Winfred P. Lehmann, who was kind enough to deliver the welcoming remarks at the conference, and, particularly, the Associate Director of the Institute, Carol F. Justus, who conceived of the conference and offered assistance and encouragement at critical stages in the planning process.

I wish also to thank the members of the Department of English as a Second Language at the University of Hawaii where I spent the spring and summer terms of 1977; they arranged my teaching duties so as to allow me to devote as much time as possible to editing tasks.

Eight of the chapters included here—those by Seliger; J. Anderson; Madden, Bailey, Eisenstein, and L. Anderson; Larsen-Freeman; Hatch; Kleinmann; Gary; and Rivers—appear in essentially the form in which they were delivered as papers at the conference. The chapter by Dulay and Burt is reprinted from an earlier publication, and Krashen's chapter is part of another, recently published work. The material presented in the Whitaker and Ritchie chapters has appeared previously though in less accessible form. The cooperation of all of the contributors was exceptional, and I hereby express appreciation for their help in making the editing of the volume much less burdensome than it would otherwise have been. I am particularly indebted to Heidi Dulay, Marina Burt, and Steve Krashen, who were extremely helpful throughout the editing process. Myron Lichtblau and Phil Peterson of Syracuse University also contributed their expert advice in several editing tasks. Any errors in editorial judgment are, of course, my own.

Finally, I wish to thank my wife, Laurie, and daughter, Jane, for their loving support and patience throughout and for putting up with my absence from a number of excursions to the beach.

1 Introduction: Theory and practice in second language research and teaching

William C. Ritchie

Workers engaged in "pure" research, as are many psycholinguists and neurolinguists, often hesitate to look to applied fields—such as, in the present case, foreign/second language teaching—for data to confirm or disconfirm hypotheses in their disciplines. Until quite recently such hesitancy would have been justified in the instance just mentioned. However, recent basic research on second language acquisition and use—carried out, in some cases, in close conjunction with the management of foreign/second language acquisition—shows considerable promise as a bridge between the masses of data available in the foreign language classroom and the consideration of such theoretical questions as the nature of the ability to acquire languages beyond the age at which first language acquisition ordinarily takes place and to use languages so acquired. This recent work thus brings the relationship between foreign/second language teaching and its basic disciplines (including psycholinguistics and neurolinguistics) closer in character than it had been previously to the relationship between, for example, clinical medicine and the biological sciences, where the interaction benefits both theory and practice. The chapters of this volume constitute a cross-section of this recent work. Before describing the contents of these chapters, it will be worthwhile to examine the theory/practice relationship in some detail in its more typical and expected forms.

1

THEORY AND PRACTICE

No one would deny that the phenomenal success achieved in medical practice over the last 100 years—particularly in the prevention and cure of infectious diseases—is due to the close interaction between basic biological research and clinical medicine.[1] Less widely recognized, perhaps, is the fact that basic research in biology has also benefited from this interaction.[2] The relationship between medicine and biology therefore provides an excellent model for the interaction of foreign/second language teaching on the one hand and basic research on the acquisition and use of second languages on the other. Exactly what is this relationship between theory and practice in medicine? The function of any theory is to provide explanations for some range of observed phenomena. In the case of the infectious diseases, a theory will provide an explanation for the symptoms of the diseases in question. Whether these symptoms are explained as a consequence of an imbalance in the four bodily humors or of the presence in the organism of large numbers of microbes of some specific sort, the relationship to practice is reasonably clear. If the symptoms are explicable as a consequence of a humoral imbalance, then the practitioner's task is to restore the balance in some way (e.g., by bloodletting). If they are explicable as a consequence of the presence of microbes, then the practitioner's task is to eliminate them (or reduce their numbers) by, say, inoculation[3] or drug therapy of some sort. A scientific theory of the phenomena to be managed thus provides the crucial descriptions and explanations required to define the tasks involved in managing those phenomena. Handler (1970) describes the consequences of the application of biological science to medical practice as follows: "No aspect of medical practice has escaped scientific attention, and for virtually all the diseases of man there are improved modes of diagnosis and therapy which, at best, are specifically curative and, at least, are supportive and relieving [p. 633]."

Conversely, the application of a particular technique for managing some range of phenomena often constitutes a test of a theory proposed to explain the phenomena. The claims that bloodletting or the administration of an antibiotic will eliminate the symptoms of a given infectious disease follow from the two quite different explanations for these symptoms described in the preceding paragraph and the use of these techniques thus provides experimental evidence for or

---

[1]See Handler (1970, Chapter 16), Beecher (1960), and Dubos (1968). See, also, Bernal (1970) for a number of instances of interaction between science and industry in the nineteenth century. The life of Louis Pasteur is particularly rich in cases of the fruitful interaction of basic research and its applications. See, specifically, Cuny (1967), Dubos (1950, 1960), and Vallery-Radot (1925).

[2]See, particularly, Handler (1970) and Beecher (1960).

[3]In cases, such as rabies, where the incubation period is of sufficient length to allow the manufacture of antibodies by the diseased organism. Note that the intelligent application of the technique of inoculation requires, in addition to an explanation for the symptoms of the disease, a theory concerning the mechanism of immunity.

against the putative explanations. Clinical medicine thus constitutes a rich source of experimental data for the testing of hypotheses proposed to explain biological phenomena.

Interaction of this sort between the disciplines basic to foreign/second language teaching and the practices of teaching themselves would require (a) a conceptual framework in terms of which alternative explanations for the specific phenomena of second language acquisition and use can be formulated and (b) systematic employment in the classroom of techniques which follow from these alternatives with a view to confirming or disconfirming them.

A review of the literature of so-called applied linguistics in the forties, fifties, and sixties reveals a relationship between language teaching and those disciplines then perceived as being basic to it—namely, learning theory and descriptive linguistics—which diverges sharply from the one described. Even the most careful and insightful attempts to "apply" learning theory to foreign language teaching (e.g., Rivers, 1964) remain at a discouragingly general and vague level when compared with the specificity of the applications of biological science in medical practice.[4] An indication of the tenuousness of the relationship between research and practice in this case is that it is simply inconceivable that foreign language teachers would have been expected to contribute at all directly to the solution of problems in learning theory.

Attempts to "apply" descriptive linguistics to language teaching through detailed contrastive analysis—that is, through comparison of the structures (utterances? rules?) of the native language of the learner with those of the language to be learned—differ little in degree of relevance to language teaching from attempts to apply learning theory. In fact, the best work of this sort (e.g., Stockwell, Bowen, & Martin, 1965) recognizes the fact that the mere comparison of the descriptions of two languages provides no explanation whatsoever for the phenomena to be managed and that some quite specific theory of second language acquisition (such as some detailed development of learning theory) is required to complete the picture. However, when the notions from learning theory deemed relevant to the explanation of the phenomena (i.e., interference, transfer, etc.) are carefully analyzed they are found to be of dubious relevance to the particular phenomena of second language learning (see Carroll, 1968; Dulay & Burt, 1974).

Mere replacement of the learning-theory/descriptive linguistics paradigm with cognitive psychology and generative grammar does not improve the situation. In a much- (perhaps over-) discussed paper, Chomsky expresses skepticism concerning "the significance, for the teaching of languages, of such insights and

[4]Consider the unavailability in 1964 (as now) of an established body of theory and research concerning, for example, the teaching of French nasal vowels or of the subjunctive in German to native speakers of English. Apparently, research of a degree of specificity parallel to this is available in medical science.

understanding as have been attained in linguistics and psychology [1966, p. 29].'' He justifies his skepticism on the basis of the claim—surely as true now as when Chomsky wrote—that "well established theory, in fields like psychology and linguistics, is extremely limited in scope [p. 31].'' Apparently, Chomsky believes that what is needed for "theory in fields like psychology and linguistics" to be applicable in language teaching is research in these fields which will render "well established" the theories formulated within them. He then discusses four "tendencies and developments within linguistics and psychology that may have some potential impact on the teaching of language . . .; the 'creative' aspect of language use; the abstractness of linguistic representation; the universality of underlying linguistic structure; the role of intrinsic organization in cognitive process [p. 32].''

Chomsky's recommendation that we be skeptical about applying the results of psychological and linguistic research to language teaching is certainly appropriate. However, there are reasons for such skepticism that go much deeper than those that Chomsky presents. Even if theory both in linguistics and in some general cognitive psychology of learning were well established, only theory and research in second language acquisition per se could determine what aspects of such theories are relevant to foreign/second language teaching. This is true because a general theory of learning would not be sufficiently specific to be applicable in foreign language teaching and a linguistic theory is simply a theory of something other than second language acquisition.

First of all, if the capacity to construct and use systems of linguistic knowledge is task specific, then there is no reason to believe that general theories of problem solving will bear on **any** aspect of language acquisition and use. Therefore, the explicability of linguistic phenomena in general and of second language phenomena in particular in terms of such theories must be demonstrated empirically.

Consider next the case of what Chomsky refers to as "linguistics." It is clear from the discussion that he regards "linguistics" to be the study of (*a*) languages acquired as first languages at the usual age for first language acquisition and (*b*) the properties shared by the grammars of such languages. There is, once again, no a priori reason to believe that "well established" theories in such a field can explain the phenomena of second language acquisition. In particular, there is no reason to believe, in advance of empirical investigation, that the use of a second language is "creative," that the "linguistic representations" in accounts of second language competence are abstract, that the underlying linguistic structures required for the explanation of second language use (assuming that there are such) are universal or that the role of intrinsic organization in cognitive processes is as significant in second language performance as it is in first. In short, Chomsky's remarks are relevant to foreign/second language teaching to precisely the extent that the phenomena of second language acquisition and use match those of first language acquisition and use.[5] The simple fact that, as Corder (1967) puts it, "the learning of the mother tongue is inevitable, whereas, alas, we all know that there is no such inevitability about the learning of a second language... [p. 163]," constitutes strong prima facie evidence against the position that theories designed to account for first languages are also valid for second. In any case, this question can only be settled by extensive empirical investigation of second language phenomena.[6] As Rivers notes (Chapter 13 of this volume) "problems of the second language learning of late adolescents and adults in formal situations... will not be solved by applying uncritically what we know about first language, or even second language, learning by children... [p. 201]."

Conversely, it would be absurd to suggest that the observations of foreign language teachers could be brought to bear on basic issues in linguistic theory in the Chomskyan sense—again, simply because they would be irrelevant. What such observations bear on is a theory of second language acquisition.

All of this is not to say that Chomskyan linguistics cannot make a contribution to the study of second language acquisition and use. In fact, it is clear that Chomsky's conceptual analysis of the tasks of research on first languages (see, e.g., Chomsky, 1965, Chapter 1; Chomsky, 1975) is just as valid as a definition of the central tasks of second language research as it is for first. An explanation of second language use surely requires an account of the user's grammar and behavioral strategies for the second language. An understanding of second language acquisition surely requires, most centrally, an account of the acquirer's "tacit linguistic theory" at the onset of the acquisition process and a set of acquisitional strategies that determine the character of the acquisition process. Obviously there are extremely important affective and nonlinguistic cognitive

[5]Chomsky may have something else in mind here; perhaps his remarks on language are intended as a description of the **desired** character of second language use at the conclusion of the acquisition process. It should be clear that such a description is precisely as relevant to the language teacher as a description of the healthy organism is to the physician treating a disease—it tells him where he wants to go but it gives no indication of how to get there. For the latter purpose, descriptions of the state of the organism in the process of acquisition (respectively, in the diseased state) and of the capacities of the organism to reach the final state (mastery of the second language, or full health) as well as an explanation of the consequences of applying various techniques (pattern practice drill, drug therapy) are required.

[6]This may be what Chomsky has in mind when he writes

It is possible—even likely—that principles of psychology and linguistics, and research in these disciplines may supply insights useful to the language teacher. But this must be demonstrated, and cannot be presumed. It is the language teacher himself who must validate or refute any specific proposal. There is very little in psychology or linguistics that he can accept on faith [1966, p. 32].

However, what is needed is an intermediate field of "second linguistics" between linguistics and psychology on one hand and foreign/second language teaching on the other. It should be added that teachers would do well to accept Chomsky's admonitions with respect to results from this latter field as well as from linguistics and psychology. See Tarone, Swain, and Fathman (1976) for discussion.

factors in language acquisition in addition to the central ones just mentioned.[7]

Given such an understanding of second language acquisition, how would it bear on the practical problems of language teaching and vice versa? Let us consider a case represented in the present volume. Schachter (1974) argues convincingly that acquirers of second languages tend to avoid in production those structures which appear, on the basis of contrastive analysis and certain minimal assumptions about the second language acquisition process, to be difficult for them in the initial stages of acquisition.[8] Madden, Bailey, Eisenstein, and L. Anderson (Chapter 7 of this volume) present some data that appear to require a similar interpretation. They suggest that some acquirers adopted a guessing strategy, others an avoiding strategy in responding to difficult structures included in their experimental instrument. Kleinmann (Chapter 10) reports a study designed specifically to uncover such "avoidance strategies." Some of his data supports (though weakly) the view that acquirers who lack confidence in their control of a given structure will prefer alternative structures.

Krashen's monitor theory of adult second language performance (Chapter 11) provides a possible general interpretation of these results. Krashen (1975) argues for a distinction between language **acquisition**—which is unconscious and results in an utterance-initiating linguistic system—and language **learning**—a conscious process which results in a "monitor," a system which takes the output of the utterance-initiating systems as input and alters it in various ways. Acquisition is typical of children and adults in informal learning environments. Learning occurs in formal situations and is limited to adults. The end of the critical period may mark a decrease in acquisition due to biological, cognitive, or affective factors. Concomitantly, the role of learning becomes more significant at that point. In Krashen's view, then, an understanding of the critical period requires an understanding of the relationship between acquisition and learning.

In his contribution to the present volume, Krashen distinguishes among monitor overusers, underusers, and optimal users. He finds that these categories imply certain personality traits: Overusers are self-conscious, underusers are outgoing. One might predict that the overusers are Madden et al.'s avoiders and the underusers their guessers, though this would, of course, have to be demonstrated empirically.

It is possible, then, that learning serves a compensatory function—at least in some cases. When the acquirer/learner fails to acquire the second language with the expected speed and agility, he or she may resort to learning as a stopgap.

Now, it might be supposed that avoidance is an essentially negative strategy

[7]See, for example, Slobin (1973) for the case of first language acquisition and Chapters 5, 7, 10, 11, 12, and 13 of this volume for the case of second language acquisition.

[8]The significance of this finding should not be underestimated. Production has been an important source of data in second language research (as in first), and the discovery that production is skewed in particular, identifiable ways is an extremely important one.

adopted by the acquirer (consciously or otherwise) to avoid appearing foolish. However, research of a more "applied" sort reported by Gary (Chapter 12) suggests a deeper, positive role for avoidance. Gary argues for the institution of courses in second languages during the initial stages of which the student is allowed to avoid oral production altogether. One rather surprising result of such courses offered in the past is that students who undergo this kind of instruction exhibit a higher level of pronunciation accuracy in the second language than those who are required to speak from the beginning of the course. In terms of Krashen's theory, pronunciation, being less subject to conscious control than morphology and syntax, is considerably less accessible to monitoring and therefore must be acquired rather than learned if it is to be developed to any appreciable extent. Apparently, a curriculum of the sort that Gary describes allows the self-conscious acquirer/learner to **acquire** much of the phonology of the second language directly without the intermediate stage of monitor learning. Should this proposed explanation be borne out by further research, the initial support for it will have come quite directly from the second language classroom. The importance of such data within the present framework of second language acquisition research should therefore be clear. (It is interesting to note in this connection that Suter [1976] found a negative correlation between amount of formal instruction— under which learning rather than acquisition is expected—and accuracy of pronunciation in a heterogeneous group of subjects.)

THE PRESENT VOLUME

The chapters in the volume are divisible into two major groups: (a) those concerned primarily with reviewing or reporting empirical results and their bearing on theoretical questions (Chapters 2–11) and (b) those concerned primarily with the implications of research and theory for language instruction and vice versa (Chapters 12 and 13). Within the first group there is a further three-way division among chapters focusing on (1) the acquirer's initial capacity for acquisition (Chapters 2–4); (2) the process of acquisition (Chapters 5–9); and (3) second language performance (Chapters 10 and 11).

The question of the first language acquirer's tacit linguistic theory (in the sense of Chomsky, 1965, Chapter 1, and elsewhere) is the central one in first language research. In view of the fact that prepubertal second language acquirers generally attain nativelike proficiency, there is no reason to believe that their tacit linguistic theories differ from those of first language learners. The case of adults is different. A possible explanation for the general failure of adults to attain nativelike proficiency in second languages is that their linguistic theories differ from those of children. The problem of the biologically determined capacity to complete acquisition is thus quite distinct in the case of the adult acquirer. Seliger (Chapter

2) and Whitaker (Chapter 3) take up the question of the neurological basis for acquisitional capacities in adults. Both take the position that there may be multiple critical periods for language acquisition rather than one as has generally been assumed in the past. In addition, Whitaker provides a concise survey of recent work bearing on localization in relation to second language acquisition and a discussion of aphasia in bilinguals. Ritchie (Chapter 4) is concerned with a possible specific cognitive correlate of the end of the critical period.

Dulay and Burt (Chapter 5) present a general overview of recent work on a number of factors in the process of acquisition, concentrating on the role of creative construction in that process. J. Anderson (Chapter 6) reports the results of a cross-sectional study of the acquisition of complement structures by adults. Madden *et al.* (Chapter 7) argue for the use of scaling techniques in the analysis of second language data on the basis that such techniques reveal learning sequences that are largely inaccessible to ordinary statistical methods. Larsen-Freeman (Chapter 8) takes up the important question of an index of development in the study of second language acquisition which would serve the purposes of, e.g., mean length of utterance in the study of first language acquisition. Hatch (Chapter 9) is concerned with the nature of the input data for child second language acquirers and, in particular, with differences between input from children and input from adults.

As already noted, Kleinmann (Chapter 10) reports the results of a study examining the problem of avoidance in second language performance and Krashen (Chapter 11) is concerned with individual differences in the use of the monitor in second language production. (Chapter 12 [Gary] was discussed earlier.) Rivers (Chapter 13) examines some recent research in adult language acquisition and reading and their bearing on the problems of teaching second language reading to post-critical-period learners.

In view of the fruitfully agitated state of current research on second language acquisition and use, it was considered wise to include as much information as possible about the empirical studies that are reported here for the first time. For this reason, those contributors reporting empirical results were invited to submit as many materials having to do with their studies (e.g., experimental instruments, accounts of raw data, etc.) as was reasonable; these have been included as appendixes to their chapters.

REFERENCES

Beecher, H. K. (Ed.). 1960. *Disease and the advancement of science*. Cambridge, Mass.: Harvard University Press.
Bernal, J. D. 1970. *Science and industry in the nineteenth century*. Bloomington, Ind.: Indiana University Press.

Carroll, J. B. 1968. Contrastive analysis and interference theory. In J. E. Matis (Ed.), *Report of the Nineteenth Annual Round Table Meeting on Linguistics and Language Studies*. Washington, D.C.: Georgetown University Press.

Chomsky, N. 1965. *Aspects of the theory of syntax*. Cambridge, Mass.: MIT Press.

Chomsky, N. 1966. Linguistic Theory. In R. G. Mead (Ed.), *Northeast Conference on the Teaching of Foreign Languages*. Menasha, Wis.: George Banta. (Reprinted in J. W. Oller & J. C. Richards [Eds.], *Focus on the learner: Pragmatic perspectives for the language teacher*. Rowley, Mass.: Newbury House Publishers, 1975. Pp. 29–35.) [Page references are to the reprinted version.]

Chomsky, N. 1975. *Reflections on language*. New York: Pantheon Books.

Corder, S. P. 1967. The significance of learners' errors. *International Review of Applied Linguistics, 5*, 161–169.

Cuny, H. 1967. *Louis Pasteur: The man and his theories*. (Patrick Evans, trans.). New York: Fawcett World Library.

Dubos, R. 1950. *Louis Pasteur, free lance of science*. Boston: Little, Brown.

Dubos, R. 1960. *Pasteur and modern science*. Garden City, N.Y.: Anchor Books.

Dubos, R. 1968. *Man, medicine and environment*. New York: The New American Library.

Dulay, H. C., & Burt, M. K. 1974. You can't learn without goofing. In J. C. Richards (Ed.), *Error analysis: Perspectives on second language acquisition*. London: Longman.

Handler, P. (Ed.). 1970. *Biology and the future of man*. New York: Oxford University Press.

Krashen, S. 1975. A model of adult second language performance. Paper presented at the annual meeting of the Linguistic Society of America, San Francisco, December.

Rivers, W. M. 1964. *The psychologist and the foreign language teacher*. Chicago: University of Chicago Press.

Schachter, J. 1974. An error in error analysis. *Language Learning, 24*, 205–214.

Slobin, D. I. 1973. Cognitive prerequisites for the development of grammar. In C. A. Ferguson & D. I. Slobin (Eds.), *Studies of child language development*. New York: Holt, Rinehart, & Winston.

Stockwell, R. P., Bowen, J. D., & Martin, J. W. 1965. *The grammatical structures of English and Spanish*. Chicago: University of Chicago Press.

Suter, R. 1976. Predictors of pronunciation accuracy in second-language learning. *Language Learning, 26*, 233–253.

Tarone, E., Swain, M., & Fathman, A. 1976. Some limitations to the classroom applications of current second language acquisition research. *TESOL Quarterly, 10*, 19–32.

Vallery-Radot, R. 1925. *The life of Pasteur*. (R. L. Devonshire, trans.). Garden City, N. Y.: Doubleday.

2 Implications of a multiple critical periods hypothesis for second language learning

Herbert W. Seliger

Research in second language acquisition has centered around the basic issue of whether adults and children are capable of the same level of achievement or not. Those who assume essential differences between adult and child learner because of biologically determined changes in the maturing organism argue that the postpubertal adult learner is unable to achieve a level of completeness in second language equal to first language competency. Many of those who assume that the differences between adult and child learning abilities are due to other factors, such as method of instruction or attitude and motivation and other affective variables, often imply that correct identification and manipulation of these variables can theoretically lead to the production of adult L_2 competence equal to that of a native speaker. The following discussion assumes the validity of the first position. That is, the biological fact of adulthood is enough to establish an insurmountable obstacle in most cases for **complete** language acquisition. The incompleteness of the adult learner's L_2 system has a physiological basis and concomitant cognitive correlates. This does not mean, of course, that no language acquisition is possible after a certain age, or that varying degrees of competence are impossible when the variables listed under the second position just presented are controlled to some extent.

It will be shown that the ability to acquire a language completely or as well as a native speaker is dependent on various changes which take place in the brain as a result of maturation. This "completeness hypothesis" claims that abilities and

11

inabilities result from a centralization of language functions in a particular hemisphere, as well as localization of specific functions within hemispheres, and a concomitant gradual loss of plasticity for the complete acquisition of specific language abilities.

Evidence from various studies in aphasia and second language acquisition for the gradually decreasing abilities in language function will be discussed. It will be shown that ability for a particular acquisition is dependent on the remaining plasticity for this acquisition in the brain. Such states of plasticity may be referred to as "critical periods." It will be shown below that studies on age-dependent aphasia indicate that the degree of remaining plasticity for the acquisition of various language abilities is a function of age. Based on this evidence, it may be claimed that there are many different critical periods for different abilities which, in turn, will determine the degree of completeness with which some aspect of language will be acquirable.

There is much evidence that the age of the learner is a factor in the ability to acquire a nativelike pronunciation of a second language. Children are able to acquire complete control of the phonological system of another language, while postpubic second language learning almost always leaves some residue of foreign accent. That is, the phonological system of the second language learner is approximative to varying degrees but almost never complete. Seliger, Krashen, and Ladefoged (1975) found that only between 6 and 8% of learners of another language in adulthood could make a claim for no accent. Similar results were found by Oyama (1973). It is clear from these studies that variables such as education, language background, years of second language study, and desire to improve accent are not as important as the age at which the learner begins to acquire the second language.

Penfield and Roberts (1959) and later Lenneberg (1967) point to the relationship between degree of acquisition of first and second languages and the age of onset of second language learning. Lenneberg infers from the extensive data which he considers that there is a link between a critical period (defined by him as the period between 2 years of age and the onset of puberty at around age 10), the completion of a lateralization process, and the emergence of foreign accent in second language learning.

It is perhaps significant that all subsequent studies regarding completeness of second language learning and the critical period have concentrated on that aspect of language mentioned almost in passing by Lenneberg—phonology—and no other. Studies concerned with adult acquisition of syntax have not been concerned with degree of completeness but rather with comparing adult sequences of acquisition with those of children and among adult learners themselves. No attempt has been made to describe the limits of adult learning of syntactic or semantic features.

The completeness hypothesis would state that there is a biological barrier to the complete acquisition of something which is brought about by changes during the maturational process. This completeness hypothesis is usually tested by comparing the adult's acquisition of a second language phonology with a child's ability to acquire this system. There are probably several good reasons why researchers have focused on phonology and not on syntactic or semantic features:

First, since phonological production can be elicited as a physically measurable response, phonological errors are more easily identifiable. Unsophisticated native speakers and even higher level nonnative speakers of a language have demonstrated an ability to distinguish native from nonnative speech (Seliger, 1976).

Second, the phonological system is the most studiable of the finite subsystems of a language, and its parts are the most easily identified and described.

Third, there is not yet any way to measure completeness of acquisition of any other aspect of language, such as syntactic or semantic features. Since these other subsystems are so vast and complex compared to the finiteness of a phonology, incomplete acquisition in syntax and semantics may exist without consequences in performance; given the size of these subsystems and possible employment of avoidance strategies, the likelihood of errors occurring is greatly reduced.

A second language learner cannot avoid using any of the sounds of a language, but he or she can easily circumlocute syntactic rules and words when unsure of their use. It is difficult to know when such avoidance behavior is taking place. There are no tests, to my knowledge, that attempt to compare a second language speaker's distribution and semantic fields for lexical items with that of native speakers. All tests thus far developed for measuring competence in these areas are sampling procedures, and there is far from complete agreement as to what is significant and what is not.

One body of research attempts to explain the incompleteness of acquisition as the result of the lateralization of language function to the left hemisphere. It is suggested that once language function becomes lateralized, further acquisition is improbable if not impossible. The concept of lateralization, however, raises more questions than it answers. What exactly is lateralized? When does it happen? Is it a genic predisposition or is it the effect of environmental stimulation? Anatomical asymmetries have been found in infants. The mere size and weight of the left hemisphere at birth would indicate that it will become the dominant hemisphere and that certain primary functions of the brain will be located there.

As stated before, Lenneberg conceived of lateralization and the ensuing domination of the left hemisphere over the right as something which takes place with the passage of time and is completed within a specified period. The process of lateralization and the critical period were thought to be co-occurring and conterminous at around puberty. Others, such as Krashen (1973), have questioned Lenneberg's chronology but not necessarily the idea that the critical period and lateralization take place at the same time.[1] Lenneberg also believed that

---

[1]Krashen has informed me that he now also questions the co-occurrence of the critical period and lateralization.

lateralization is a **function** of language. That is, in order for the process to take place, language stimulation was necessary. Much the same has been suggested by the authors of the Genie studies in attempting to explain why there seems to be left brain atrophy (see, e.g., Fromkin, Krashen, Curtiss, Rigler, & Rigler, 1974).

However, in opposition to the traditional view that lateralization and the critical period are coinceptive and conterminous, many recent studies indicate that lateralization may be independent of the concept of critical period. In fact, the brain may already be lateralized **before** the onset of language. Experiments by Molfese, Freeman, and Balermo (1975) using auditory-evoked response have shown that infants with a mean age of 5.8 months have similar lateralized responses to both verbal and nonverbal stimuli as older children and adults. If anything, their data show a decrease for the degree of lateralization with increasing age, which they explain on the basis of increased myelinization and thickening of the corpus callosum and thus more communication between the two hemispheres. In contradiction to Lenneberg, they feel that the effects of left brain damage or hemispherectomy on language abilities cannot be determined by the extent of prior lateralization since this seems to be present already at birth. Rather, the ability of children to recover from such damage is indicative of remaining plasticity in the brain. That is, plasticity, and not lateralization, is responsible for such recovery.

Another possible interpretation of the concepts of lateralization and the critical period is suggested by research in aphasiology. In this view, lateralization is part of some more inclusive process which continues much later than that time span which Lenneberg proposed, while the term "critical period" may be interpreted as the gradual loss of plasticity in various parts of the brain for different functions over **most** of one's lifetime. Under this view, the localization effects known as lateralization are both interhemispheric and intrahemispheric.

In a study of 32 children ages 6 to 15, Alajouanine and L'hermitte (1965) found that while the cerebral lesions were on the whole similar, the aphasic disorders were different from those suffered by adults with similar lesions and different according to the ages of the children. Alajouanine and L'hermitte divided the children into two subgroups: 9 children aged 5 to 9 years, and 23 children aged 10 to 15 years. In the group under 10, the reduction of verbal expression was severe; disorders of articulation and phonetic disorders were almost always present. In the group of 10- to 15-year-olds, disorders of articulation were less frequent (only 13 of the 23 in this group). Of further interest is the fact that in terms of recovery, the authors found no significant difference between the below 10 and the above 10 age groups. Within a year, 75% of the children had regained normal or nearly normal language.

Brown and Jaffe (1975) have interpreted the phenomenon of age-dependent aphasia as indicating that lateralization is a continuing process. According to them, age-dependent aphasia, as found by Alajouanine and L'hermitte and others, is the result of the continued specialization within the wider left hemisphere speech zone. What is of interest for those concerned with the effects of lateralization and the critical period on second language learning is that Brown and Jaffe found not only that different age groups exhibited different aphasias, but also that the types of aphasia went from those where language dysfunction was general and widespread at younger ages of onset to more specific types of language dysfunction in later life **when the lesion was in the same area of the brain.** For example, the same lesion in Wernicke's area may produce motor aphasia in a child, anomia or phonemic paraphasia (conduction aphasia) in youth and middle age, and jargon aphasia in later life.[2]

To Brown and Jaffe, this indicates that there is a continuing process of specialization which is revealed by the type of aphasia. In other words, in the case of the child, no matter where the damage occurs, the disturbance to language will be much the same. In the case of the adult, the type of disturbance depends on where the lesion occurs.

As another example, when young children suffer aphasia it usually takes the form of mutism or agrammatism. This can occur whether the lesion is in the frontal, temporal, or parietal lobe. By age 10, while left hemisphere lesions still produce mutism or agrammatism, anomia and paraphasia also appear. This is especially interesting in light of views which claim that lateralization is complete by age 5 or by puberty. Studies that show lateralization by age 5 may be looking at interhemispheric effects while apparently further intrahemispheric differentiation is going on.

Brown and Hecaen (1976) found that in terms of the interaction of age and type of aphasia, anomalous dextrals—that is, right-handers who were mixed dominant or not clearly left lateralized for language—as well as about 30% of left-handers, according to their estimate, showed similar aphasia profiles as those found for children. This, in addition to similarities in fluent and nonfluent types of aphasia, led them to conclude that these abnormal groups are childlike in the sense that their aphasia type indicates an incomplete state of lateralization of function and specification in the left hemisphere. Such a finding would also indicate that such populations as anomalous dextrals and some sinistrals would maintain the state of plasticity necessary for certain kinds of acquisition far beyond what would be found in the normal population of right-handers. This finding may help to explain why certain learners well into adulthood succeed in completely acquiring such language subsystems as a second language phonology, while the vast majority do not.

To summarize to this point, a review of the relevant literature indicates first,

---

[2]Recent cases examined by Brown (personal communication) indicate incidence of jargon aphasia as early as age 40.

the concentration of most language functions in the left hemisphere, and second, further specificiation or localization of particular language functions in specific areas of the left hemisphere, as evidenced by age-dependent aphasia. While the process of localization is going on, there remains plasticity for those functions not yet localized, as evidenced by different recovery potentials for different ages. The longer the localization process continues, the longer plasticity remains for that particular function. According to Brown and Hecaen (1976), each type of aphasia is determined by the state of the localization process at the moment of brain damage. By the same token, it can be argued, as already demonstrated in studies of adult acquisition of second language phonology, that particular inabilities in second language acquisition may, like age-dependent aphasia, indicate the state of remaining plasticity.

Because localization does not take place at once, but affects different aspects of language at different periods of life, one would expect a different timetable to evolve in terms of different language abilities. That is, there would be many critical periods, successive and perhaps overlapping, lasting probably throughout one's lifetime, each closing off different acquisition abilities.

This may explain why phonology is acquirable beyond the age 5 cutoff for lateralization but not much beyond the onset of puberty in most cases, and why other aspects of the language system, at least in some form, are acquirable throughout most of life.

Given this observation, what kind of model is suggested for second language learning? What happens, for example, in cases where incomplete second language learning is the result of the closing off by a critical period of complete acquisition of some aspect of language?

Kinsbourne (1972) suggests that there exists an attentional asymmetry in the brain. That is, stimuli selectively activate the left or the right hemisphere depending on which is the functionally appropriate one for processing. Since the left is functionally dominant for language, stimuli having languagelike characteristics are processed there. However, depending on the state of interhemispheric and intrahemispheric localization, some of what is presented to the left will be incorporable as part of a new language system and some will not. That is, without relating to the problems of aptitude and intelligence, owing to the loss of plasticity and the closing of critical periods for whatever language functions, the learner will not be able to incorporate some aspect of the second language. Such a situation would be true regardless of whether the language was being acquired in natural or formal learning environments.

In natural learning environments, no matter what the age of the learner, that which is acquirable and for which cerebral capabilities still exist will be acquired. Some learning may be impossible owing to the closing of critical periods. This may explain, in addition to the usual psycholinguistic and sociolinguistic explanations, why second language learning in adults increases at a particular rate and then slows down to a point where further increments, while continuing, are almost imperceptible.

In addition, there does seem to be some kind of universal hierarchy of acquisition, indicating that variations in language background, strength of motivation, etc., are not the relevant variables. Even the untrained can detect common problem areas, such as the meaning and distribution of common prepositions, rules for the use of articles, tense and aspect distribution rules, and so on. Because of the seeming universality of these "fossilizations," one is led to suspect some psychocerebral mechanism underlying them.

What happens in the language classroom? Two kinds of learning apparently take place. First, there is the continued acquisition of meaningful propositional language, facilitated by the isolation and structured feedback of formal or artificial learning environments (see Krashen & Seliger, 1975, for a fuller discussion of this). Second, there is a type of classroom learning, however, which may be a response to the continuing localization process taking place. What is done in the classroom with language material which, because of the loss of plasticity, is no longer easily acquirable? A natural tendency of any teaching–learning system is to try to overcome such natural obstacles or to compensate for natural weaknesses. When it was found, for example, that the learner could not acquire a phonology simply by being exposed to primary language data, the phonetic segments were isolated to the point where form was divorced from meaning, as in minimal pair drills.

It was found early in modern language teaching, much to everyone's delight, that isolation and drill consisting of imitation and repetition of language bits that were usually semantically discrete were "successful" in getting the learner to do things he couldn't do naturally. That is, he could imitate holistically presented segments of language. However, it was also found that learners who performed associative and imitative tasks well in the language laboratory and the language classroom were not able to integrate these imitations into propositional language. That is, these holistically learned units could not be assimilated into the language system.

What seems to have brought about the second kind of learning is that, in order to overcome left hemisphere deficits due to the loss of plasticity, we have unwittingly utilized right brain capabilities for memorizing whole units, such as phonetic segments, and perhaps whole sentences where these are associated with automatic speech. We are all familiar with Genie's ability to imitate such phonetic segments, while it is reported that she was unable to incorporate these into her speech. Levy (1969) claims that the right brain is characterized by abilities for "immediately abstracting the stimulus gestalt." This ability is actively counteracted by a strong analytic propensity in the language hemisphere.

Studdert-Kennedy (1975) assigns to the right hemisphere the ability to decode written and spoken input having integrated whole graphologies and phonologies which are tied to their appropriate meanings. However, he concludes that only the dominant left hemisphere can perform truly linguistic tasks of the separation and sorting of complex auditory parameters into phonetic features.

It is for this reason that the second type of learning based on behaviorist methodologies cannot succeed. Training right brain language capabilities provides no more than an illusion of learning. The inabilities which are brought about by the successive and gradual loss of plasticity cannot be overcome.

However, the work on age-dependent aphasia and the concept of multiple critical periods indicates that language acquisition abilities are not lost at once. What we witness is an ever gradual reduction of such abilities. Much language can still be acquired by adults, but not to the same degree possible for children or those in a childlike state of lateralization.

With the development of more sensitive tools in the study of second language learning abilities and inabilities, more light will be shed on the qualitative differences between the right and the left brain. Such further research may also shed light on a language model that is more closely correlated with cerebral function. It may be that rather than a model consisting of discrete subsystems of phonology, syntax, morphology, and semantics, we shall find strata of language which localize as integrated layers or levels consisting of features of all these subsystems at once. The end of a critical period for phonology may only be for some features of that system together with some aspects of the other subsystems.

In conclusion, on the basis of various studies of age-dependent aphasia, it is hypothesized that there is a continuous long-term process of interhemispheric and intrahemispheric localization of function. The type of language dysfunction, either aphasic or as evidenced by universal second language inabilities, is taken to be indicative of both the state of the localization process and the amount of remaining plasticity. Since different aspects of language are affected at different stages in this process, it is hypothesized that there are multiple critical periods which correlate with localization and the gradual loss of plasticity. In addition, some formal language teaching procedures may be reactive to these cerebral conditions and seek to subvert them by unwittingly activating nonpropositional language functions in the minor hemisphere.

REFERENCES

Alajouanine, Th. & L'hermitte, F. 1965. Acquired aphasia in children. *Brain, 88,* 4, 653–662.
Brown, J. W. & Hecaen, H. 1976. Lateralization and language representation. *Neurology, 26,* 183–189.
Brown, J. W., & Jaffe, J. 1975. Hypothesis on cerebral dominance. *Neuropsychologia, 13,* 107–110.
Fromkin, V., Krashen, S., Curtiss, S., Rigler, D., & Rigler, M. 1974. The development of language in Genie: A case of language acquisition beyond the "critical period." *Brain and Language, 1,* 81–107.

Kinsbourne, M. 1973. The control of attention by interaction between the cerebral hemispheres. In Sylvan Kornblum (Ed.), *Attention and performance IV*. North Holland Publishing Co. Pp. 239–256.

Krashen, S. D. (1973. Lateralization and the critical period: Some new evidence. *Language Learning, 23,* 1, 63–74.

Krashen, S. D., & Seliger, H. W. 1975. The essential contributions of formal instruction in adult second language learning. *TESOL Quarterly, IX,* 2, 173–183.

Lenneberg, E. H. 1967. *Biological foundations of language*. New York: Wiley.

Levy, J. 1969. Possible bases for the evolution of lateral specialization of the human brain. *Nature, 224,* 614–615.

Molfese, D. L., Freeman, R. B., & Balermo, D. S. 1975. The ontogeny of brain specialization for speech and non-speech stimuli. *Brain and Language, 2,* 356–358.

Oyama, S. C. 1973. A sensitive period for the acquisition of a second language. Unpublished Ph.D. dissertation, Harvard Univ.

Penfield, W., & Roberts, L. 1959. *Speech and brain mechanisms*. Princeton, New Jersey: Princeton Univ. Press.

Seliger, H. W. 1976. Two experiments in foreign language testing and acquisition. Proceedings of the Fourth International Congress in Applied Linguistics (AILA), Stuttgart.

Seliger, H. W., Krashen, S. D., & Ladefoged, P. 1975. Maturational constraints in the acquisition of second language accent. *Language Sciences, 36,* 20–22.

Studdert-Kennedy, M. 1975. Two questions. *Brain and Language, 2,* 2, 123–130.

3

Bilingualism:

A neurolinguistics

perspective[1]

Harry A. Whitaker

Several lines of investigation in neurolinguistics can be related to issues in second language acquisition research. The first is the evidence that the components of language (**performance grammar** is a more useful designation) are not equally distributed through the brain; there is a degree of modality independence (speaking, hearing, reading, writing) and a degree of linguistic structures independence (syntactic and semantic features, lexical and grammatical formatives, for example). The second is the evidence from brain-damaged bilingual or multilingual speakers that, in the typical case, all of a person's languages are similarly represented in the brain, in the same manner as in a monolingual speaker, although there are some interesting exceptions to this situation. The third is the evidence from maturation studies of brain-damaged children suggesting what relationships exist between hemispheric lateralization, the efficacy of the right hemisphere versus the left for language acquisition, and the optimal period for language acquisition; it would be reasonable to conclude that this evidence applies to bilingual as well as to monolingual acquisition.

[1]This chapter is based upon a presentation made at "A Bilingual Symposium—Building a Research Agenda," sponsored by the National Institute of Education and held at the Linguistic Society of America's annual meeting, San Francisco, December 27–28, 1975. The chapter was completed while the author was a Senior Research Fellow in the Department of Neurological Surgery, University of Washington, supported in part by NINCDS Fellowship number 1-F32-NS05580-01.

21

Over a century and a half of research on man's nervous system and its behavioral correlates has established beyond doubt that the brain is not an undifferentiated tissue mass equally capable in all regions of supporting all behaviors that the organism exhibits. Different regions of the brain have characteristically different structures and each makes a different contribution (or none) to different behaviors. As is popularly known, the left hemisphere in man contains the major anatomical substrates for language in such a high proportion of human beings (over 90%) that in fact one should look for causes and explanations for the few instances of right hemisphere language dominance. Within the left hemisphere, there is further localization of the anatomic regions of the performance grammar (PG); the majority of the frontal lobe and significant portions of the parietal, temporal, and occipital lobes simply do not play a role in the PG. In Figure 1 the shaded area indicates the typical cortical extent of the PG in the left hemisphere. The particular zones of the PG which subserve the various modalities through which language is perceived or expressed are indicated in Figure 2. HAND and WRITING denote the areas for motor control of the right hand; TACTILE denotes the area which processes sensory information from the skin, muscles, and tendons of the right hand; SPEECH and FACE denote the areas which control the vocal tract musculature; AUDITORY denotes the area which processes spoken language (with preference given to the right ear); and VISUAL denotes the area which

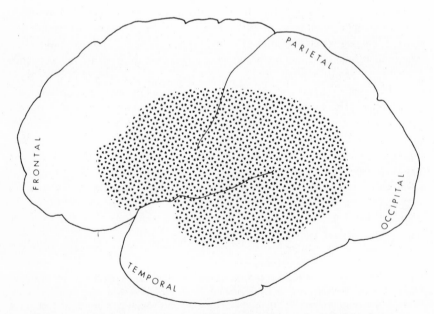

Figure 1. Typical cortical extent of the performance grammar in the left hemisphere.

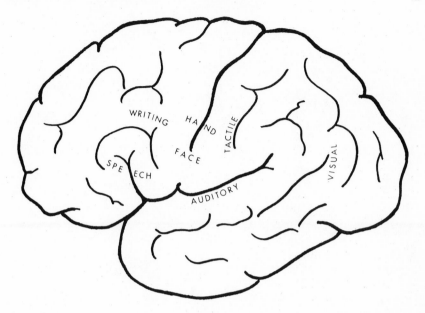

Figure 2. Zones of the performance grammar subserving the various language modalities.

processes written language. The classical names for the cortical regions of the language area are given in Figure 3.

An extended discussion of localization would not be appropriate here, but it would be worthwhile to review the position with which most researchers would agree (Dingwall & Whitaker, 1974; Luria, 1964; Whitaker, 1971). Just as complex behaviors may be analyzed into components, the brain substrates of these behaviors will involve a number of different, interconnected areas. The vocal production of an appropriate (in context) utterance in some language is obviously not just a matter of properly sequencing the activity of the muscles of the vocal tract; if such a vocal production is called "speech," then it is quite clear that "speech" is not localized to one area of the brain. As one breaks down such a vocal production into the component words, their phonological organization, the articulatory program, visual and auditory inputs regarding the context, the syntactic organization of the utterance, and other discourse parameters, one typically finds more discrete areas of the brain contributing to the language system. On the other hand, a single region of the brain such as the supramarginal gyrus (itself a somewhat vague anatomical designation), clearly one of the major components of the PG, controlling syntactic categorization of lexical items (cf. Kehoe & Whitaker, 1973), does not have just one functional property. In order to find a structure in the brain which has a single functional property, it is probably necessary to go to the microscopic level, but certainly at the very least to the .4

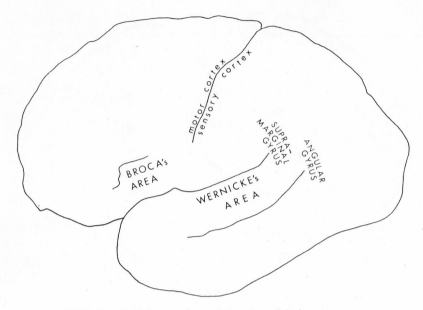

Figure 3.   Classical names for cortical regions of the language area.

mm wide columnar structures of cortical neurons. In the case of human speech
and language, however, the linguistic analysis of performance does not yet seem
to be sufficiently refined to begin to look for correlates at the level of microscopic
anatomy.

What we can do is analyze the linguistic dissociations that occur following
brain damage and take them as prima facie evidence that these linguistic elements
are represented differently in the neural substrate. For example, one of the most
common observations of brain-damaged adults is the dissociation between lexical
and grammatical formatives; some subjects have great difficulties with nouns,
verbs, adjectives, etc., while others have equally great difficulties with articles,
certain prepositions that are basically syntactic in function, pronouns with minimal semantic content, etc. Another common observation is an impairment of the
syntactic categorization of lexical items in spite of no problem with the semantic
values; a subject may know the meaning of *perceive* but be unable to put the
lexical item into its proper syntactic form as a verb, noun, or adjective—
perceive, perception, perceptible—or he may attach an inappropriate derivational affix *-ness or *-ity. In subjects whose native language is Japanese, it has
been found that the syllabic writing systems, Katakana and Hiragana, may be
dissociated from the logographic writing system, Kanji, as a result of brain
damage (Sasanuma, 1975). This shows that phonetically based writing systems
may be differently represented than visually based ones in the neural substrate.

The separation of the modalities for expressing or comprehending language has already been remarked upon; it is these dissociations which in large part led to the classification of the aphasia syndromes. Any of the basic four language modalities—speaking, hearing, reading, and writing—may be severely impaired while the others are relatively intact following brain damage. It is important to emphasize that such impairments are not in the basic motor or sensory systems but are in the linguistic or PG aspect of these systems. Thus, a brain lesion may render a subject unable to process spoken language auditorily but still able to hear sounds normally within the frequency range of spoken language. A person may be able to see but be unable to read, or a person may be able to chew, swallow, and even sing but be unable to speak.

The second line of evidence of relevance to second language acquisition research—that is, the effects of brain damage on bilingual or multilingual speakers—has been reported on occasion in the literature since the mid-nineteenth century. What would have been a formidable task of collecting and analyzing this body of research has fortunately been done in a review by Paradis (1977). The discussion which follows is based on his review of 138 cases reported in the world's literature since 1866. It should be noted at the outset that the cases reported in the literature are generally the unique cases which have some interest because they differ from the typical state of affairs. Usually, brain damage affects all of a subject's languages in the same manner and to an equal degree, if the subject has equal skills in the languages and if the languages are linguistically comparable. The reason for this is that additional languages are organized and represented in the brain in a comparable manner. The only exception to this principle is the potential involvement of the right hemisphere's homologous areas, to be discussed below.

Because the type of aphasia is a function of the locus and extent of the lesion, research on bilingual aphasia has tended to focus on the modes of restitution of the different languages. Paradis identified four such modes or patterns of recovery as follows:

1. **Synergistic**   Recovery in one language is accompanied by recovery in the other languages. There are two forms.
   a. Parallel: All languages are similarly impaired by the lesion; all languages recover to a similar degree.
   b. Differential: Each language is impaired differently by the lesion; recovery may be to a similar level or may differentially reflect the original impairments, but the degree of recovery that occurs, occurs at the same rate for all languages.
2. **Antagonistic**   One language recovers to some point and then as the next language begins to recover, the first-recovered language regresses.

3. **Successive**   One language recovers almost fully, at which time the
                       next language first begins to recover.
4. **Selective**   One or more languages do not recover at all or remain
                       permanently severely impaired.

Only 6 of the 138 reported cases exhibited the antagonistic mode of recovery, slightly more than 4% of the cases considered to be sufficiently unique or interesting to be worth reporting. In view of this, there seems to be little point in attempting an explanation of what is surely a very unusual phenomenon. There were also very few cases of successive recovery reported, a total of 11. However, successive recovery appears to be a special instance of the synergistic–differential pattern, the difference between them a matter of temporal variability. And, since both synergistic (parallel and differential) modes of recovery are the predominant as well as the predicted types, one explanation will account for all three.

Parallel, differential, and successive recovery of more than one language following brain damage can be fairly well accounted for by the natural events of recovery from aphasia: the nature of the lesion, its size, the extent to which distant cortical regions are impaired in function, whether or not the lesioned area is permanently destroyed or only temporarily dysfunctional, the location of the lesion, and factors pertaining to the subject's cognitive–intellectual level prior to brain damage. An additional factor in multilingual aphasia is the degree of proficiency in the different languages. Although it is not yet an established fact, there is reasonable evidence to indicate that the degree of recovery in each language is proportional to the degree of proficiency in that language prior to the brain damage.

Selective recovery—the permanent impairment of one or more of the languages known to the subject prior to his brain damage—is obviously the type which is most difficult to explain. Thirty-two cases, over 23%, of this type have been reported in the literature. Selective recovery, of course, does not imply that the recovered languages reach their former level; in fact, most of the cases of this type exhibit a residual aphasia. The recovery is selective because even though aphasic, these subjects are able to control some language modalities in the recovered language in contrast with virtually none in the lost languages. Paradis identifies three factors which have been invoked to explain this phenomenon: The first is a group of sociological, physiological, and psychological factors; the second is a visual factor; and the third is a hemispheric laterality factor. A variety of "laws" have been proposed in the first group of factors: Retention of the native language, retention of the most recently acquired language, retention of the most familiar language, retention of the language most frequently used, retention of the language used in the recovery context, retention of the language for which the subject has the greatest emotional attachment, and the like, have all been invoked at one time or another to explain why one language recovered to some degree while another language remained permanently lost or severely impaired. As one might expect, for each case proposed as an example of one of these physio–psycho–social factors, there are counterexamples. However, it is well known that brain damage can be associated with such a retrograde and anterograde amnesia. It would not be unreasonable to infer that a number of personal, social, or environmental factors would significantly influence the manner in which and the degree to which second languages were acquired. The evidence used to support these factors as explanations for selective recovery thus may have a degree of validity.

Several cases have been reported in which the selectively lost language was one in which the subject had only auditory–verbal skills but no reading and writing, whereas the selectively retained language was one in which the subject had both auditory–verbal and reading–writing skills. Such subjects have been observed to note that their ability to visualize words in the one language made it easier to recall and the lack of this rendered the other language inaccessible. The degree to which a visual representation can influence recovery in multilingual aphasia is perhaps best seen in the case of the English classics scholar who recovered, in sequence, Greek, Latin, then French, and last, his native English. The Greek and Latin, of course, were acquired virtually exclusively through reading and writing; at the peak of his impairments, the Greek was proportionately less affected than this subject's English reading and writing. The probable explanation of this visual factor is that the lesion was situated in the regions of the PG subserving the auditory–verbal modalities. In the case of English and French, reading and writing involved reference to the phonetic features of those languages; in the case of Greek and Latin, this was not the case. Although such evidence from individual case histories should be treated with caution, it does seem to correspond well to the differential impairments of syllabic and logographic writing systems in Japanese, cited earlier. Consistent with differences in the components of the PG in different parts of the language area, lesions restricted to these parts will have selective effects that relate to differences in the language proficiencies. One would predict that analogous differences would obtain in a case in which the two languages had markedly different syntactic or phonological rule systems.

The hemispheric laterality factor has not been well studied in bilingual aphasia research. Some studies using the dichotic paradigm, by which the manifestation of an ear preference is taken as evidence for language dominance in the opposite hemisphere, suggest that there are bilingual subjects who have one language in the left and the other in the right hemisphere, or one language in the left and the other language bilaterally represented, but the weight of this evidence actually points to the same conclusion reached by studies of brain-damaged subjects: For most bilinguals, as with most monolinguals, all languages are represented predominantly in the left hemisphere. In the few cases in which the question of right hemisphere dominance for one of the languages can be raised, one usually finds one or more of the following aspects of the case: left-handedness or ambidextrousness, early damage to the left hemisphere, or late (postpuberty) acquisition of the second language. While none of these situations will insure a transference of language dominance to the right hemisphere by either the native or the second language, all of them have been associated with right hemisphere language dominance in monolinguals. It should be reiterated that, even if language dominance shifts to the right hemisphere or even if there is one language in the left and the other language in the right hemisphere, the same areas of the right hemisphere subserve language as in the left.

Although one might expect that mixing or interferences between languages would be a common feature of bilingual aphasia—it is observed frequently in the non-brain-damaged bilingual subject—it is, in fact, not reported that often. Paradis notes that only 10 of the 138 cases in the literature discuss this phenomenon. As in non-brain-damaged bilinguals, mixing may comprise phonological blends from semantically equivalent lexical items, or combinations of a stem from one language and an affix from the other, and the like. In view of the rarity of report of mixing or interference in this body of literature, little would be gained by speculating on its significance.

Although the most frequent sequelae of brain damage in the bilingual subject are the equal impairment, parallel recovery, and equal restitution of both languages, proportionate to the degree of mastery or proficiency in each language, this fact does not necessarily point to a type of bilingualism such as those proposed by Weinreich (1966). It is true that this fact is consistent with the notion of compound bilingualism—one set of lingustic rules and different sets of lexical items (Wald, 1974). On this line of reasoning, the cases of differential or partial recovery, successive recovery, and particularly, selective recovery, would be consistent with the notion of coordinate bilingualism—separate linguistic systems for each language (Wald, 1974). The problem is that the first set of facts— parallel recovery—is also consistent with the notion of coordinate bilingualism, for the simple reason that it is almost certain that all languages are represented and organized similarly in the same anatomical structures. Therefore, a lesion in one of these structures would affect all languages similarly regardless of whether there was a single set of linguistic rules or not, provided that one takes account of different proficiencies and/or different modalities of representation. And, as already noted, there are a number of factors relating to the individual's social and psychological experiences and his internalization of these experiences, which very well might account for the less often observed situation of selective recovery. From the evidence at hand, it is not clear that a case can be made from these data for these two types of bilingualism, let alone the third type postulated by Weinreich, the subordinate.

The third line of evidence comes from studies of the maturation of the brain and the acquisition of language. The classical, and now popularized, view that the left and the right hemispheres are equally good substrates for language from early in life (the potential for shifting from the left to the right diminishes with age) is simply untrue. Dennis and Whitaker (1977) reviewed the clinical litera- ture from 1868 to the present on the effects of early damage to the right or the left hemisphere on the subsequent development of speech and language. The results are clear: The two hemispheres are not equally at risk from birth with respect to the eventual effects of unilateral lesions. Early and even neonatal damage to the left hemisphere will, in the majority of cases, lead to impairments in speech and language. By the age of 5, the proportions of left hemisphere damage producing language impairment are virtually the same as in adults (Krashen, 1975).

Dennis and Whitaker (1976) have also studied the linguistic skills of several children who underwent complete hemispherectomy prior to 4 1/2 months of age and who are now 10 years old. We compared the linguistic abilities of the isolated and normal right hemisphere to the isolated and normal left hemisphere on a variety of phonological, syntactic, and semantic tasks. Their composite I.Q. scores were identical (and equivalent to normal children of this age), their auditory–verbal skills were identical, and there were few differences on the semantic tests; however, consistent and striking differences were found on the syntactic tasks. The isolated right hemisphere is notably deficient in processing sentences in which word order is an important variable, for example. The evi- dence we have obtained in this research is consistent with a substantial body of research that shows that the two cerebral hemispheres differ from each other along a number of dimensions and that these differences are present as early in life as they can be measured (cf. Kinsbourne & Smith, 1974). It is thus not surprising that the left hemisphere is typically the language hemisphere in both monolinguals and bilinguals.

There is a fairly extensive and rapidly expanding literature on the maturation of the nervous system (both animal and human studies), some of which is directly pertinent to the ontogeny of speech and language. It is not clear, however, how much of this would be pertinent to educators, in a practical sense that is, in view of the fact that children do not typically enter educational systems before 4 years of age.

By most accounts, the human brain has reached 80–90% of its adult values at around 4 to 5 years of age. Biochemical, electrophysiological, and morpho- logical criteria all point to this same conclusion. It has been noted that the plasticity of the nervous system, its ability to compensate for left hemisphere brain damage by shifting language to the right hemisphere, begins to decline noticeably after 5 years of age. This does not imply that there are no further maturational milestones—developmental psychologists and linguists have documented a number of such steps. What it does seem to imply is that the basis for acquisition and learning, the neural basis, is undergoing some as-yet-unspecified shift to an adult type. Although there is evidence that under unusual circumstances language acquisition may occur after puberty (Fromkin, Krashen, Curtiss, Rigler, & Rigler, 1974), possibly by the right hemisphere, it is neither as rapid nor as successful as normal language acquisition. Although the differences would be more subtle, the same would probably be true of primary language acquisition after 5 years of age. What all this seems to speak to is that second language acquisition in the school setting should probably be initiated as soon as possible in order to capitalize on the residual language readiness of the brain.

Although the brain is well on the way to maturity at the age of 5, as measured by currently available techniques, it does not reach this stage by a uniform progression in its several parts. Just as there are clear structural and functional differences in different parts of the central nervous system, the rate of maturity varies also. It is of some interest to note that most of these maturational markers—the degree of myelinization, the thickness of cerebral cortex, the degree of branching and connectivity in the dendritic structures of cortical neurons, the internal structure of nerve cell bodies, or the frequency and amplitude of electrical activity from the cortical neurons—indicate that the last cortical area to mature is the region of the supramarginal and angular gyri. Since we know that this region subserves the visual language modality among other functions, this would imply that the acquisition of reading and writing skills would naturally follow the acquisition of auditory–verbal skills. This would apply to the acquisition of the first language, certainly, and is quite obviously the actual case. It would be intuitively plausible that second language acquisition, in the school setting and after 5 years of age, would be accomplished more quickly and more successfully if it were done in the same order: first the auditory–verbal modalities and then the visual–manual modalities. However, it should be emphasized that this is only plausible intuition; the neurolinguistic evidence does indicate something of what the final neural organization will be like, but does not provide unequivocal support for any method of achieving that final organization.

Research on adult monolingual aphasics has provided evidence that a variety of linguistic structures and components of the performance grammar are separately represented in the brain (Whitaker & Whitaker, 1977); this must be true for the bilingual speaker as well. One may reasonably conclude that for bilingual and multilingual speakers, the observed interlanguage differences of proficiency, context of use, or other psychosocial factors, are correlated with different representations (not necessarily different localizations) in the brain. Research on maturational correlates of language acquisition would lead one to conclude that the earlier a second language is introduced, the more likely the neural substrate for it will parallel that of the native or first language. One might argue on intuitive grounds by analogy to the way in which the brain matures that learning to read a second language would best follow learning auditory–vocal control over it. Experience, and therefore education, modifies the brain; bilingual education modifies the brain in a manner that seems to be quite analogous to first language acquisition.

An important lacuna in our understanding of the maturation of the brain as it relates to the acquisition both of language and of other cognitive functions is the characterization of what physical changes occur from about 7 to 9 years of age. Developmental evidence clearly indicates that there are both cognitive and linguistic milestones during this age period. Identifying the neural correlates of these milestones would enable us better to understand the relations between later second language acquisition and changes in the brain. Other directions which neurolinguistic research should take with reference to multilingualism include both the brain-damaged and the non-brain-damaged subject. The brain-damaged bilingual patient will continue to be an important source of information on the ways in which different languages are learned and thus represented in the brain. Comparing simultaneous and successive acquisition of a second language with sophisticated analyses of bilingual aphasic impairments may shed light on theories that claim that there are compound, coordinate, and subordinate bilinguals. Study of such patients could also shed light on the effects of different types of acquisition: auditory–verbal only, visual–written only, or both. Study of such patients, as well as study of non-brain-damaged bilinguals, may also clarify the role of the right hemisphere in second language acquisition. Dichotic listening techniques and averaged evoked potential techniques may provide evidence of the role of each hemisphere in language processing. Comparing the data from such techniques with information on the age of acquisition of different languages may shed some light on the question of the role of the right hemisphere in late language acquisition.

REFERENCES

Dennis, M., & Whitaker, H. A. 1976. Language acquisition following hemi-decortication: Linguistic superiority of the left over the right hemisphere. *Brain & Language, 3,* 404–433.

Dennis, M., & Whitaker, H. A. 1977. The acquisition of language by the right and by the left hemispheres. In S. Segalowitz & F. Gruber (Eds.), *Language development and neurological theory.* New York: Academic Press.

Dingwall, W. O., & Whitaker, H. A. 1974. Neurolinguistics. In B. J. Siegel, A. R. Beals, & S. A. Tyler (Eds.), *Annual Review of Anthropology, 3.* Palo Alto: Annual Reviews.

Fromkin, V. A., Krashen, S. D., Curtiss, S., Rigler, D., & Rigler, M. 1974. The development of language in Genie: A case of language acquisition beyond the "critical period." *Brain & Language, 1,* 81–107.

Kehoe, W. J., & Whitaker, H. A. 1973. Lexical structure disruption in aphasia: A case study. In H. Goodglass & S. Blumstein (Eds.), *Psycholinguistics and aphasia.* Baltimore: Johns Hopkins Univ. Press.

Kinsbourne, M., & Smith, W. L. (Eds.) 1974. *Hemispheric disconnection and cerebral function.* Springfield, Illinois: Thomas.

Krashen, S. D. 1975. The critical period for language acquisition and its possible bases. In D. Aaronson & R. W. Rieber (Eds.), *Developmental psycholinguistics and communication disorders*. New York: New York Academy of Sciences.

Luria, A. R. 1964. Neuropsychology in the local diagnosis of brain damage. *Cortex, 1,* 3–18.

Paradis, M. 1977. Bilingualism and aphasia. In H. Whitaker & H. A. Whitaker (Eds.), *Studies in neurolinguistics, 3*. New York: Academic Press.

Sasanuma, S. 1975. Kana and kanji processing in Japanese aphasics. *Brain & Language, 2,* 369–383.

Wald, B. 1974. Bilingualism. In B. J. Siegel, A. R. Beals, & S. A. Tyler (Eds.), *Annual Review of Anthropology, 3*. Palo Alto: Annual Reviews.

Weinreich, U. 1966. *Languages in contact*. The Hague: Mouton.

Whitaker, H. A. 1971. Neurolinguistics. In W. O. Dingwall (Ed.), *A survey of linguistic science*. College Park: Univ. of Maryland Press.

Whitaker, H., & Whitaker, H. A. 1977. Language disorders. In R. Wardhaugh & H. D. Brown (Eds.), *A survey of applied linguistics*. Ann Arbor: Univ. of Michigan Press.

4 The Right Roof Constraint in an adult-acquired language

William C. Ritchie

Expanding slightly on Chomsky's familiar formulation (e.g., Chomsky, 1965, Ch. 1), we may consider the minimal task of a theory of language acquisition/learning[1]—whether by child or by adult, whether of a first language or of a second—as the specification of the internal structure of the abstract input–output device diagrammed in 1.

1.
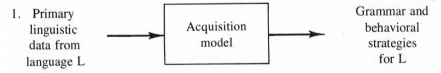

Primary linguistic data from language L → Acquisition model → Grammar and behavioral strategies for L

[1] I assume Krashen's distinction between acquisition—an unconscious, natural process that typically takes place in informal settings—and learning—a conscious process that typically occurs in formal classroom environments (see Krashen, 1975, 1977, this volume). Though I can give no strong arguments at this point, I suspect that the topics covered in this paper are more relevant to acquisition than to learning. On the basis of this suspicion, I shall use the terms "acquisition" and "acquirer" rather than "learning" and "learner" as cover terms for the cumbersome "acquisition/learning," etc. In addition, I recognize that an account of the capacity for language use requires more than an account of the user's grammar and behavioral strategies. In particular, a more complete account will include a hypothesis about what has been called the user's "communicative competence [Hymes, 1964, and elsewhere]." Considerations of the latter appear not to be relevant to the issues raised in this paper—I therefore restrict my attention throughout the paper to the minimal model given here.

Since the result of language acquisition is, minimally, an internalized grammar and a set of behavioral (that is, perceptual and productional) strategies, and since language acquisition does not occur instantaneously, an empirically adequate account of the device of 1 must include, again minimally, the theories of 2 and the strategies of 3.

2.   a. A theory of linguistic competence, which specifies, among other things, the class of candidate grammars available to the acquirer as hypotheses about the structure of L and an account of how these grammars function (Chomsky, 1965, 1973).
       b. A theory of linguistic performance which specifies the class of behavioral strategies available to the acquirer as possible optimal strategies for L (Bever, 1970, pp. 311–312).

3. A set of acquisitional strategies that specifies which grammar/behavioral-strategy-set combinations made available by 2 will be entertained as hypotheses about L early in the acquisition process and which will be entertained later.

Particular hypotheses about 2 and 3 are thus hypotheses about the structures and strategies that language acquirers incorporate a priori into the systems of linguistic knowledge and language use that they acquire and into the process of acquisition itself.

A great deal of research has been done recently on the specification of 3 for both child and adult second language acquirers.[2] On the other hand, detailed investigations of 2 for second language acquirers—either children or adults—are virtually nonexistent. For the critical-period (child) language acquirer of a first language, 2 consists of the tacit universal theories of first language competence and performance which it is the linguist's and psycholinguist's central task to discover. In view of the fact that children generally attain native proficiency in second languages, it seems safe to adopt these same theories as accounts of the capacity of the child second language acquirer—at least as working hypotheses. In the case of the adult (post-critical-period) acquirer, one logical possibility is that 2 is identical to 2 for children.[3] However, the very fact of the critical period (see, e.g., Oyama, 1973; Seliger, Krashen, & Ladefoged, 1975) leaves open the

[2]This literature is quite extensive. The following are representative works: Dulay and Burt, 1974; Krashen, Sferlazza, Feldman, and Fathman, 1976; Larsen-Freeman, 1976; Schacter, 1974; Taylor, 1975. See also the papers in the present volume by J. Anderson, Gary, Hatch, Larsen-Freeman, Kleinmann, and Madden, Bailey, Eisenstein, and L. Anderson.

[3]Under the assumption that this possibility is actually the case, the failure of adults to attain full proficiency in second languages would be due to factors other than loss of intrinsic language acquisition capacity—that is, unsuitable learning environments, lack of motivation, differences from the child in general learning style, etc. See, e.g., Corder, 1967; Diller, 1971; Krashen, in press; Macnamara, 1975; Palmer, 1964, for expressions of this position.

possibility that 2 for adults is different from 2 for children—that is, that it is different from the universal theories of first language competence and performance.

The purpose of this paper is to report a preliminary empirical investigation of this last possibility with respect to a specific syntactic principle which has been discussed in the linguistic and psycholinguistic literature as part of 2 for children acquiring first languages. The question investigated is whether or not this principle is also part of 2 for adults—that is, whether or not adults incorporate the principle a priori into the grammars/strategies they construct for second languages independent of their experience with particular primary data from that language.

PRELIMINARIES

It is a truism in the study of second language acquisition that the grammars/strategies constructed for second languages by adults are, at some stage in the process of acquisition, determined (at least in part) by the grammar/strategies of the acquirer's first language. In investigating 2 for adults, we are interested in establishing what principles constitute the capacity of **any** adult to acquire **any** language regardless of his first language. In order to reduce the effects of the first language to a minimum, it is necessary to choose for investigation a principle (P), a first language (L_1), and a second language (L_2), such that P is not incorporated in the (natively acquired) grammar/strategies of L_1 but **is** present in the (again, natively acquired) grammar/strategies of L_2. Given such a case, the source of P—should it be found to be present in adult-acquired grammars/strategies for L_2— must be the acquirer's general capacity for language acquisition rather than the "transferred" grammar/strategies of L_1.[4]

In the present study, these requirements are met by the choice of a constraint on right movement rules—the Right Roof Constraint: see below—as P, the choice of Japanese—the grammar of which does not contain right movement rules (Kuno, 1972)—as L_1, and the choice of English—the grammar of which **does** contain right movement rules—as L_2.

The Right Roof Constraint

Ross (1967) notes the existence in English of pairs of syntactically related sentences such as 4–6 and proposes the rule of Extraposition from NP (henceforth, ExfrNP), as stated in 7, to account for this relationship.

---

[4]Other possible sources for P are informal exposure to data from L_2 and formal instruction in L_2. In the present case, neither alternative seems particularly plausible.

4. a. *A gun which I had cleaned* went off.
    b. *A gun* went off *which I had cleaned*.

5. a. *I gave **a gun which I had cleaned*** to my brother.
    b. *I gave **a gun*** to my brother *which I had cleaned*.

6. a. *He let **some cats which were meowing*** out.
    b. *He let **some cats*** out *which were meowing*.

7. ExfrNP (optional)
    SD: X [$_{NP}$ NP – S $_{NP}$] – X
           1   2   3 $\Longrightarrow$
    SC: 1 $\emptyset$ 3 + 2

The examples 4–6 show that the rule must move a clause over **whatever** forma-
tive sequence intervenes between its original position and its surface position at
the end of the sentence. If the formalization of the rule is to capture this apparently significant generalization, then its third term must be a variable. However,
as Ross notes, the string 8c below, putatively related to 8a, is the result of
applying 7 to the underlying structure of 8a, whereas it is clear that 8b rather than
8c should be the result of such an application.

8. a. [$_s$ *That **a gun which I had cleaned*** went off $_s$] *surprised no one*.
    b. [$_s$ *That **a gun*** went off *which I had cleaned* $_s$] *surprised no one*.
    c. *[$_s$ *That **a gun*** went off $_s$] *surprised no one **which I had cleaned***.

It is thus necessary to constrain ExfrNP so that it will apply to the structure
underlying 8a to give not 8c but 8b. Ross (1967, p. 307) proposes a constraint on
right movement rules—the Right Roof Constraint (henceforth, the RRC)—which
has the content of 9.

9. *The Right Roof Constraint*[5]
    Surface strings in which an element has been moved to the right out of the
    sentence in which the element originated are ill formed.

As stated, the RRC has the effect of constraining not only ExfrNP but all right
movement rules including Extraposition (Extrap), the rule which relates the

[5]The term "Right Roof Constraint" is due to Grosu (1973). The observational statement 9 has been
given descriptive content in two ways in the literature. Ross (1967) and Chomsky (1973) propose that
RRC facts be accounted for by imposing a condition on the functioning of the grammar of English; in
Chomsky's proposal, the RRC is subsumed under a more general principle, the Subjacency Condition
(Chomsky, 1973, pp. 270–272). On the other hand, the well-known fact that interrupted structures
are difficult to process perceptually suggests that the RRC may be a grammatized behavioral principle. In fact, Grosu (1973) has argued for this view. For our purposes, the question of whether or not
the RRC is behaviorally motivated is immaterial—the important question is whether it is incorporated
a priori in grammars/strategies by the child or acquired on the basis of experience with particular
primary linguistic data. An argument for the former position appears below in the text.

sentences in 10. The examples in 11 illustrate the need for the RRC to be generalized in this way.

10.   a. *That John had left surprised Mary.*
      b. *It surprised Mary that John had left.*

11.   a. [s *That it surprised Mary that John had left* s] *amused Alice.*
      b. *[s *That it surprised Mary* s] *amused Alice that John had left.*

There is good reason to believe that the RRC, whatever its precise nature, is not acquired by children in the process of first language acquisition on the basis of exposure to particular primary linguistic data but is, rather, incorporated a priori in the grammars/strategies which they construct for their first languages. Typically, the ontogenetic history of acquired constraints on rules includes an early period during which the constraint is violated in production, followed by a process of refinement leading eventually to production conforming almost entirely to the constraint. (See, e.g., Slobin, 1973, pp. 204–206, for a discussion of this sort of "overregularization" and refinement.) If the RRC were acquired rather than incorporated a priori, one would expect an early stage of acquisition in which utterances like 8c and 11b were produced, followed by a gradual refinement to the production of utterances like 8b and 11a, respectively, in their place. Though, to my knowledge, no attempt has been made to investigate the question directly, it seems implausible that the RRC would develop in this way. It is, therefore, a reasonable candidate for inclusion in either 2a or 2b, at least for critical-period first language acquirers.

Two Hypotheses

Given that the RRC is present in the organism as a potential constraint during the critical period, the central question for the study of adult (post-critical-period) second language acquisition is whether the RRC continues to be present after the close of the critical period: Do adults retain the RRC or have they lost it? In order to determine whether the first possibility (henceforth, "retention") or the second (henceforth, "loss")—or neither—is supported empirically, the study described below was conducted.

METHOD

Subjects

Two groups of subjects were used: a control group of native speakers of General American English and an experimental group of native speakers of Japanese. All subjects were graduate students or faculty members (or their spouses) at Syracuse University and all were naive with respect to linguistic theory.

The control group consisted of six subjects. Their performance in the study was taken as a test of the materials used.

There were 20 experimental subjects: 12 males and 8 females. All except one (Subject 18—see Appendix A) could be considered as having acquired/learned English only in a formal classroom setting until arrival in the United States (range of age at arrival: 21 to 40 years). The age of initial exposure to English ranged from 8 to 13 years (mean = 11.9 years).[6] (Other characteristics of the experimental subjects—both of individuals and of the sample as a whole—are given in Appendix A.)

Materials

The subjects were administered a questionnaire made up of 120 items. (See Appendix B.) Each item consisted of two strings of English words of varying degrees of grammaticality, one marked a and the other b. The subject's task was to indicate whether: (1) the string marked a was more grammatical than that marked b ($a > b$); (2) strings a and b were the same in grammaticality ($a = b$); or (3) b was more grammatical than a ($b > a$).[7]

The tasks required by the items were classifiable into four different types in accordance with different combinations of well-formed and ill-formed strings, as indicated in Table 1A. For each item there was an "expected" response—that is, a response which accorded with the investigator's judgment as a native speaker of General American English—and two "unexpected" responses. In the case of tasks of Types A–C, the unexpected responses were further differentiable into "neutral" and "contrary." The possibilities are summarized in Table 1B.

The questionnaires and instructions were given to subjects in printed form. No time limit was imposed, though subjects were asked to give their "initial, intuitive" responses. Instructions for the questionnaire were printed in Japanese for the Japanese subjects. The questionnaire tested for the presence or absence of the RRC with respect to two sets of right movement phenomena: strings involving

---

[6]Estimates concerning the age of termination for the critical period vary from approximately 11 years (Lenneberg, 1967) to 15 years (Bever, 1975). Seventeen of the 20 subjects were within this age range at initial exposure to English; the others were 8 years old (two subjects) and 10 (one subject). The results indicate no significant difference between the latter 3 subjects and the former 17 with respect to loss or retention. "Exposure" for all but Subject 18 was limited to a maximum of 5 hours a week in a formal classroom setting. Subject 18 attended a private school where English was used as a medium of instruction.

[7]When grammaticality judgments are used as linguistic data (whether in the study of first or of second languages), it appears advantageous whenever possible to use relative rather than absolute judgments in order to compensate for the "law of contrast." See Bever (1970, pp. 346–348) for discussion.

Table 1.   Description of Questionnaire Items

A. Classification

Task type	Explanation	Example from questionnaire
A	One string is well formed the other violates constraints on word order.	1. a. *John had climbed a hill.* b. *Hill a climbed had John.* (Expected response: $a > b$)
B	One string is well formed, the other is semantically anomalous.	4. a. *John had climbed a hill.* b. *John had climbed a letter.* (Expected response: $a > b$)
C	Both strings are ill formed; one is semantically anomalous, the other violates constraints on word order.	7. a. *Mary had built a letter.* b. *Letter a built had Mary.* (Expected response: $a > b$)
D	Both strings are well formed or ill formed in the same way.	10. a. *Mary had built a boat.* b. *Bill had sent a letter.* (Expected response: $a = b$)

B. Response Types

Task type	Expected response	Subject's response	Subject's response will be called:
A–C	$a > b$	$a > b$	Expected
		$a = b$	Neutral } Unexpected
		$b > a$	Contrary }
	$b > a$	$b > a$	Expected
		$a = b$	Neutral } Unexpected
		$a > b$	Contrary }
D	$a = b$	$a = b$	Expected
		$a > b$ }	Unexpected
		$b > a$ }	

the application of Extrap and strings involving the application of ExfrNP. Since the two sets of strings involved were different in structure, the presence or absence of the RRC and confirmation or disconfirmation of alternatives to retention and loss as explanations for presence or absence of the RRC (see below) were treated independently for Extrap and ExfrNP strings.

CRITERIA AND ALTERNATIVE HYPOTHESES (RETENTION)

Items 103–108 tested for the presence in the subjects of the RRC (confirming **retention**) for Extrap strings, and Items 112–117 did so for ExfrNP strings. A subject was provisionally considered as having the RRC for either Extrap or ExfrNP strings if he gave at least five (of six) expected responses on the relevant items in each case ($p = .038$, binomial distribution).

There is an alternative explanation for a subject's reaching criterion on these items—namely, that he lacks the RRC (which makes crucial mention of the **structure** of the string over which elements can be moved by Extrap and ExfrNP) but has, instead, a principle which specifies that, given two sentences exhibiting right movement, the sentence in which the moved element has been shifted a greater **linear** distance to the right (where the linear distance is measured in morphemes) is less acceptable or grammatical than the one in which the linear distance over which the element has been moved is smaller. In order to provide evidence to test this alternative, items 109–111 and 118–120 were included. In each case, the sequence over which the element has been moved is longer in the string that does **not** violate the RRC than it is in the string that **does** violate the RRC. This alternative to true retention was considered falsified for a subject if he gave three (of three) expected responses in the relevant items in each set—Extrap and ExfrNP—of strings ($p = .037$).

A subject who met criterion for both sets of items was considered as confirming retention; otherwise, as not confirming retention.

Notice that contrary responses to Items 109–111 and 118–120 might be based on the judgment that sentences containing the longer predicates (that is, 109b, 110b, etc.) are ungrammatical—or at least less grammatical than their short-predicate counterparts—thus indicating that the linear-distance constraint mentioned above was not the basis for presence-of-RRC judgments and that the RRC in its structural form might still be present. A number of items were included to test for this possibility. (See Table D-4, Appendix D, for a full list.)

CRITERIA AND ALTERNATIVE HYPOTHESES (LOSS)

Confirmation of the **loss** hypothesis for the RRC with respect to a given subject required that all nine items in each of the two sets of sentence types—Items 103–111 for Extrap and 112–120 for ExfrNP—be taken into account. The criterion for confirmation of loss was set at nine (out of nine) unexpected responses in each case ($p = .039$).

Assuming that a subject met criterion for confirmation of loss, there were a number of alternative hypotheses in addition to loss itself that could account for this fact. The following appear to be the major ones.

Alternative I: The subject was unable to do the tasks required in responding to the questionnaire in general.

Alternative II: The subject had not acquired the basic structures and lexicon required to give responses that would disconfirm loss.

Alternative III: The rules of Relative Clause Formation, Extrap, and ExfrNP, all of which are required for expected judgments on Items 103–120, were not sufficiently well established in the subject for him to make the judgments that would disconfirm loss.

Items were included in the questionnaire to test each of these alternatives. These items and criteria for confirmation of Alternatives I–III are discussed in detail in Appendix C.

SUMMARY

In summary, there are five possible outcomes for each subject with respect to each set (Extrap and ExfrNP) of strings as indicated in 12.

12.   1. Presence of RRC confirmed (retention confirmed).
      2. Absence of RRC confirmed (loss confirmed).
      3. Neither absence nor presence of RRC confirmed:
         a. Criterion for presence of RRC met but basis was linear distance, not structure.
         b. Criterion for absence of RRC met but one or more of Alternatives I–III were viable.
         c. Criteria for neither presence nor absence of RRC met.

RESULTS AND DISCUSSION

Results

CONTROL GROUP (TEST OF QUESTIONNAIRE)

The control group was used to test the items in the questionnaire. The same type of criterion was used for each item as was used in determining the viability of Alternatives I–III for each subject in the experimental group (Appendix C)—the responses to items were assigned the same values as for the experimental subjects: 2 points for an expected response, 1 point for a neutral, and no points for a contrary response in items involving tasks of Types A–C, and 1 point for expected, none for unexpected responses on items of Type D. Since there were six subjects in the control group, there were either 12 or 6 total points for each item and criterion was set at 10/12 points ($p = .038$, multinominal distribution) for items of Types A–C and 5/6 points ($p = .018$) for items of Type D.

On this analysis, there were eight items which failed to meet criterion: 85, 86, 91–93, 100–102. All eight of these items tested for grammaticality of the longer predicates used in both Extrap and ExfrNP Items 106–111, and 115–120. (The specific consequences of the failure of these items to meet criterion in interpreting the experimental results are discussed in footnote *b*, Table D-4, Appendix D.)

EXPERIMENTAL GROUP

The number of experimental subjects exhibiting each of the five outcomes listed in 12 is given in Table 2.

Table 2. **Number of Subjects Confirming Retention and Loss of the RRC for Extrap and ExfrNP Strings** ($N = 20$)

Outcome	1. Retention	2. Loss	3. Neither		
			3a[a]	3b[a]	3c[a]
Sentence types					
Extrap	16	0	2	0	2
ExfrNP	13	2	1	2	2

[a] See 12 in the text, p. 41.

Discussion

For Extrap strings, of the 16 subjects confirming either retention or loss, all 16 confirmed retention. Of the 15 subjects who confirmed either retention or loss for ExfrNP strings, 13 confirmed retention. Taking into account just the 18 items that tested directly for the presence or absence of the RRC and structure rather than distance as the basis of RRC judgments, the probability of this result is extremely small. Retention is therefore very strongly supported by the results of this study.

A closer examination of the results (see Appendix D) shows even stronger support for retention than does the summary given above. In the case of Extrap sentences, there were two subjects (12 and 13) who failed to meet criterion for the presence of the rule of Extrap itself and yet succeeded in confirming presence of the RRC for Extrap strings. These subjects had thus incorporated an a priori principle (the RRC) in their grammars/strategies for English that had the effect of constraining the application of a rule which itself was not firmly established in their grammars for English.

Even stronger evidence is provided by the results from ExfrNP strings. In this case, a total of five subjects who confirmed retention (01, 04, 11, 12, 17) failed to reach criterion for presence of ExfrNP alone (11, 17) or for both Relative Clause Formation and ExfrNP (01, 04, 12). Of these five subjects, two (11, 17) met criterion for **absence** of ExfrNP. That is, even though a transformation constrained by the RRC was absent from these subjects' grammars for English, they judged strings involving the application of the rule as though they possessed the RRC as a **potential** condition on that (apparently absent) rule.

CONCLUSION

This preliminary study provides strong evidence for the presence of the Right Roof Constraint—an independently proposed and justified universal for child-acquired first languages—among the principles which constitute the post-critical-period language acquirer's capacities for language acquisition, thus lending preliminary empirical support to the assumption of the authors listed in footnote 3 that linguistic universals are intact in the adult and that the end of the critical period is determined by factors other than loss of universal constraints.

However, since only one universal has been investigated here, these results are hardly conclusive—it may be that universals other than the RRC are lost to the adult. This question can be resolved only by an exhaustive investigation of first-language universals with respect to their presence or absence in the grammars/strategies that adults construct for second languages.

APPENDIX A   SUBJECTS

Table A-1.   Characteristics of Individual Subjects

Subject	Sex	Age of initial exposure to English	Length of period of study of English (years)	Time spent in English-speaking country (months)	Estimated percentage of time speaking English	Age of first arrival in English-speaking country	Age at administration of questionnaire	Outcome[a] Extrap	ExfrNP
01	F	12	14	32	90	31	34	1	1
02	F	10	10	47	18	31	35	1	1
03	M	13	8	42	22	32	36	1	3c
04	F	12	12	5	80	24	24	1	1
05	M	8	14	42	60	21	25	1	3b
06	M	13	7	109	100	25	34	1	1
07	F	13	7	106	100	25	34	1	1
08	F	12	8	12	15	27	28	3c	2
09	M	12	8	15	60	29	30	3c	2
10	F	12	9	84	10	22	29	1	3c
11	M	13	10	100	50	31	39	1	1
12	M	12	8	5	30	28	28	3a	1
13	F	13	10	27	50	22	24	1	3b
14	F	13	8	15	35	40	41	1	1
15	M	12	8	36	30	27	30	1	1
16	M	12	7	58	25	22	29	1	3a
17	M	13	8	17	99	24	26	1	1
18	M	8	14	16	30	30	31	1	1
19	M	12	11	39	50	23	26	1	1
20	M	12	8	51	15	26	30	3a	1
Mean		11.9	9.5	42.9	46	27.0	30.7		
Range		8–13	7–14	5–109	10–100	21–40	24–41		

[a] 1 = Retention confirmed

2 = Loss confirmed

3a = Criterion for retention met but alternative is viable

3b = Criterion for loss met but alternative(s) are viable

3c = Criteria for neither retention nor loss met.

APPENDIX B   THE QUESTIONNAIRE

Background Information

The accompanying questionnaire is part of an informal research program on adult foreign language learning that is being conducted by members of the Linguistics Department of Syracuse University. Since the program is unsponsored and unfinanced, we have called upon our friends to act as participants. Needless to say, we very much appreciate your assistance in this.

The purpose of the study is to find out in exactly what ways the knowledge of the syntactic structure of English that a **nonnative** speaker of English has either differs from or resembles the knowledge that a **native** speaker has of this structure. In order to do this, we are asking both nonnative and native speakers to make a large number of judgments about sentences in English—specifically, judgments about whether or not two sentences are equally good sentences of English. The sentences have been chosen so that we will find out from your judgments some very basic facts about how adults learn foreign languages in general and why they so often have more difficulty learning languages than children do.

The ultimate goal of our research, then, is to make it easier for adults to learn foreign languages.

One final remark to the native speakers of Japanese who are participating: We have reason to believe that many of the judgments that you will be asked to make on this questionnaire are among the most difficult judgments about English sentences for Japanese speakers to make. Therefore, if you find them difficult, it is not because you have not learned English well—it is simply because they are very difficult judgments. Also: Be assured that these questionnaires and the answers that you give will remain confidential.

If you like, we will send you a copy of your corrected answer sheet and a copy of the questionnaire when the study is over. Please indicate on the answer sheet if you would like to receive these things.

Again, we wish to express our deepest gratitude for your participation in this study.

WILLIAM C. RITCHIE
Assistant Professor of Linguistics
Syracuse University

Instructions

Fill out the first page of the answer sheet. If you would like to receive your corrected answer sheet and a copy of the questionnaire after the study is over, please indicate this at the bottom of the first page of the answer sheet.

The questionnaire is made up of 120 items. Each item consists of two sentences—an *a* sentence and a *b* sentence. Your task will be to decide whether (1) the *a* sentence is more grammatical in English than the *b* sentence (that is, whether the *a* sentence is a better sentence in English than the *b* sentence), or (2) the *a* sentence and the *b* sentence are the same in grammaticality (that is, neither is a better sentence than the other), or (3) the *b* sentence is more grammatical than the *a* sentence.

As examples, consider A, B, and C below.

A.   a. *The statement frightened the boy.*
       b. *Boy the frightened statement the.*

B.   a. *The man surprised the statement.*
       b. *The man surprised the boy.*

C.   a. *The boy frightened the man.*
       b. *The man surprised the child.*

In A, the *a* sentence is more grammatical than the *b* sentence. In cases like this, mark the first column opposite the number of the item as indicated on the second page of the answer sheet. In B, the *b* sentence is more grammatical than the *a* sentence. Cases like this require a mark in the third column on the answer sheet as indicated. In C, *a* and *b* are the same in grammaticality (namely, they are both completely grammatical). As indicated on the answer sheet, mark the center column for these cases.

There will be some items in which neither sentence will be completely grammatical but it will be possible to say that one is more grammatical than the other. For example, consider D and E below.

D.   a. *Man the frightened statement the.*
       b. *The man frightened the statement.*

E.   a. *The boy surprised the proposal.*
       b. *Surprised proposal the boy the.*

In D, *b* is more grammatical than *a* and in E, *a* is more grammatical than *b*. Again, these answers are registered on the answer sheet.

You may become tired of making judgments in the process of doing the questionnaire. If so, rest for a moment before you continue.

Do not think for very long about individual items—we want your initial, intuitive response.

Part I

1. a. *John had climbed a hill.*
   b. *Hill a climbed had John.*
2. a. *Letter a sent had Mary.*
   b. *Mary had sent a letter.*
3. a. *Boat a built had Bill.*
   b. *Bill had built a boat.*
4. a. *John had climbed a hill.*
   b. *John had climbed a letter.*
5. a. *Bill had built a letter.*
   b. *Bill had built a boat.*
6. a. *Mary had sent a letter.*

   b. *Mary had sent a hill.*
7. a. *Mary had built a letter.*
   b. *Letter a built had Mary.*
8. a. *Hill a sent had John.*
   b. *John had sent a hill.*
9. a. *Letter a climbed had Bill.*
   b. *Bill had climbed a letter.*
10. a. *Mary had built a boat.*
   b. *Bill had sent a letter.*
11. a. *John had climbed a hill.*
   b. *Mary had sent a letter.*

12. a. *Bill had built a boat.*
    b. *John had climbed a hill.*
13. a. *The answer was orange.*
    b. *The ball was orange.*
14. a. *The woman was tall.*
    b. *The thought was tall.*
15. a. *The man was fat.*
    b. *The idea was fat.*
16. a. *The answer was surprising.*
    b. *Surprising was answer the.*
17. a. *Disturbing was thought the.*
    b. *The thought was disturbing.*
18. a. *The idea was amusing.*
    b. *Amusing was idea the.*
19. a. *The answer was amusing.*
    b. *The answer was fat.*
20. a. *The thought was disturbing.*
    b. *The thought was orange.*
21. a. *The idea was tall.*
    b. *The idea was amusing.*
22. a. *The idea was fat.*
    b. *The idea was amusing to all of the boys.*
23. a. *The thought was disturbing to some of the girls.*
    b. *The thought was orange.*
24. a. *The answer was tall.*
    b. *The answer was surprising to a few of the students.*
25. a. *The idea was surprising to some of the boys.*
    b. *The thought was amusing.*
26. a. *The answer was disturbing.*
    b. *The idea was amusing to a few of the girls.*
27. a. *The thought was disturbing to all of the students.*
    b. *The answer was surprising.*
28. a. *A boat had sunk.*
    b. *Sunk had a boat.*
29. a. *Collapsed had hill a.*
    b. *A hill had collapsed.*
30. a. *A letter had arrived.*
    b. *Arrived had letter a.*
31. a. *A boat had sunk three weeks afterwards.*
    b. *A letter had collapsed.*
32. a. *A letter had arrived three months afterwards.*
    b. *A hill had arrived.*
33. a. *A letter had collapsed.*

    b. *A hill had collapsed three years afterwards.*
34. a. *That John had climbed a hill was surprising.*
    b. *The idea was tall.*
35. a. *The thought was orange.*
    b. *That John had sent a letter was amusing.*
36. a. *The answer was fat.*
    b. *That Mary had built a boat was disturbing.*
37. a. *The thought was fat.*
    b. *That Bill had climbed a hill was amusing to a few of the boys.*
38. a. *That John had sent a letter was disturbing to all of the girls.*
    b. *The answer was tall.*
39. a. *The idea was orange.*
    b. *That Mary had built a boat was surprising to some of the students.*
40. a. *That Bill had sent a letter was fat.*
    b. *That Bill had sent a letter was disturbing.*
41. a. *That Mary had climbed a hill was surprising.*
    b. *That Mary had climbed a hill was orange.*
42. a. *That John had built a boat was amusing.*
    b. *That John had built a boat was tall.*
43. a. *That Bill had sent a letter was obvious.*
    b. *That Bill had sent a letter was fat.*
44. a. *That Mary had climbed a hill was orange.*
    b. *That Mary had climbed a hill was clear.*
45. a. *That John had built a boat was tall.*
    b. *That John had built a boat was apparent.*
46. a. *That Bill had climbed a hill was disturbing to a few of the girls.*
    b. *That Bill had climbed a hill was fat.*
47. a. *That Bill had built a boat was orange.*
    b. *That Bill had built a boat was amusing to all of the students.*
48. a. *That John had sent a letter was tall.*
    b. *That John had sent a letter was disturbing to some of the boys.*
49. a. *A letter had collapsed.*
    b. *A hill that John had climbed had collapsed.*

50. a. *A boat that Bill had built had sank.*
    b. *A hill had arrived.*
51. a. *A hill had elapsed.*
    b. *A letter that Mary had sent had arrived.*
52. a. *A letter that John had built had arrived.*
    b. *A letter that John had sent had arrived.*
53. a. *A hill that Mary had sent had collapsed.*
    b. *A hill that Mary had climbed had collapsed.*
54. a. *A boat that John had elapsed had sunk.*
    b. *A boat that John had built had sunk.*
55. a. *A letter that Mary had sent had collapsed.*
    b. *A letter that Mary had sent had arrived three weeks afterwards.*
56. a. *A boat that John had built had sunk three months afterwards.*
    b. *A boat that John had built had elapsed.*
57. a. *A hill that Bill had climbed had collapsed three years afterwards.*
    b. *A hill that Bill had climbed had arrived.*

Part II

58. a. *It was surprising that John had climbed a hill.*
    b. *The idea was orange.*
59. a. *The thought was tall.*
    b. *It was amusing that Bill had sent a letter.*
60. a. *The answer was fat.*
    b. *It was disturbing that Mary had built a boat.*
61. a. *The idea was tall.*
    b. *It was amusing that Bill had climbed a hill.*
62. a. *It was disturbing that Mary had sent a letter.*
    b. *The thought was fat.*
63. a. *It was surprising that Bill had built a boat.*
    b. *The answer was orange.*
64. a. *It was obvious that Bill had sent a letter.*
    b. *The idea was fat.*
65. a. *The thought was orange.*
    b. *It was clear that Bill had sent a letter.*
66. a. *The answer was tall.*

    b. *It was apparent that Mary had climbed a hill.*
67. a. *That Bill had sent a letter was fat.*
    b. *It was disturbing that Bill had sent a letter.*
68. a. *It was surprising that Mary had climbed a hill.*
    b. *That Mary had climbed a hill was orange.*
69. a. *It was amusing that John had built a boat.*
    b. *That John had built a boat was tall.*
70. a. *It was obvious that Bill had sent a letter.*
    b. *That Bill had sent a letter was fat.*
71. a. *That Mary had climbed a hill was orange.*
    b. *It was clear that Mary had climbed a hill.*
72. a. *That John had built a boat was tall.*
    b. *It was apparent that John had built a boat.*
73. a. *That John had built a boat was disturbing.*
    b. *It was fat that John had built a boat.*
74. a. *It was orange that Bill had sent a letter.*
    b. *That Bill had sent a letter was surprising.*
75. a. *It was tall that Mary had climbed a hill.*
    b. *That Mary had climbed a hill was amusing.*
76. a. *It was fat that Mary had sent a letter.*
    b. *It was disturbing to all of the boys that Mary had sent a letter.*
77. a. *It was amusing to some of the girls that John had built a boat.*
    b. *It was orange that John had built a boat.*
78. a. *It was surprising to a few of the students that Bill had climbed a hill.*
    b. *It was tall that Bill had climbed a hill.*
79. a. *A hill had collapsed that John had climbed.*
    b. *John had climbed a letter.*
80. a. *Bill had built a letter.*
    b. *A boat had sunk that Bill had built.*
81. a. *A letter had arrived that Mary had sent.*
    b. *Mary had built a letter.*
82. a. *A hill had collapsed that Bill had climbed.*
    b. *A hill had collapsed that Bill had sent.*

83. a. *A boat had sunk that John had built.*
    b. *A boat had sunk that John had elapsed.*
84. a. *A letter had arrived that Mary had climbed.*
    b. *A letter had arrived that Mary had sent.*
85. a. *A boat had sunk three weeks afterwards that John had built.*
    b. *A boat had sunk that John had elapsed.*
86. a. *A hill had collapsed that Mary had sent.*
    b. *A hill had collapsed three months afterwards that Bill had climbed.*
87. a. *A letter had arrived that Bill had climbed.*
    b. *A letter had arrived three years afterwards that Bill had sent.*

Part III

88. a. *That Mary had climbed a hill was fat.*
    b. *That it was surprising to all of the boys that Mary had climbed a hill was obvious.*
89. a. *That it was disturbing to some of the girls that Bill had built a boat was clear.*
    b. *That Bill had built a boat was tall.*
90. a. *That John had climbed a hill was orange.*
    b. *That it was amusing to a few of the students that John had climbed a hill was apparent.*
91. a. *That it was surprising that John had built a boat was obvious.*
    b. *That it was surprising to all of the boys that John had built a boat was obvious.*
92. a. *That it was disturbing that Bill had sent a letter was clear.*
    b. *That it was disturbing to some of the girls that Bill had sent a letter was clear.*
93. a. *That it was amusing to a few of the students that John had climbed a hill was apparent.*
    b. *That it was amusing that John had climbed a hill was apparent.*
94. a. *That a letter that Bill had sent had arrived three days afterwards was obvious.*
    b. *That a letter that Bill had built had arrived was clear.*
95. a. *That a boat that Mary had elapsed had sunk was apparent.*
    b. *That a boat that Mary had built had sunk three months afterwards was clear.*
96. a. *That a hill that Bill had climbed had collapsed three years afterwards was apparent.*
    b. *That a hill that Bill had sent had collapsed was obvious.*
97. a. *That a letter had arrived three days afterwards that Bill had sent was obvious.*
    b. *That a letter that Bill had built had arrived was obvious.*
98. a. *That a boat that Mary had elapsed had sunk was apparent.*
    b. *That a boat had sunk three months afterwards that Mary had built was clear.*
99. a. *That a hill had collapsed three years afterwards that Bill had climbed was apparent.*
    b. *That a hill that Bill had sent had collapsed was apparent.*
100. a. *That a hill had collapsed that Bill had climbed was clear.*
     b. *That a hill had collapsed three years afterwards that Bill had climbed was clear.*
101. a. *That a boat had sunk that John had built was obvious.*
     b. *That a boat had sunk three months afterwards that John had built was obvious.*
102. a. *That a letter had arrived three months afterwards that Mary had sent was apparent.*
     b. *That a letter had arrived that Mary had sent was apparent.*
103. a. *That it was surprising that Mary had built a boat was obvious.*
     b. *That it was surprising was obvious that Mary had built a boat.*
104. a. *That it was disturbing was clear that Bill had sent a letter.*
     b. *That it was disturbing that Bill had sent a letter was clear.*
105. a. *That it was amusing that John had climbed a hill was apparent.*

b. *That it was amusing was apparent that John had climbed a hill.*

106. a. *That it was surprising to all of the boys that Mary had built a boat was obvious.*

    b. *That it was surprising to all of the boys was obvious that Mary had built a boat.*

107. a. *That it was disturbing to some of the girls that Bill had sent a letter was clear.*

    b. *That it was disturbing to some of the girls was clear that Bill had sent a letter.*

108. a. *That it was amusing to a few of the students was apparent that John had climbed a hill.*

    b. *That it was amusing to a few of the students that John had climbed a hill was apparent.*

109. a. *That it was surprising was obvious that Mary had built a boat.*

    b. *That it was surprising to all of the boys that Mary had built a boat was obvious.*

110. a. *That it was disturbing was clear that Bill had sent a letter.*

    b. *That it was disturbing to some of the girls that Bill had sent a letter was clear.*

111. a. *That it was amusing to a few of the students that John had climbed a hill was apparent.*

    b. *That it was amusing was apparent that John had climbed a hill.*

112. a. *That a hill had collapsed that Bill had climbed was clear.*

    b. *That it was amusing was apparent that John had climbed a hill.*

113. a. *That a boat had sunk that John had built was obvious.*

    b. *That a boat had sunk was obvious that John had built.*

114. a. *That a letter had arrived was apparent that Mary had sent.*

    b. *That a letter had arrived that Mary had sent was apparent.*

115. a. *That a hill had collapsed three weeks afterwards that Bill had climbed was obvious.*

    b. *That a hill had collapsed three weeks afterwards was obvious that Bill had climbed.*

116. a. *That a boat had sunk three months afterwards that Mary had built was apparent.*

    b. *That a boat had sunk three months afterwards was apparent that Mary had built.*

117. a. *That a letter had arrived three days afterwards was obvious that John had sent.*

    b. *That a letter had arrived three days afterwards that John had sent was obvious.*

118. a. *That a hill had collapsed was clear that John had climbed.*

    b. *That a hill had collapsed three years afterwards that John had climbed was clear.*

119. a. *That a boat had sunk was obvious that Bill had built.*

    b. *That a boat had sunk three months afterwards that Bill had built was obvious.*

120. a. *That a letter had arrived three days afterwards that Mary had sent was apparent.*

    b. *That a letter had arrived was apparent that Mary had sent.*

Extraposition Study—Answer Sheet

Name _____Sex: Female _____, Male _____

Syracuse address _____Phone _____

What is your native language? _____

For nonnative speakers of English:

Present Age _____

At what age did you begin to learn English? _____

Was it in a school? Yes. _____ No. _____

If so, how many years did you study? _____

How many months have you spent in an English-speaking country in all? _____

Approximately what percent of the time during the day do you use English either in speaking or listening? _____

	a is more grammatical than b	a and b are the same in grammaticality	b is more grammatical than a
A.	X	___	___
B.	___	___	X
C.	___	X	___
D.	___	___	X
E.	X	___	___

Part I

	a is more grammatical than b	a and b are the same in grammaticality	b is more grammatical than a
1.	___	___	___
2.	___	___	___
3.	___	___	___
4.	___	___	___
5.	___	___	___
6.	___	___	___
7.	___	___	___
8.	___	___	___
9.	___	___	___
10.	___	___	___
11.	___	___	___
12.	___	___	___
13.	___	___	___
14.	___	___	___
15.	___	___	___
16.	___	___	___
17.	___	___	___

	a is more grammatical than b	a and b are the same in grammaticality	b is more grammatical than a
18.	___	___	___
19.	___	___	___
20.	___	___	___
21.	___	___	___
22.	___	___	___
23.	___	___	___
24.	___	___	___
25.	___	___	___
26.	___	___	___
27.	___	___	___
28.	___	___	___
29.	___	___	___
30.	___	___	___
31.	___	___	___
32.	___	___	___
33.	___	___	___
34.	___	___	___
35.	___	___	___
36.	___	___	___
37.	___	___	___
38.	___	___	___
39.	___	___	___
40.	___	___	___

	a is more grammatical than b	a and b are the same in grammaticality	b is more grammatical than a
41.	___	___	___
42.	___	___	___
43.	___	___	___
44.	___	___	___
45.	___	___	___
46.	___	___	___
47.	___	___	___
48.	___	___	___
49.	___	___	___
50.	___	___	___
51.	___	___	___
52.	___	___	___
53.	___	___	___
54.	___	___	___
55.	___	___	___
56.	___	___	___
57.	___	___	___

Part II

	a is more grammatical than b	a and b are the same in grammaticality	b is more grammatical than a
58.	___	___	___
59.	___	___	___
60.	___	___	___
61.	___	___	___
62.	___	___	___

⋮

APPENDIX C   ALTERNATIVES TO LOSS

The items testing for Alternatives I–III (pp. 40–41 in the text) varied with respect to the grammatical complexity of the strings contained in them. Since relative complexity of items entered into setting the criteria for confirmation or disconfirmation of these hypotheses, it is important at this point to make explicit the notion of relative complexity used. An item was considered more complex than another if the number of embeddings in the strings included in it was greater. The various possible combinations of strings are listed below in order of relative complexity.

13.   a. Both strings simplex; e.g., Items 1–12.   (Simp/Simp)
         b. One string simplex, the other singly complex; e.g., 34–39.   (Simp/SComp)
         c. Both strings singly complex; e.g., 40–48.   (SComp/SComp)
         d. One string singly complex, the other doubly complex; e.g., 88–90.   (SComp/DComp)
         e. Both doubly complex; e.g., 91–120.   (DComp/DComp)

Items of the various degrees of complexity testing each of the three alternative hypotheses are given in Table C-1.

Table C-1. Items Testing Alternatives to Loss

	Simp/Simp	Simp/SComp	SComp/SComp	SComp/DComp	DComp/DComp
I. Ability to do tasks					
Type A	1-3, 16-18, 28-30	—	—	—	—
Type B	4-6, 13-15, 19-21, 31-33	34-39	40-42, 46-48	—	—
Type C	7-9	—	—	—	—
Type D	10-12	25-27	—	—	91-93, 100-102
II. Basic structures and lexicon[a]					
S_1: Verb–Object	4-6	—	—	—	—
S_2 (Extrap only): Subject–Adjective	19-24	34-39	40-42, 46-48	—	—
S_2 (ExfrNP only): Subject–Verb	31-33	—	—	—	—
S_3: Subject–Adjective	—	43-45	—	—	—
III. Transformations[a]					
Relative Clause Formation	—	49-51	52-57, 82-84	—	94-96
Extraposition	—	58-66	67-78	88-90	—
Extraposition from NP	—	—	79-81	—	97-99

[a] See text, p. 55.

54

The items testing for Alternative II (basic structures and lexicon) and for Alternative III (transformations) require some discussion.

Each of the items testing for basic structures and lexicon consisted of, first, a string violating semantic constraints on "selectional relations" such as Subject–Verb, Verb–Object, or Subject–(Adjectival)Predicate, and, second, a string which did not violate such constraints. It was considered that items of this sort would provide a sufficient test to indicate mastery of both the selectional relations and the lexical items involved. The particular structures and lexical items tested were, of course, those used in Items 103–120; these items, it will be recalled, tested directly for the presence or absence of the RRC. The underlying structures of Items 103/106 and 112/115 are given below as examples of the underlying structures of all the Extrap and ExfrNP strings of 103–120.

14.   Items 103 and 106

   [$_{s_3}$ [$_{s_2}$ *that* [$_{s_1}$ *that Mary had built a boat* $_{s_1}$] *was surprising (to all of the boys)* $_{s_2}$] *was obvious* $_{s_3}$]

15.   Items 112 and 115

   [$_{s_3}$ [$_{s_2}$ *that a boat* [$_{s_1}$ *John had built a boat* $_{s_1}$] *had sunk (three years afterwards)* $_{s_2}$] *was obvious* $_{s_3}$]

(Phrases like *to all of the boys* in 14 and *three years afterwards* in 15 were absent in Items 103–105 and 112–114 respectively, and present in 106–108 and 115–117, also respectively.) The selectional relations tested for are listed in 16 .

16.   S$_1$:   Verb–Object (*build a boat, climb a hill, send a letter*)

   S$_2$ (Extrap strings only): Subject–Predicate (*that S be surprising, that S be disturbing, that S be amusing*)

   S$_2$ (ExfrNP strings only): Subject–Verb (*a boat sink, a hill collapse, a letter arrive*)

   S$_3$:   Subject–Predicate (*that S be obvious, that S be apparent, that S be clear*)

All of the items testing for presence of Extrap or ExfrNP are interpretable in either of two ways: (*a*) If the subject has the rule in question, then the items consist of a string that violates semantic conditions on selectional relations and a string that is well formed (that is, they are tasks of Type B). (*b*) If, however, the subject does not have the rule, then the string in the derivation of which either rule has applied will (for the subject) violate constraints on the order of elements in the sentence, and the item will be interpreted as constituting a Type C task—one in which the subject must judge a string violating just semantic constraints as more grammatical than a string violating constraints in order of elements. An expected response to one of these items was therefore interpreted as indicating presence of the rule in question, a contrary response as indicating absence of the rule

Criteria for presence of a given structure, rule, etc., were determined in accordance with two measures: (*a*) the number of points accrued by a given subject on items testing the structure, based on a point system to be discussed immediately below; and (*b*) the degree of grammatical complexity of the items.

Each subject was assigned points on items in accordance with the scheme given in Table C-2. The number of points obtained by a subject was calculated separately for the items relevant to each hypothesis at each level of complexity. Criteria were set for each such class of items so that the probability of the subject's obtaining that number of points was less than .05 (multinomial distribution). For example, there were 12 Simp/Simp items testing the subjects' ability to do tasks of Type B. Since, for Type B tasks, the maximum total points that could be obtained by a subject on each item was 2, the maximum for all 12 items was 24. The smallest number of points such that $p < .05$ was

18. Therefore, the criterion for mastery of tasks of this Type (B) at this level of complexity (Simp/Simp) was set at 18/24 points ($p = .025$).[8]

Table C-2.   Point Assignment Scheme

Task type	Subject's response	Points
A–C	Expected	2
	Neutral	1
	Contrary	0
D	Expected	1
	Unexpected	0

The items were ordered in the questionnaire in terms of the grammatical complexity of their included strings with the simpler items placed earlier. Complexity entered into determining presence of a structure in the following way: If a subject failed to meet criterion on an early, simple set of items testing for the structure but succeeded in meeting criterion on a later, more complex set, then he was considered as having met criterion for the structure on the whole on the grounds that the early failure to meet criterion must have been due to some extraneous factor, such as nonfamiliarity with the task of making relative grammaticality judgments, etc. It was thus necessary for a subject to fail on the most complex items testing a structure to be considered as having failed to meet criterion for that structure in general. For example, suppose a subject failed to meet criterion for presence of Relative Clause Formation on Items 49–51 (all Simp/SComp) but succeeded in meeting it on Items 94–96 (all DComp/DComp). Such a subject would be considered as possessing Relative Clause Formation.

[8]One would ordinarily consider loss to be supported if Alternatives I–III are not confirmed at, say, $p < .05$. The criteria set here are stated as criteria for **confirmation** (at $p < .05$) of the **denials** of Alternatives I–III. The effect is to make confirmation of loss less probable since it makes it easier for subjects to meet criterion for these alternatives (strictly speaking, easier to **fail** to meet criterion for their denials).

APPENDIX D   INDIVIDUAL RESULTS

All results are given in terms of the point scheme of Table C-2 (Appendix C) unless otherwise noted.

Table D-1.   Ability to Do Tasks

Task type	A	B			C	D		
Complexity	Simp/Simp	Simp/Simp	Simp/SComp	SComp/SComp	Simp/Simp	Simp/Simp	Simp/SComp	DComp/DComp
Items	1–3 16–18 28–30	4–6 13–15 19–21 31–33	34–39	40–48	7–9	10–12	25–27	91–93 100–102
Criterion	14/18	18/24	10/12	14/18	6/6	3/3	3/3	5/6
p	.032	.025	.038	.032	.037	.037	.037	.018
Subject								
01	18	23	12	18	3	3	3	5
02	18	24	12	18	6	3	3	6
03	18	22	12	18	4	3	3	4
04	14	23	10	18	6	3	3	3
05	18	23	12	18	6	3	0	6
06	18	24	12	18	6	3	0	3
07	18	24	12	18	6	3	3	4
08	18	23	12	18	6	3	3	6
09	18	24	12	16	6	3	3	6
10	18	23	11	18	6	3	3	6
11	18	23	12	18	6	3	3	6
12	18	24	12	18	6	3	3	6
13	18	24	12	18	6	3	3	6
14	18	24	12	18	6	3	3	6
15	18	24	12	18	6	3	3	2
16	18	23	12	18	6	3	3	0
17	17	23	12	18	6	3	3	3
18	18	23	12	18	6	3	3	6
19	18	24	12	18	6	3	3	6
20	18	23	12	18	6	3	0	6

Table D-2. Basic Structures and Lexicon[a]

Structure	S_1 verb–object	S_2 (Extrap Ss) subject–adjective			S_2 (ExfrNP Ss) subject–verb	S_3 subject–adjective
Complexity	Simp/Simp	Simp/Simp	Simp/SComp	SComp/SComp	Simp/Simp	Simp/SComp
Items	4–6	19–21 22–24	34–36 37–39	40–42 46–48	31–33	43–45
Criterion	6/6	10/12	10/12	10/12	6/6	6/6
p	.037	.038	.038	.038	.037	.037
Subject						
01	6	12	12	12	5	6
02	6	12	12	12	6	6
03	6	11	12	12	5	6
04	6	12	10	12	5	6
05	6	12	12	12	6	6
06	6	12	12	12	6	6
07	6	12	12	12	6	6
08	6	12	12	12	6	6
09	6	12	12	10	6	6
10	6	12	11	12	6	6
11	6	12	12	12	6	6
12	6	12	12	12	6	6
13	6	12	12	12	6	6
14	6	12	12	12	6	6
15	6	12	12	12	6	6
16	6	12	12	12	5	6
17	6	12	12	12	6	6
18	6	12	11	11	5	6
19	6	12	12	12	6	6
20	6	12	12	12	6	6

[a] See 16 in text, p. 55.

Table D-3. Transformations

Rule	Relative Clause Formation				Extraposition			Extraposition-from-NP	
Complexity	Simp/ SComp	SComp/ SComp	SComp/ SComp (ExfrNP)[a]	DComp/ DComp	Simp/ SComp	SComp/ SComp	SComp/ DComp	SComp/ SComp	DComp/ DComp
Items	49–51	52–54 55–57	82–84	94–96	58–60 61–63 64–66	67–69 70–72 73–75 76–78	88–90	79–81	97–99
Criterion	6/6	10/12	6/6	6/6	14/18	18/24	6/6	6/6	6/6
p	.037								
Subject									
01	5	10	5	4	18	22	6	4	5
02	4	12	6	6	18	24	6	0	6
03	6	12	6	6	18	24	6	6	4
04	6	12	4	5	18	24	6	6	5
05	5	10	6	5	16	24	6	6	3
06	0	12	6	6	18	24	6	0	6
07	0	12	6	6	18	24	6	0	6
08	6	12	6	6	18	24	6	6	6
09	6	12	6	6	18	24	6	6	6
10	6	12	3	6	15	24	6	0	3
11	6	12	6	6	18	24	6	0	0
12	6	12	3	4	18	24	6	2	2
13	6	12	6	6	18	24	6	0	0
14	6	12	6	6	18	24	6	6	6
15	6	12	6	6	18	24	6	0	6
16	5	12	6	6	18	24	6	6	6
17	6	12	6	6	18	24	6	0	0
18	6	12	6	6	18	24	6	6	6
19	6	12	6	6	18	24	6	6	6
20	6	12	6	6	18	24	6	6	6

[a] Items 82–84 required the subject to make judgments in keeping with the presence or absence of Relative Clause Formation in sentences i
from-NP had applied.

Table D-4. Alternatives to Distance (Rather Than Structure) as the Basis of RRC Judgments[a]

	Extraposition sentences						Extraposition-from-NP sentences		
Condition	Long predicates grammatical in general				Long predicates as grammatical as short predicates		Long predicates grammatical in general		Long predicates as grammatical as short predicates
Complexity	Simp/ Simp	Simp/ SComp	SComp/ SComp	SComp/ DComp	Simp/ Simp	DComp/ DComp	Simp/ Simp	SComp/ SComp	DComp/ DComp
Items	22–24	37–39	46–48 76–78	88–90	25–27	91–93	31–33	55–57 85–87	100–102
Criterion	6/6	6/6	10/12	6/6	*b*		6/6	10/12	*b*
p	.037	.037	.038	.037			.037	.038	
Subject									
01	6	6	10	6	+	+	5	11	−
02	6	6	12	6	+	+	6	12	+
03	6	6	12	6	+	+	5	9	−
04	6	6	12	6	+	+	6	12	−
05	6	6	12	6	+	+	6	10	+
06	6	6	12	6	−	+	6	12	+
07	6	6	12	6	−	+	6	12	−
08	6	6	12	6	+	+	6	12	+
09	6	6	12	6	+	+	6	12	+
10	6	5	12	6	+	+	6	9	+
11	6	6	12	6	+	+	6	8	+
12	6	6	12	0	+	+	6	12	−
13	6	6	12	0	+	+	6	9	+
14	6	6	12	6	+	+	6	12	+
15	6	6	12	6	+	+	6	8	+
16	6	6	12	6	+	+	5	12	+
17	6	6	12	6	+	+	6	6	−
18	6	6	12	6	+	+	5	12	+
19	6	6	12	6	+	+	6	12	+
20	6	6	12	6	−	+	6	12	+

[a] These results are relevant to the confirmation of retention only if the subject exhibits outcome 3a. (See section on Results, pp. 41–42.
[b] The criterion here was met if the subject judged the string with the long predicate to be as grammatical as or more grammatical than the string containing the shorter predicate. + = criterion met. − = criterion not met. Recall that Items 85, 86, 91–93, 100–102 failed to meet criterion when test constituted evidence that distance-rather-than-structure was **not** a satisfactory explanation for a subject's failure to meet criterion on structure-not-distance items (Table D-5) if they had tested out with control subjects. Since they did not, this alternative to distance-rather-than-structure was not testable.

Table D-5. **Presence or Absence of the RRC: Structure Rather Than Distance as the Basis for the RRC**

	Extrap sentences			ExfrNP sentences		
	Presence of RRC		Absence of RRC	Presence of RRC		Absence of RRC
Condition	Direct	Structure not distance	Direct	Direct	Structure not distance	Direct
Items	103–105 106–108	109–111	103–105 106–108 109–111	112–114 115–117	118–120	112–114 115–117 118–120
Criterion	10/12 points	6/6 points	9/9^a Neutral or contrary	10/12 points	6/6 points	9/9^a Neutral or contrary
p	.038	.037	.039	.038	.037	.039
Subject						
01	12	6	0	10	6	2
02	12	6	0	12	6	0
03	12	6	0	8	3	6
04	12	6	0	12	6	0
05	12	6	0	6	3	9
06	12	6	0	12	6	0
07	12	6	0	12	6	0
08	7	3	8	6	3	9
09	7	3	8	6	3	9
10	12	6	0	7	3	8
11	12	6	0	12	6	0
12	12	0	3	12	6	0
13	12	6	0	6	3	9
14	12	6	0	12	6	0
15	12	6	0	12	6	0
16	12	6	0	12	3	3
17	12	6	0	12	6	0
18	12	6	0	10	6	1
19	12	6	0	12	6	0
20	12	5	1	12	6	0

^{a}The criterion in this case is nine (of nine) unexpected responses. The number given in the column is the number of such responses.

ACKNOWLEDGMENTS

I wish to acknowledge gratefully the contribution of the 28 subjects of this study, without whose unremunerated and voluntary participation it would have been impossible. I wish also to thank Ms. Masako Katoh for her assistance in contacting subjects, translating instructions into Japanese, and tabulating results—all of which made the study considerably less difficult and more enjoyable than it would have been otherwise.

The results of this study appeared in a highly preliminary form in a paper entitled "Constraints on Adult-Acquired Syntax" delivered before the winter meeting of the Linguistic Society of America, December, 1972, Atlanta, Georgia.

REFERENCES

Bever, T. 1970. The cognitive basis for linguistic structures. In J. Hayes (Ed.), *Cognition and the development of language*. New York: Wiley. Pp. 279–352.

Bever, T. 1975. Psychologically real grammar emerges because of its role in language acquisition. In D. Dato (Ed.), *Developmental psycholinguistics: Theory and applications*. Georgetown University Round Table on Languages and Linguistics. Washington, D.C.: Georgetown Univ. School of Languages and Linguistics. Pp. 63–75.

Chomsky, N. 1965. *Aspects of the theory of syntax*. Cambridge, Massachusetts: MIT Press.

Chomsky, N. 1973. Conditions on transformations. In S. Anderson & P. Kiparsky (Eds.), *A festschrift for Morris Halle*. New York: Holt. Pp. 232–286.

Corder, S. 1967. The significance of learner's errors. *IRAL, 5*, 161–170.

Diller, K. 1971. *Generative grammar, structural linguistics, and language teaching*. Rowley, Massachusetts: Newberry House.

Dulay, H., & Burt, M. 1974. A new perspective on the creative construction process in child second language acquisition. *Language Learning, 24*, 253–278.

Grosu, A. 1973. On the status of the so-called right roof constraint. *Language, 49*, 294–311.

Hymes, D. 1964. Introduction: Toward ethnographies of communication. In J. Gumperz & D. Hymes (Eds.), The ethnography of communication. *American Anthropologist, 66* (2), 1–34.

Krashen, S. 1975. A model of adult second language performance. Paper presented at the winter meeting of the Linguistic Society of America, San Francisco, California, December.

Krashen, S. 1977. Language acquisition and language learning in the late entry bilingual education program. In E. Briere (Ed.), *Language development in a bilingual setting*. Los Angeles: Language Development and Assessment Center, California State University.

Krashen, S., Sferlazza, V., Feldman, L., & Fathman, A. 1976. Adult performance on the SLOPE test: More evidence for a natural sequence in adult second language acquisition. *Language Learning, 26*, 145–151.

Kuno, S. 1972. Natural explanations for some syntactic universals. In *Report No. NSF-28 to the National Science Foundation*. Cambridge, Massachusetts: Computation Laboratory of Harvard Univ.

Larsen-Freeman, D. 1976. An explanation for the morpheme acquisition order of second language learners. *Language Learning, 26*, 125–134.

Lenneberg, E. 1967. *Biological foundations of language*. New York: Wiley.

Macnamara, J. 1975. Comparison between first and second language learning. In *Working Papers on Bilingualism, no. 7*. Toronto: Ontario Institute for Studies in Education. Pp. 71–95.

Oyama, S. 1973. A sensitive period for the acquisition of a second language. Unpublished Ph.D. dissertation, Harvard Univ.

Palmer, H. 1964. *The principles of language-study*. New York: Oxford Univ. Press.

Ross, J. 1967. *Constraints on variables in syntax*. Unpublished Ph.D. dissertation, MIT.

Schachter, J. 1974. An error in error analysis. *Language Learning, 24,* 205–214.

Seliger, H., Krashen, S., & Ladefoged, P. 1975. Maturational constraints in the acquisition of second language accent. *Language Sciences, 36,* 20–22.

Slobin, D. 1973. Cognitive prerequisites for the development of grammar. In C. Ferguson & D. Slobin (Eds.), *Studies of child language development*. New York: Holt. Pp. 175–208.

Taylor, B. 1975. The use of overgeneralization and transfer learning strategies by elementary and intermediate students in ESL. *Language Learning, 25,* 73–107.

5 Some remarks on creativity in language acquisition[1]

Heidi Dulay
Marina Burt

It may seem superfluous to devote a chapter to general remarks on creativity since it appears that virtually no one today would deny the creative participation of the learner in the acquisition process. The combined effects of Chomsky's revival of the "creative aspects of language use" as a major focus of theoretical linguistics, along with the complementary efforts of Piaget in developmental psychology, have given creativity a central place in contemporary psycholinguistics.

Thus far in psycholinguistic research, however, we have not been able to specify with much clarity or precision the ways in which the learner is creative. While analyses of developing learner speech generally support the view of the learner as an active and creative participant in the acquisition process, the absence of specific principles to explain all the facts that have been accumulating in journals and anthologies is perhaps the greatest difficulty apparent in the "creative" approach to language acquisition. It seems important, therefore, to attempt to operationalize at least some of the aspects of creativity that seem basic to an explanation of language learning behavior.

[1]H. Dulay and M. Burt, "Remarks on Creativity in Language Acquisition," in M. Burt, H. Dulay, and M. Finocchiaro, Eds., *Viewpoints on English as a Second Language* (New York: Regents Publishing Co., 1977), reprinted by permission.

We briefly review two widely used and different notions of creativity and present a partial model of certain creative aspects of second langugage (L_2) acquisition. A variety of facts collected from the existing empirical literature are then gathered together to demonstrate (a) the mediating (creative) role of affective and cognitive structures on input during the acquisition process, and (b) the role of input factors in a creative construction framework. Special emphasis is given to frequency of occurrence of grammatical structures in the learner's input. In light of the apparent interaction between learner and environment, we suggest how frequency might be viewed within a creative construction framework.

DEFINITION OF CREATIVITY

The term **creativity** has been used in several disciplines—education, psychology, linguistics, and language acquisition—in two distinct and, in some respects, contradictory ways. Although in both senses of the term some notion of independence is implied, the notion of creativity often used in education and psychology is substantially different from that used in linguistics and language acquisition.

In education, "creative thinking" and "creative writing" often connote an ability to produce ideas, solutions to problems, or twists of words and phrases that do not conform to what is most frequently produced by most people. For example, using cooked rice as glue would.be considered a creative use of rice. And the phrase *as cold as a polar bear's whiskers* would be considered more creative than *as cold as ice* (cf. Renzulli, 1973). Creativity in this sense refers to the independence of some individuals from some tendency or norm set by the majority.

This use of the term derives much of its theoretical basis from the thinking and empirical research on creativity in psychology, largely inspired by the work of J. P. Guilford and his associates on a structure-of-the-intellect model (cf. Wallach, 1970). Guilford introduced the notion of creativity as "divergent thinking"—a cognitive process that involves coming up with many different possible alternatives in response to a problem or to the task of processing information—as opposed to "convergent thinking," which refers to zeroing in on the one correct answer (cf. Guilford, 1967).[2] For example, to answer the question *Which state*

---

[2]Torrance (1966a) extends Guilford's concept of creativity to include any problem-solving or hypothesis-generating activity whether it be convergent or divergent in nature. He defines creative thinking as

a process of becoming sensitive to problems, deficiencies, gaps in knowledge, missing elements, disharmonies, and so on: identifying the difficulty; searching for solutions, making guesses, or formulating hypotheses about the deficiencies; testing and retesting these hypotheses and possibly modifying and retesting them; and finally communicating the results [Torrance, 1966a, p. 6].

borders California on the north? one would simply employ convergent thinking skills in order to arrive at the one correct answer (Oregon). However, the request *Name as many uses of a shovel as you can* taps divergent thinking skills. Someone who offered 20 uses of a shovel would be considered more creative than one who offered only 5, and the less conventional the use, the more creative. An artist's use of a shovel as a "found object" to display in an art gallery might be considered highly creative. In this sense of creativity not everyone is creative, and those who are exhibit a certain independence from conventional thinking and behavior.

In linguistics, on the other hand, the essence of creativity is the use of rules and conventions of a language. Speakers can express an indefinite and infinite number of thoughts using sentences never heard before because they have internalized a system of rules that governs ordinary language use (cf. Chomsky, 1965, p. 6). Because speakers regularly produce and understand sentences never heard before, they are said to use the language creatively. For example, *Grandmother had a hair transplant yesterday* or *Ed is overjoyed that his paper is finally done* are ordinary sentences. They are creative in the linguistic sense, however, because the speaker generated such sentences from an internalized rule system rather than as a result of having heard, imitated, and memorized them. Linguistic creativity then is not the privilege of a select few who might be poets. It is characteristic of all normal speakers of any language.

Creativity in language acquisition derives from the linguistic notion; it is also attributed to all normal learners. It too refers to **a degree of learner independence from external input factors** such as the exact form of modeled utterances, frequency of occurrence, or rewards for correctness. While for mature speakers, creativity stems from a control of the rules of the language they speak, for language **learners,** creativity stems from the structure of those mental mechanisms responsible for learning the rules of a new language. Thus, as has been suggested elsewhere, "creative construction" in language acquisition refers to the process by which learners gradually reconstruct rules for speech they hear, guided by innate mechanisms which cause them to formulate certain types of hypotheses about the language system being acquired, until the mismatch between what they are exposed to and what they produce is resolved.

Examples of this creativity abound. Valdman (1974), for example, studied American college students in a beginning French class who had little opportunity to hear French outside the classroom. He states that the "most striking feature of the data . . . is the relatively high incidence of the WH-fronting type of question, e.g., *Où Jean va?* [in spite of the fact that] the subjects were exposed only to the inversion and *est-ce que* types of question [e.g., *Où va Jean?* and *Qu'est-ce que*

This construct is operationalized in a battery of instruments he designed to measure individual creativity (Torrance, 1966b).

vous étudiez ici? respectively]." He concludes that "it can be asserted with confidence that the WH-fronting type questions they produced were generated by some sort of reconstructing process rather than direct imitation [p. 14]." He also points out that the "corresponding structure in L1 can be rapidly eliminated as a potential source [p. 15]." Examples of this sort from children learning a first or second language have been presented in numerous papers, as we shall see later. In sum then, creativity in language learning refers to the human learner's predisposition to organize input in ways that exhibit a certain independence from external environmental characteristics. This aspect of language acquisition is believed to be rooted in innate and universal structural properties of the mind.

The last discussed notion of creativity is the sense in which we use the term in this chapter. It has inspired both first and second language acquisition researchers to undertake extensive investigations of learners' developing speech in order to determine whether learners were in fact creative—whether their verbal behavior could be considered reflections of universal cognitive structure. Much of the research supports the position that creativity is an essential factor in explaining language acquisition behavior, though some of the recent research indicates a discomfort with attributing much of the learner's progress to internal processing mechanisms, to the neglect of input factors. It seems timely, therefore, to place into perspective the role of internal "creative" mechanisms vis-à-vis input in language acquisition. One might simply ask: When does input—its form, its frequency, and its intensity—**not** affect learning, and when does it exert its influence? We begin with the first half of the question: In what specific ways does the human mind mediate input? In other words: In what ways is language acquisition creative?

Given the myriad conscious and unconscious internal factors interacting with input to produce learner speech, it may not be possible to isolate these entirely. Nonetheless, given the data available at the present time, it appears we may attribute certain discrepancies between input and learner output to at least five very general but distinct sources: a **socioaffective filter,** a **cognitive organizer,** a **monitor, personality,** and **past experience** (the first language).

The socioaffective filter refers to conscious or unconscious motives or needs, attitudes or emotional states of the learner. As the term suggests, these filter the input and affect the rate and quality of language acquisition. Among other things, the socioaffective filter contributes to (*a*) individual preferences for certain input models over others; (*b*) prioritizing aspects of language to be learned; and (*c*) determining when language acquisition efforts should cease. For example, depending on various criteria, a learner will "tune in" more to certain speakers of the language rather than others.

In addition to learning from certain models rather than from others, learners acquire certain types of verbal routines or vocabulary items rather than others, and some stop acquiring the target language at a point before they reach nativelike proficiency. All these types of behavior may be attributed to affective factors interacting with external sociolinguistic factors. These delimit to a significant extent the input data which is made available to the cognitive organizers.

The importance of taking into account the possible effects of socioaffective filtering of input on child verbal performance cannot be overemphasized. When child speech is not entirely consonant with that of the speakers to whom the child is being compared (say, the teacher or certain other children in the community), one may not simply assume that the discrepancy is the result of delayed or incorrect learning; it is entirely possible that due to certain sociolinguistic circumstances, the child prefers to acquire forms other than those used as the norm. This very important distinction between **cannot** learn versus **prefers not** to learn must be made before it is justifiable to conclude that the child's speech is the result of learning disabilities.

The cognitive organizer refers to the internal data processing mechanisms responsible for the construction of the grammar we attribute to the learner. It is what Chomsky has referred to as the "Language Acquisition Device," and what others have called the "black box." The cognitive organizer contributes, among other things, to (a) the error types that occur systematically in developing speech; (b) the progression of rules that learners use before a structure is mastered; and (c) the order in which structures are acquired.

Slobin (1971a), for instance, provides a classic example of the development of the past tense morpheme in English: The past tense of *break* and *drop* are first expressed as *broke* and *drop*; then when the child acquires the -*ed* rule for past tense formation, the forms *breaked* and *dropped* are used. As the child learns that the long form of the past tense ending -*ed* is used with words ending in *t* and *d,* the two words are further regularized to *breakted* and *dropted,* and only in the final stage are the correct forms sorted out. These kinds of examples, as well as others, make it obvious that children do not learn their language by successive approximations to the adult norm through a process of more and more correct imitations. Rather, they actively and creatively build up the rules of the emerging grammar, constructing hypotheses about the form that it should take.

A third source of creative activity is the monitor (Krashen, 1977), which may be defined as the conscious editing of one's own speech. The degree to which speech is edited depends upon individual criteria as well as the nature and focus of the task being performed. Concern over grammatical correctness is an individual criterion operating in many individuals. This concern often results in a great deal of editing, as seen in numerous hesitations or constant self-correction. On the other hand, tasks which cause speakers to focus on communication tend to bring on less self-editing, while tasks whose focus is linguistic analysis (such as fill-in-the-blank or translation) seem to invite more editing.

It seems useful to think of the internal processing of language input as the successive operation of the socioaffective filter, the cognitive organizer, and the

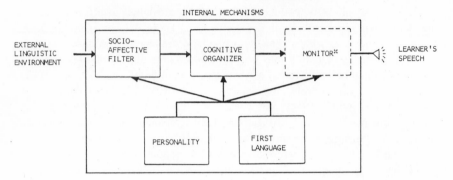

Figure 1.   Working model for some aspects of creative construction in second language acquisition. The monitor is enclosed in a broken-line box to indicate that it is not always active in language production.

monitor, in that order, with personality factors and first language experience influencing the operation of all three. For example, persons with outgoing, uninhibited personalities have been observed to monitor their speech infrequently, while self-conscious, introverted persons are more likely to overmonitor their speech (Krashen, 1977). Similarly, the past experience of having learned one's first language is integrated into some of the organizing strategies used by a learner to acquire a second language. This is evident for example, in certain aspects of the acquisition of phonology and the use of code alternation as a second language learning device.

Although our current knowledge of the L_2 acquisition process is far from detailed or complete, it is sufficient to begin to sketch the general outlines suggested by available research. The operation of internal factors in the language acquisition process just discussed is illustrated in Figure 1. As indicated in the figure, learners screen out certain linguistic input to which they are exposed, and organize the input they "tune in" to into a system of rules which gradually evolves as the learner continues to be exposed to natural speech in the target language. From their developing rule systems, learners generate the utterances we study, diagnose, and hope will soon give way to the grammatical sentences of proficient speakers.

A detailed discussion of the operation of the monitor and of other internal factors such as personality and experience, including the role of first language acquisition experience and knowledge on second language acquisition,[3] is beyond the scope of this paper. We simply wish here to indicate their suggested place in this scheme. We shall discuss in greater detail, however, research data that point to affective filtering and cognitive organization of input.

[3]For a detailed discussion of issues on this topic, see Dulay and Burt, 1972, 1974a, 1975a; Hernández-Chávez, 1977a.

EVIDENCE FOR AFFECTIVE FILTERING OF INPUT

A review of the second language research literature shows that the clearest examples of affective filtering of input involve an apparent preference for certain speaker models over others under certain circumstances, for example, preference for peers over teachers, peers over parents, and own ethnic group members over nonmembers.

Preference for certain models is clearly demonstrated by learners acquiring one of two dialects to which they are exposed in daily communication. Milon (1975) reports that a 7-year-old Japanese-speaking child who had immigrated to Hawaii learned the Hawaiian Creole English of his agemates rather than the Standard English of his teachers during his first school year. When he moved to a middle-class neighborhood the following year, however, he quickly picked up the Standard English that his new friends spoke. In explaining this phenomenon, Milon states that "there is no question that the first dialect of English these young immigrant children learn is the dialect of their peers, and that they learn it from their peers. If they learn productive control of the dialect of their teachers it is not until later . . . [Milon, 1975: p. 159]."

A similar example—in this case showing L$_1$ learners' preference for peers' speech over parents'—is provided by Stewart (see Dale, 1976, p. 281) who reports that the black children he studied in Washington, D.C., learn the dialect used by their peers (a dialect of Black English that is most different from Standard English), rather than the dialect used by their parents (a dialect of Black English closest to Washington, D.C., Standard English). Likewise, Labov (1972) finds that both black and white children in a middle-class area of northeastern New Jersey learn to pronounce the r's before consonants as their New Jersey friends do, rather than drop the r's as their New York raised parents do. These data too show "that children learn more language behavior from members of their own peer group than from their parents . . . [Dale, 1976, p. 281]."

Finally, Benton (1964) reports that Maori children learn the English dialect of their own ethnic group rather than standard New Zealand English. In some cases this model preference is consciously articulated:

> One teacher reported that a Maori child had told her: "Maoris say *Who's your name,* so that's what I say." Maori English is often an important sign of group membership and a source of security for these children [Benton, 1964, p. 93; Richards, 1974, p. 169].

The examples we have presented here demonstrating the individual's affective filtering of input through model preference represent only one of many types of end products whose source lies in the basic psychological need to identify with and belong to a social group (peers over nonpeers, etc.). Since language is an important identification marker of social groups, it is to be expected that language learners and users should show the kinds of preferences we have seen for speaker models representing their preferred group.[4]

More in-depth investigations of affective filtering of input would probably be closely tied to the study of sociolinguistic features of primary linguistic data. A full treatment of these important issues is unfortunately beyond the scope of this chapter. Here we simply suggest that affective factors cause learners to filter their linguistic input in particular ways, resulting in various observed differences between learner speech and that of the total input. We are suggesting that such differences cannot be explained by appealing to a description of linguistic input alone; rather, such descriptions must be accompanied by a specification of the various kinds of internal forces which operate on linguistic input and the conditions under which they operate. These are just beginning to receive serious attention.

EVIDENCE FOR COGNITIVE CREATIVITY

As was mentioned earlier, the notion of creativity in language acquisition entails the assumption that internal processors make a contribution to learning progress that is independent of the contribution made by input. Part of the evidence for cognitive creativity, therefore, involves demonstrating discrepancies between the actual characteristics of the learner's output and what might be predicted if input factors alone were responsible for the learner's progress (taking into consideration, of course, possible effects of affective filtering of input). The research findings summarized here are grouped according to the input factors which have been shown to be mediated in systematic ways. They include the form, perceptual salience, and frequently of input structures; corrective feedback; and reinforcement.

Form of Input Structures: Contiguity of Elements in Speech Patterns

The systematic deviations from the structure of the sentences learners hear in their environment comprised the initial glimpses of creativity in language acquisition. Researchers noticed that language learners systematically produced constructions they could not have heard before, and which could thus be explained only by an appeal to human cognitive organization. Utterances such as *Adam hit ball* (Brown, 1973b), *No wipe finger* (Klima & Bellugi, 1966), and *Mommy sock* (Bloom, 1970) have become part of the standard repertoire of first language

[4]There are many examples, of course, of proficient speakers who interact at a variety of levels and with more than one social group. These speakers typically control the languages, dialects, or styles appropriate for interaction with the particular group at the appropriate time.

acquisition researchers, as have "overgeneralizations" such as *digged, goed,* and *childs,* which have even found their way into papers on adult foreign language learning as well as child second language acquisition. The observed deviations from well-formed sentences are not haphazard lapses of memory or poor attempts at imitation. Rather, the occurrence of systematic errors comprises "the best evidence we have that the child possesses construction rules [Brown, 1973a]."

Countless first language (L_1) acquisition studies have made this point, including L_1 research on some 33 languages other than English (cf. Brown, 1973a, Ch. 1). See, for example, Klima and Bellugi (1966), Cazden (1972), Brown (1973a), among others, and Dale (1976) for a comprehensive review of that literature.

Second language acquisition research, following closely on the heels of the advances made in first language studies, provides similar evidence. Since this research has been summarized elsewhere (cf. Dulay & Burt, 1975a, b), suffice it to mention here that error types that can best be explained by positing some creative restructuring process on the part of the learner have been observed in child second language speech (Dulay & Burt, 1972, 1974a; Ervin-Tripp, 1974; Hernández-Chávez, 1972; Venable, 1974, among others), as well as in adult second and foreign language performance (Richards, 1971, 1974; Taylor, 1975; Valdman, 1974, among others). Additionally, L_2 learners, like L_1 learners, pass through certain steps in the acquisition of negatives and interrogatives. (For negation see Gillis & Weber, 1976; Hernández-Chávez, 1972. For Wh-questions, see Ravem, 1974.)

Learners' systematic use of novel construction rules during the process of acquiring syntactic structures makes up the bulk of the research evidence for the role of cognitive organizers in language acquisition.

Perceptual Salience

Perceptual salience is an input factor that has not as yet been precisely defined, though general descriptions such as "amount of phonetic substance, stress level, usual serial position in a sentence, and so on [Brown, 1973a:, p. 409]" have been used to give it a general meaning in the research literature. Salience may be defined solely in terms of input characteristics (in which case it would be analogous to the notion of "stimulus intensity" in behaviorist learning theory); or its definition may include internal processing factors which cause certain features in the learner's input to **become** salient. This discussion refers only to the former sense of the term which is implied in most of the relevant literature.

Perceptual salience is commonly mentioned by some L_2 researchers as a potential predictor of order of acquisition; that is, the more perceptually salient an item is, the sooner it should be learned if its effects remain unmitigated. There is evidence, however, that learners do indeed regulate potential effects of perceptual salience: They do not acquire grammatical morphemes that are equally salient at the same time, nor are the potential effects of the different degrees of salience of certain structures realized.

Consider, for example, some of the s morphemes whose order of acquisition in oral production has been studied extensively for both first and second language learners. In L_2 research, it has been found repeatedly that the contracted form of the singular copula (as in "He's fat") and the short plural morpheme (as in "windows") are learned early. The short possessive (as in "the king's") and the third person indicative (as in "sees") are learned much later, however. (See, for example, Dulay & Burt, 1974b, 1975a; Burt, Dulay, & Hernández-Chávez, 1976; Fathman, 1975, for children; and Krashen, Madden, & Bailey, 1975; and Larsen-Freeman, 1976a for adults.) It is clear that perceptual salience, generally defined, cannot underlie this acquisition order, since the phonetic substance and stress levels of these s morphemes are virtually the same. The early acquisition of the contractible singular copula is especially interesting, since its sentence medial position presumably makes it less salient than it would be in, say, final position. (The differential acquisition of these morphemes was also found by Brown for his L_1 learners, although some of the specific items were ordered differently.)

The last example we will mention in this context (though there are many more) is the late acquisition of the long plural morpheme -es relative to the short plural -s. Even though the long plural is syllabic and the short plural is not, the long plural is acquired much later than the short plural. (Burt et al., 1976, or Dulay & Burt, 1974b, 1975b). The opposite order would be predicted by perceptual salience.

Frequency of Occurrence

When frequency is discussed as an input variable in language acquisition research, it refers to the number of times a given structure has presumably occurred in a learner's immediate linguistic environment. For example, one might count how many times Wh-questions occurred in the speech of a mother to her child during some discourse situations that might be representative of the child's total input. The count would be considered the frequency of Wh-questions in the child's input. The relation of this input variable to learner speech has received considerable attention in language acquisition research.

Perhaps the most systematic and extensive evidence of the unpredictable relationship between external frequency and language learning comes from first language acquisition research. It is now well known that the order of acquisition of morphemes found by Brown for his three children learning English barely correlated with the frequencies with which those morphemes occurred in the speech of the children's parents in parent–child discourse. The Spearman rank order correlation (ρ) between the rank order of acquisition (averaged across the children) with the rank order of frequency (averaged across the pairs of parents) was very low (+.26) leading to Brown's conclusion that "no relation has been demonstrated to exist between parental frequencies and child's order of acquisition [Brown, 1973a, p. 362]."

A second example of the mitigation of external frequency pressures—this time in second language acquisition—may be extracted from the data presented in Wagner-Gough and Hatch (1975). In their observations of a child learning English as a second language, they report that although two types of questions occurred with equal frequency in their subject's linguistic input, only one type of question was produced correctly and not the other. The Wh-questions *What's X?* and *Where's X?* were produced correctly, whereas the question which required copula inversion (*Is this X?*) was not. Thus we observe the selective learning of one question type, in spite of the equal frequency of occurrence of two types in the input data.

Of course, all of the novel constructions and systematic errors found in learner speech (see above) remain the most pervasive phenomena that cannot possibly be attributed to input frequency. Recall, for example, Valdman's finding, described earlier, that a significant number of American college students learning French in his class (in the United States) produced an intermediate question form which did not occur in their input at all.

Finally, consider the well-known fact that specific grammatical morphemes in English occur more frequently than specific major content words; and yet, "the early absence and long delayed acquisition of those more frequent forms has always thrown up a challenge to the notion that frequency is a major variable in language learning . . . [Brown, 1973a, p. 362]." The relatively late acquisition of grammatical morphemes compared to content words has also become an established fact for second language learners. Here again it seems as though factors other than frequency are operating to determine learning priorities.

Corrective Feedback

Experienced language teachers have long known that providing students with the correct forms of their imperfect utterances can be immensely frustrating. Although students say they want corrective feedback (Cathcart & Olson, 1976) and teachers try to provide as much as they can, it is all too obvious, and painful for both teachers and students, that many errors are impervious to correction. In fact, Cohen and Robbins (1976) found that the effects of correction in the written work of university ESL students in the United States did not actually influence the production of errors. Although the authors believe this lack of influence was caused by factors relating to the quality and systematicity of the corrections, we see no justifiable reason to expect significantly different results with better or more systematic correction techniques.

In first language acquisition, Cazden's experiment (Cazden, 1965) on the effect of **expansions** is the classic study along these lines. It was hypothesized that systematic modeling of the grammatically correct versions of children's utterances (expansions) might be a major force in acquisition progress. To most everyone's surprise, Cazden found that expansions had no effect whatsoever on the speech of the children she studied.

These findings suggest that more "systematic" feedback may not be the answer. More **selective** feedback, tailored to the learner's internal level of linguistic development, may be more effective.[5] We return to this later.

Reinforcement

Another input factor that has received some attention, albeit only in the first language literature so far, is reinforcement. Although Chomsky (1959) has shown that an examination of the notion of reinforcement in the psychological literature reveals no consistent definition of "reinforcing behavior," the appeal of intuitive notions of reinforcement is so widespread that some pertinent research results may be worth mentioning here.

Using Skinner's notion that any sign of approval constitutes reinforcing behavior (Skinner, 1953, p. 78), Brown and Hanlon (1970) studied the effects of positive and negative reinforcement on children's developing speech. They used parental approval (determined by responses such as *That's right, Correct, Very good,* and *Yes*), and disapproval (as indicated by *That's wrong, That's not right,* or *No*) as indicators of positive and negative reinforcement. Brown and Hanlon report that there was not even "a shred of evidence that approval and disapproval are contingent on syntactic correctness [p. 47]," but rather that these are linked to the truth value of the proposition contained in the child's utterance.

Brown and Hanlon found a similar result when they studied a different form of reinforcement, namely "relevant and comprehending reactions" to the child's utterances, as opposed to irrelevant reactions, or no reaction at all. Here again, they found that reinforcing input does not affect the child's progress in acquiring grammatical forms.

Summary

So far, we have summarized available empirical data that indicate the influence of human cognition and affect on the course of language acquisition. Specifically, we have presented cases where certain input factors alone cannot possibly account for the speech produced. As we have seen, frequency, perceptual sa-

---

[5]A criterion for selective correction, based on ease of comprehension, has been suggested and worked out by Burt and Kiparsky (1972). See also Burt (1974).

lience or intensity, corrective feedback, reinforcement, and contiguity of elements in a structure cannot, by themselves, account for specific learning outcomes.

These observations must not be taken to imply that input factors are unimportant or negligible, rather that any theory or account of language acquisition, whether first or second, must take into account the independent and central contribution of internal mechanisms to the construction of the new language system.

Within this framework, and given the data presented so far, one might well ask with due concern, "What then is the role of input factors in the acquisition of productive syntactic rules?"

ROLE OF INPUT FACTORS

An increasing number of studies have attempted to describe the external environment of the language learner and have suggested input variables that affect the learning of syntax and morphology. What is usually presented are cases where certain learner outcomes mirror input factors, such as the observation that the relative frequency of *What's this?* and *Where's that?* matches their early use. The interpretation of such observations is typically that the given input factor is an "important determinant" of progress in language acquisition. However, as discussed earlier, high frequency or highly salient items, etc., are not always learned first. This dilemma leads one to suggest that the formulation of accurate and predictive principles concerning the effects of input factors on progress in acquisition might best be accomplished **by specifying conditions under which external factors will have an effect.** Such conditions may have to do with relationships among several input factors operating at the same time, and between input variables and internal processing factors.

A clear and important example of such an effort is the recent series of investigations conducted by Piagetian psychologists B. Inhelder, H. Sinclair, and M. Bovet (1974), who studied the effects of certain training procedures on children's progress in cognitive development. Although the study does not investigate language development per se, its assumptions, procedures, and findings should be extremely useful to language acquisition researchers interested in the effects of input factors.

Inhelder *et al.* conducted a series of learning experiments on the acquisition of the process of conservation and class inclusion. They selected 34 children aged 5:1 to 7:0 from the Genevan State nursery and primary schools. The children were selected on the basis of cognitive developmental levels; they ranged from those who never made a conservation judgment (Level 1) to those tho made such judgments most of the time (Level 4). The experimenters then provided various types of training sessions to see what their effect on the children's learning would be.

The training sessions "resembled the kind of situation in which [cognitive developmental] progress takes place outside an experimental set-up," that is, where children interact naturally with features of the environment provided by the experimenters, observing characteristics of objects and making judgments about them. "Experimental situations that might almost automatically elicit the correct answers were avoided [Inhelder *et al.*, 1974, p. 24]."

The training sessions (which were the same for all the children) had virtually no effect on the 15 children at the nonconservation level (only 2 of those children improved substantially), while most of the 19 intermediate level children progressed substantially. In other words, the more advanced children made real progress in cognitive development while the less advanced children did not, despite the fact that the input provided in the experimental conditions was the same (pp. 51–52). The authors take pains to point out that **all** the children noticed **all** the relevant observable features presented to them; however, only the more advanced children were able to use the information for solving the problem at hand. The beginners simply did not know how to use the observations they had made (p. 53). Apparently then, the effects of the "observable features" of the input help children develop their reasoning insofar as these features can be integrated into their developing cognitive system. The provision of appropriate input, therefore, accelerates cognitive development when the learner has reached a certain cognitive level that permits the formulation of certain kinds of judgments.

Although the findings of Inhelder *et al.* do not deal specifically with second language acquisition, they illustrate the importance of specifying principles of interaction between input factors and mental factors (rather than suggesting a conflicting relationship between internal mental mechanisms and external input or environment) in the explanation of learning. This approach makes it possible to predict when a certain type of input—in this case a type of training procedure will significantly affect learning, and when it will not.

Another treatment of input along these lines is included in E. Hernández-Chávez's 17-month longitudinal study of a Spanish-speaking child's acquisition of English grammatical structures and semantic relations (Hernández-Chávez, 1977a and b). Hernández made biweekly tape recordings of his subject Güero's verbal interactions with his nursery school classmates and the adults at the school. He found that a large portion of Güero's utterances during the first 8 months seemed to be composed, at least in part, of imitated elements of modeled utterances, for example,

Adult: You don't want it?
Güero: No want–it. I no want–it.

(where *want–it* is the reproduced portion of the modeled utterance). These he called "quasi-spontaneous utterances," since part of the utterance was freely produced and part was imitated from the model.

Upon closer examination and analysis of the discourse transcripts, Hernández noticed that there was much speech addressed to the child that was not integrated in quasi-spontaneous utterances until much later in the study, if at all. For example, although the imperative subject *you* (in the context of an imperative sentence such as *You look at me, OK?*) occurred regularly in the speech addressed to the child in every successive taping from month 2 on,[6] Güero did not make any attempt to use it until month 5.5, when it finally appeared in a quasi-spontaneous utterance:

Model: you read it
Guero: you read that

The structure was produced totally spontaneously shortly thereafter (in month 6). Many other examples of this sort are discussed at length in Hernández (1977b), where he demonstrates that for the 10 grammatical functions analyzed, a similar order of emergence in spontaneous and quasi-spontaneous utterances was evident.

From such observations, Hernández argues that the child was imitating input **selectively** based at least in part on the state of his developing grammar.[7] The only exceptions seemed to be a few "stretches of speech that were memorized and associated with very specific nonlinguistic contexts, such as games." He suggests that the child's apparent memorization and imitation of input must be placed into a wider creative context if these phenomena are to be fully understood.[8] Here again, as with the Inhelder *et al.* studies, the specification of an interaction between internal states and external input serves to increase the predictive power of a statement on the effects of input.

From these kinds of findings, it is clear that the investigation of the explanatory power of input in a theory of language acquisition is an important undertaking for both basic psycholinguistic research and for pedagogical advancement. Others share this view. For example, Hatch and Wagner-Gough (1976), Larsen-Freeman (1976a), and Wagner-Gough and Hatch (1975) attempt

[6]Hernández, personal communication. As frequency information was not reported in this paper, Hernández provided us with this information.

[7]The state of the child's construction of the new grammar also influences the structures used in code switches. For example, Güero produced *Este es yours* at the time he was "trying out" English possessives.

[8]Other researchers have also described the incorporation of apparently imitated portions of input by language learners (Clark, 1974, L_1; Hakuta, 1974, L_2; Wagner-Gough & Hatch, 1975, L_2, among others). Hernández is unique, however, in going beyond the description of the phenomenon to an attempt to relate the child's level of grammatical development to what is likely to be imitated.

to link various input factors with the order in which syntactic and morphological structures are learned. It is unfortunate, however, that these efforts have not resulted in a clear description of the role, weight, or precise functioning of the factors proposed. Characteristics of the input language, such as semantic value, communicative function, salience, frequency, number of forms, etc., are proposed to "account" for the early or late production of specific structures. For example, high frequency is suggested to account for early acquisition of *What's X?* and *Where's X?* while the later acquisition of *be* inversion questions, e.g., *Is this a book?* (which occur with the same frequency as the *What's X* and *Where's X* questions) is attributed to the low "semantic value" of *be* and its number of variant forms (Wagner-Gough & Hatch, 1975, p. 299). It is not the case, however, that the semantic value and potential number of forms of the copula in the first acquired structures are the same as those in the later to be acquired structures. Moreover, if the *'s* in the Wh-questions cited is not a productive part of the child's grammar but, rather, part of an unanalyzed fragment, the Wh-questions cannot be said to have been productively acquired yet. Even without these difficulties, one would expect a discussion of why these factors operate only some of the time.

It has been pointed out by others who have attempted to explain language learning behavior that input is the "other side" of the learning process. The unresolved question is the exact nature of the contribution of input. Brown and Hanlon ask, for example, "Why do data have an impact at some times and at other times no effect at all [1970, p. 50]?" Brown (1973a), Chomsky (1959, 1975, Ch. 4), Piaget (1970, Ch. 4), and others discuss various aspects of the possible role of input at some length. It seems, however, that these discussions have gone largely unnoticed in the papers mentioned above. For example, consider the following suggestion concerning how we might prioritize explanations of language learning data:

> Everyone of us has our biases and could assign priority to our favorites. For example, I happen to think that low semantic value, number of forms, number of functions, and perceptual salience account for late acquisition of the English definite article much more clearly than language universals or contrastive analysis. Most people who have taught students from Japan, Korea and China would disagree. . . . Perhaps an interesting experiment might be set up where we ask everyone who is working on second language learning . . . to look at sets of data and give explanations for each. Finally, they could rank or weight their explanations as they like [Hatch & Wagner-Gough, 1976, pp. 54–55].

Surely such an approach does not represent the kind of methodology required to advance our understanding of language acquisition. It seems more likely that attempts to deal with input factors in relation to learner factors within a cohesive theoretical framework and a well-developed methodology (such as Inhelder *et al.* and Hernández have done) may prove more productive.

Correlations and Causality

Another potential weakness in the study of input effects on learning is the erroneous treatment of statistical correlations as **causal** relationships between factors studied. For example, Larsen-Freeman (1976a, b) found that the frequency order of nine morphemes based on the speech of (a) the parents of Brown's three young children learning English as a first language, and (b) university ESL teachers, correlated significantly with the morpheme acquisition order found for child and adult L_2 learners. These correlations led her to conclude that "morpheme frequency of occurrence in native-speaker speech is the principal determinant for the oral production morpheme order of second language learners [1976a, p. 132]." It is erroneously assumed, however, that because two things go together (e.g., Brown's parents' morpheme frequency and L_2 learners' acquisition order), one causes or determines the other. This type of assumption is a well-known source of erroneous beliefs (see, for example, Huff, 1954; Hays, 1963). The error lies in assuming that if B goes together with A, then A has caused B. Clearly, it could easily be the other way around; or perhaps neither caused the other; they may both be the result of some third factor, etc. Brown (1973a), in reporting "no relationship" between parental frequency and child order of L_1 acquisition, was of course aware of this basic distinction when he added that even "if a relation had been demonstrated to exist, it would still have been necessary to make a case for causality or determination [p. 362]." In the study under consideration, no such case has been made.

The tenuous value of the use of correlations in the investigation of cause and effect is clearly illustrated in Larsen-Freeman's own findings: While the frequency of morphemes in the speech of Brown's parents to their 2- to 4-year-old children correlates significantly with the acquisition order of **university level** ESL students (the three ρ values were $+.79$, $+.80$, $+.93$), the parents' morpheme frequency hardly correlates with the acquisition order of their own children ($\rho = .26$)! Additionally, the morpheme frequency in the speech of teachers of **university** ESL students correlates more highly with acquisition orders of public school **children** learning English as a second language (the six ρ values range from $+.70$ to $+.78$) than with university ESL students (the six ρ values range from $+.43$ to $+.73$, the two lowest not reaching acceptable significance levels). Since it is well known that adults' speech addressed to children differs from that addressed to other adults[9] (e.g., correlations between Brown's parents' morpheme frequency and that of the ESL teachers studied were relatively low: The six ρ values ranged from .42 to .63, with two not reaching .05 significance levels), the meaning of such correlations is far from clear.

The confusion of a statistical correlation with a cause-and-effect relationship is not uncommon. It seems important, therefore, to remind the untrained reader that

[9]See, for example, Wagner-Gough (1975) and Landes (1975) for a review of the relevant studies.

even though a given relationship "has been shown to be [statistically] real, the cause and effect nature of it is only a matter of speculation [Huff, 1954, p. 98]."[10]

The preceding discussion is not intended to imply that input frequency has no effect on language acquisition, only that its effects remain largely unspecified in the L_2 research literature to date.

Some Effects of Very High Frequency

There are items, phrases, and utterances whose frequency is extremely high in general discourse, or which are primarily associated with specific and frequent functions, such as certain types of social interaction. These appear to have a variety of effects on learner speech.

Although Brown (1973a) found no general correlation between frequency and acquisition order, he did find a relationship between very frequently used items and certain speech behavior (also reported in Cazden, 1972). When the parents of his three children produced certain Wh-questions (e.g., *What's that?*) at a very high rate during a period when the children did not yet know the structure of Wh-questions, the children learned to produce the two most frequently repeated ones on "roughly appropriate occasions" (*What's that* and *What are you doing?*). When, much later,

> the children began to produce all manner of *wh*-questions in the preposed form (such as *What he wants?*), it was interesting to note that *What's that?* and *What are you doing?* were not at first reconstructed in terms of the new analysis. . . . In terms of [the children's] new rules, they ought to have said *What that is?* and *What you are doing?* but instead, they at first, persisted with the old forms [Brown & Hanlon, 1970, p. 51].

Thus, one effect of very frequently occurring forms is that at least some of them somehow will be represented in the child's performance "even if its structure is far beyond him." The child will render a version of it and will form a notion of the circumstances in which it is used. Such constructions will, in Brown and Hanlon's words, "become lodged in his speech as an unassimilated fragment [p. 51]."[11] Furthermore, they suggest that extensive use of such unanalyzed or mistakenly analyzed fragments probably protects them, for a time,

---

[10]As one of the more amusing examples of this difficulty, Huff cites the close relationship found between the salaries of Presbyterian ministers in Massachusetts and the price of rum in Havana. "Which is the cause and which the effect . . . ? Are the ministers benefiting from the rum trade or supporting it?" Of course, it is much more likely that both figures are growing because of "the influence of a third factor: the historic and world-wide rise in the price level of practically everything [p. 90]."

[11]These should not be confused with the quasi-spontaneous utterances discussed earlier, whose occurrence does not depend on high frequency but probably on the state of the child's developing grammar together with the availability of the structure in the child's input.

from reanalysis. Here then, especially high frequency seems to interfere with the learners' productive integration of certain structures into their grammatical system.

We found a similar type of phenomenon in a recent study we conducted on the acquisition of English by Keres-speaking Indian children and Spanish-speaking Mexican American children. Using the ordering theoretic method described in our earlier studies (Burt *et al.*, 1976, Dulay & Burt, 1975b), we analyzed the natural speech protocols of elementary school children collected by speech clinicians in New Mexico,[12] and speech collected with a structured conversation technique similar to the *Bilingual Syntax Measure* (Burt *et al.*, 1976). The following progression was obtained for a subset of related Wh-questions structures:

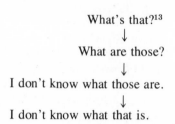

What's that?[13]

↓

What are those?

↓

I don't know what those are.

↓

I don't know what that is.

where ↓ indicates that the acquisition of the structure at the top of the arrow precedes the acquisition of the one at the bottom.

Focusing on the order of the copula and demonstrative pronoun in the Wh-constructions alone, we see that *What's that?* was acquired first. Its correct use preceded the correct production of *What are those?* which differs only in number. (Its intermediate form, *What those are?* however, appeared together with *What's that?*) Both correctly formed simple Wh-questions preceded the acquisition of the two types of embedded Wh-questions (plural and singular). Finally, and of special interest here, we observe that the correct form of the embedded plural Wh-question precedes the acquisition of the embedded singular Wh-question, i.e., *I don't know what's this* persisted even while *I don't know what those are* had been acquired. This evidence too suggests a "protected" status for the *What's X?* sequence.

It appears then that Brown's suggestions concerning the effects of high frequency on first language learning are applicable to second language learning as well.

---

[12]Under the direction of Professor Dolores Butt of the Department of Communicative Disorders at the University of New Mexico, Albuquerque, New Mexico.

[13]*This* and *that* appeared interchangeably in the singular context and *those* and *these* in the plural context for these constructions.

Frequency in Creative Construction

The effects of frequency on the acquisition of syntactic and morphological structures seem to be far from clear or simple. We have seen some cases where certain structures are produced and not others, despite equal input frequency; other cases where structures are produced that did not even occur in the input; and still others where some very high frequency phrases are memorized before the child knows their internal structure, apparently to the temporary detriment of their productive integration into the child's developing target language system.

These findings are not entirely mysterious if one assumes that the developmental state of the learner's cognitive organizers is of major importance in determining how linguistic input data will affect it; and further, that a defining characteristic of the developmental state is the organizational level of the (learner's) internal grammar of the target language.[14] Given these assumptions, we might expect that the potential effects of input frequency on learning are directly related to the state of the learner's internal target language grammar. In this view, one might suggest that **frequency serves primarily to increase the probability that those structures which the learner is ready to process will occur, thus increasing the chances that the learner will be able to attend to and process them.**[15]

If this is the case, one might expect that the rate at which acquisition takes place may be increased if maximal exposure of a precise sort at specific times over an appropriate period of time is provided. This assumes of course that the affective filters will "let the input through." And that the critical characteristics of the "right sort" of exposure have been determined.

These kinds of suggestions, which receive some support from experiments such as those conducted by Inhelder et al., assume some knowledge of the developmental steps in the learning process. That is, to the extent that the right kind of exposure depends on the level of grammatical development of the learner, to that extent we must know what the developmental steps are. Although a great deal of research and experimentation has been devoted to this end in cognitive psychology, similar investigations intended to uncover steps in the development of a second language have just begun. The results obtained by Inhelder et al., however, are cause for optimism. They suggest the correctness of recent attempts to learn about the acquisition process by careful observation of those who are in the process of acquiring a second language.

---

[14]See Pylyshyn (1973) for a careful and exhaustive treatment of the role of competence theories in cognitive psychology.

[15]It is important to distinguish at least three different ways in which a language learner might use a structure in speech: (a) as a productive rule that has been integrated into the learner's target language grammar; (b) as a quasi-spontaneous utterance where the learner is "getting ready" to use the structure productively; and (c) as an unanalyzed fragment. The effects (or noneffects) of frequency on the first two may be similar, but effects on the third may differ from the first two.

SUMMARY AND CONCLUSIONS

The ultimate source of creativity in language acquisition is the structure of the human mind. Because the mind in action is not directly observable (recent advances in neuropsychology notwithstanding), creativity will remain, at least for the foreseeable future, an inference from observable fact. This chapter has attempted to gather the empirical evidence available in the current literature which points to the necessity of positing the independent contribution of the mind to the language acquisition process—in particular, L_2 acquisition.

We reviewed evidence that learners do not necessarily acquire a variety of speech to which they are exposed regularly—not because they are somehow lacking in language learning ability, general intelligence, or social class, but because they tune in to certain models over others. Internal affective forces, such as the need to identify with a social group, filter the input to the learner in important respects, i.e., affective filters narrow down what will be admitted for cognitive processing.

Evidence for the independent effects of cognitive organizing mechanisms on the learning process consists of empirical findings that demonstrate discrepancies between the characteristics of the learner's output and what might be predicted if input factors alone were responsible for the learner's progress. Examples of the mitigation of the potential effects of the form, the frequency, and the perceptual salience of linguistic structures in a learner's environment, and of the potential effects of corrective feedback and reinforcement, all point to the force of creative mental factors on learning outcomes. If one assumes a creative construction framework to account for language acquisition, input factors take on a specific role. They provide the raw material which the mind digests and alters in accordance with its structure. In this view, (external) frequency serves to increase the probability that the learner will encounter in the environment what he or she is "ready for" or "needs to be exposed to" in order to continue development.

To know what the learner is ready for or needs to be exposed to requires a description of the developmental levels that reflect the process of language acquisition (where certain characteristics may differ for L_1 and L_2 or for the child and adult L_2 learners).

So far we have information on the acquisition orders for certain structures of English.[16] The linguistic structures themselves do not constitute the defining

---

[16]Despite differences in age, language, and formal instructional background, there are strikingly similar acquisition orders in oral production for groups of grammatical morphemes across child second language learners when their focus is communication (Dulay & Burt, 1975a, b; Burt *et al.*, 1976; Fathman, 1975). Orders of acquisition similar to those found for children learning L_2 have been observed for adults' oral production (Krashen *et al.*, 1975; Larsen-Freeman, 1976a). Finally, d'Anglejan and Tucker (1975) have found a developmental order for the comprehension of linguistically complex English structures by French-speaking adults. The order was similar to that found by C. Chomsky (1970) for English first language acquisition by children 5 to 10 years old.

characteristics of the levels; they are, so to speak, symptomatic of the levels—instances of more general characteristics. For example, in the development of cognition, a child's perception that there is the same amount of water in a tall slender glass as there is in a short wide glass is but an instance of the general operation of conservation in the child. Other instances of conservation of quantity abound.

The task of specifying the defining characteristics of levels or steps in the L_2 acquisition process still remains before us. In L_1 acquisition research, one of the few serious hypotheses advanced to attempt to explain acquisition order was Brown's derivational complexity hypothesis. It relied on the early (1965) model of transformational grammar that grew out of the basic framework of mental creativity that Chomsky had outlined. The actual derivational history proposed by transformational grammarians, coupled with a metric of semantic complexity, was used to try to explain order of acquisition. (Cf. Brown, 1973a; Dulay & Burt, 1975b, for a critical review.) From the vantage point of hindsight, one might think that the ultimate fate of the derivational complexity hypothesis was predictable, given the still evolving status of transformational grammar and Chomsky's own cautionary remarks concerning its function (cf. Chomsky, 1965, p. 9). At the time, however, the lack of even a hint of a working model of speech perception, production, or acquisition that seriously acknowledged the learner's independent contributions left few serious alternatives. Generative grammar was such a long overdue departure from both the linguistic and verbal learning theories available in the 1950s that the instant canonization by psycholinguists of even its narrowest aspects was almost inevitable.

It is now clear, however, that the initial hope on the part of psycholinguists that aspects of a model of generative grammar might predict language acquisition behavior has dissipated (see Fodor & Garrett, 1966; Fodor, Bever, & Garrett, 1974; Dulay & Burt, 1975b, for discussion). Not only has research along these lines been relatively unproductive, but the 1965 "Aspects model" used in most of the psycholinguistic research has undergone significant change (see Chomsky, 1975, Ch. 2; Bresnan, 1976). It is also becoming more and more apparent that although theories or models appropriate for generative grammar, speech perception–production, first language acquisition, and second language acquisition might all fall within a framework of human creativity, the specific models for each will probably be quite different.

It is to be hoped, however, that the immensity of the task before us will not stifle but rather inspire continued and creative (in the educational–psychological sense) research into these important areas of inquiry.

REFERENCES

Benton, R. 1964. *Research into the English language difficulties of Maori school children, 1963–1964.* Wellington, New Zealand: Maori Education Foundation.

Bloom, L. 1970. *Language development: Form and function in emerging grammars.* Cambridge, Massachusetts: M.I.T. Press.

Blumenthal, A. L. 1970. *Language and psychology.* New York: Wiley.

Bresnan, J. 1976. Toward a realistic model of transformational grammar. Paper presented at the M.I.T.-A.T.&T. Convocation on Communications, M.I.T., Cambridge, Massachusetts, March.

Brown, R. 1973a. *A first language.* Cambridge, Massachusetts: Harvard Univ. Press.

Brown, R. 1973b. Development of the first language in the human species. *American Psychologist, 28,* February, 97-102.

Brown, R., & Hanlon, C. 1970. Derivational complexity and order of acquisition in child speech. In John R. Hayes (Ed.), *Cognition and development of language.* New York: Wiley.

Burt, M. 1974. Error analysis in the adult EFL classroom. *TESOL Quarterly, 9,* 53-63.

Burt, M. Dulay, H., & Hernández-Chávez, E. 1976. *Bilingual syntax measure: Technical handbook.* New York: Harcourt.

Burt, M., & Kiparsky, D. 1972. *The gooficon: A repair manual for English.* Mowley, Massachusetts: Newbury House.

Cathcart, R. & Olson, J. 1976. Preferences for correction of classroom conversation errors. Paper presented at TESOL Convention, New York.

Cazden, C. B. 1965. *Environmental assistance to the child's acquisition of grammar.* Unpublished Ph.D. dissertation, Harvard Univ., Cambridge, Massachusetts.

Cazden, C. B. 1972. *Child language and education.* New York: Holt.

Chomsky, C. 1970. *The acquisition of syntax in children age 5 to 10.* Cambridge, Massachusetts: M.I.T. Press.

Chomsky, N. 1959. A review of B. F. Skinner's *Verbal behavior. Language, 35,* 26-58.

Chomsky, N. 1965. *Aspects of the theory of syntax.* Cambridge, Massachusetts: M.I.T. Press.

Chomsky, N. 1975. *Reflections on language.* New York: Random House.

Clark, R. 1974. Performing without competence. *Journal of Child Language, 1,* 1-10

Cohen, A. D., & Robbins, M. 1976. Toward assessing interlanguage performance: The relationship between selected errors, learner's characteristics and learner's explanations. *Language Learning, 26,* 45-66.

Dale, P. S. 1976. *Language development: Structure and function.* New York: Holt.

d'Anglejan, A., & Tucker, G. R. 1975. The acquisition of complex English structures by adult learners. *Language Learning, 25,* 281-296.

Dulay, H., & Burt, M. 1972. Goofing: An indicator of children's second language learning strategies. *Language Learning, 22,* 235-252.

Dulay, H., & Burt, M. 1974a. Errors and strategies in child second language acquisition. *TESOL Quarterly, 8,* 129-136.

Dulay, H., & Burt, M. 1974b. A new perspective on the creative construction process in child second language acquisition. *Language Learning, 24,* 253-278.

Dulay, H., & Burt, M. 1975a. Creative construction in second language learning and teaching. In M. Burt & H. Dulay (Eds.), *New directions in second language learning, teaching and bilingual education.* Washington, D.C.: TESOL. Pp. 21-32.

Dulay, H., & Burt, M. 1975b. A new approach to discovering universals of child second language acquisition. In D. Dato (Ed.), *Developmental psycholinguistics: Theory and applications.* Washington, D.C.: Georgetown Univ. Press. Pp. 209-233.

Dulay, H., & Burt, M. 1977. Remarks on creativity in language acquisition. In M. Burt, H. Dulay, & M. Finocchiaro (Eds.), *Viewpoints on English as a second language.* New York: Regents.

Ervin-Tripp, S. 1974. Is second language learning like the first? *TESOL Quarterly, 8,* 111-127.

Fathman, A. 1975. Language background, age and the order of acquisition of English structures. In M. Burt & H. Dulay (Eds.), *New directions in second language learning, teaching and bilingual education.* Washington, D.C.: TESOL. Pp. 33-43.

Fodor, J. A., Bever, T. G., & Garrett, M. F. 1974. *The psychology of language*. New York: McGraw-Hill.

Fodor, J. A., & Garrett, M. F. 1966. Some reflections on competence and performance. In J. Lyons & R. Wales (Eds.), *Psycholinguistic papers*. Edinburgh Univ. Press. Pp. 135–162.

Gillis, M., & Weber, R. 1976. The emergence of sentence modalities in the English of Japanese-speaking children. *Language Learning, 26,* 77–94.

Guilford, J. P. 1967. *The nature of human intelligence*. New York: McGraw-Hill.

Hakuta, K. 1974. Prefabricated patterns and the emergence of structure in second language acquisition. *Language Learning, 24,* 287–298.

Halle, M. 1975. Confessio grammatici. *Language, 51,* 525–535.

Halle, M. 1976. New Approaches to a realistic model of language. Paper presented M.I.T.-A.T.& T. Convocation on Communications, M.I.T., Cambridge, Massachusetts, March.

Hatch, E., & Wagner-Gough, I. 1976. Explaining sequence and variation in second language acquisition. *Language Learning, Special Issue No. 4,* 39–57.

Hays, W. L. 1963. *Statistics*. New York: Holt.

Hernández-Chávez, E. 1972. Early code separation in the second language speech of Spanish-speaking children. Paper presented at the Stanford Child Language Research Forum, Stanford Univ., Stanford, California.

Hernández-Chávez, E. 1977a. The development of semantic relations in child second language acquisition. In. M. Burt, H. Dulay, & M. Finocchiaro (Eds.), *Viewpoints on English as a second language*. New York: Regents.

Hernández-Chávez, E. 1977b. The acquisition of grammatical structures by a Mexican American child learning English. Unpublished Ph.D. dissertation, Univ. of California, Berkeley, California.

Huff, D. 1954. *How to lie with statistics*. New York: Norton.

Inhelder, B., Sinclair, H., & Bovet, M. 1974. *Learning and the development of cognition*. Cambridge, Massachusetts: Harvard Univ. Press.

Klima, E. S., & Bellugi, U. 1966. Syntactic regularities in the speech of children. In J. R. Lyons & R. J. Wales (Eds.), *Psycholinguistic papers*. Edinburgh: Edinburgh Univ. Press.

Krashen, S. D. 1976. Formal and informal linguistic environments in language acquisition and language learning. *TESOL Quarterly, 10,* 157–168.

Krashen, S. D. 1977. The monitor model for adult second language performance. In. M. Burt, H. Dulay, & M. Finocchiaro (Eds.), *Viewpoints on English as a second language*. New York: Regents.

Krashen, S. D., Madden, C. & Bailey, N. 1975. Theoretical aspects of grammatical sequencing. In M. Burt & H. Dulay (Eds.), *New directions in second language learning, teaching and bilingual education*. Washington, D.C.: TESOL. Pp. 44–54.

Labov, W. 1972. *Language in the inner city: Studies in the Black English vernacular*. Philadelphia: Univ. of Pennsylvania Press.

Landes, J. E. 1975. Speech addressed to children: Issues and characteristics of parental input. *Language Learning, 25,* 355–380.

Larsen-Freeman, D. 1976a. An explanation for the morpheme acquisition order of second language learners. *Language Learning, 26,* 125–134.

Larsen-Freeman, D. 1976b. ESL teacher speech as input to the ESL learner. *Workpapers in TESL,* UCLA.

Milon, J. P. 1975. Dialect in the TESOL program: If you never you better. In M. Burt & H. Dulay (Eds.), *New directions in second language learning, teaching and bilingual education*. Washington, D.C.: TESOL.

Piaget, J. 1970. *Structuralism*. New York: Basic Books.

Pylyshyn, Z. W. 1973. The role of competence theories in cognitive psychology. *Journal of Psycholinguistic Research, 2,* 21–50.

Ravem, R. 1974. The development of *wh*-questions in first and second language learners. In J. Richards (Ed.), *Error analysis: Perspectives on second language learning.* New York: Longmans, Green.

Renzulli, J. 1973. *New directions in creativity.* New York: Harper.

Richards, J. C. 1971. Error analysis and second language strategies. *Language Sciences, 17,* 12–22.

Richards, J. C. 1974. *Error analysis: Perspectives on second language learning.* New York: Longmans, Green.

Skinner, B. F. 1953. *Science and human behavior.* New York: Macmillan.

Taylor, B. 1975. The use of overgeneralization and transfer learning strategies by elementary and intermediate university students learning ESL. In M. Burt & H. Dulay (Eds.), *New directions in second language learning, teaching and bilingual education.* Washington, D.C.: TESOL. Pp. 55–69.

Torrance, E. P. 1966a. *Torrance tests of creative thinking: Norms—technical manual.* Princeton, New Jersey: Personnel Press.

Torrance, E. P. 1966b. *Torrance tests of creative thinking: Directions manual and scoring guide: verbal test and figural test.* Research ed. Princeton, New Jersey: Personnel Press.

Valdman, A. 1974. Error analysis and pedagogical ordering. Reproduced by Linguistic Agency University at Trier, D-55 Trier, West Germany.

Venable, G. P. 1974. *A study of second-language learning in children.* 641 M. Sc. (Appl) II Project, McGill Univ.

Wagner-Gough, J. 1975. Comparative studies in second language learning. Unpublished M.A. thesis, Univ. of California, Los Angeles, California.

Wagner-Gough, J., & Hatch, E. 1975. The importance of input data in second language acquisition studies. *Language Learning, 25,* 297–308.

Wallach, M. A. 1970. Creativity. In P. H. Mussen (Ed.), *Carmichael's manual of child psychology.* Vol. 1. New York: Wiley. Pp. 1211–1272.

6 Order of difficulty in adult second language acquisition

Janet I. Anderson

Studies on learning sequences have received considerable attention in first language acquisition research. In a longitudinal study on the acquisition of 14 grammatical morphemes, R. Brown (1973) established an order approaching invariance. A cross-sectional study by de Villiers and de Villiers (1973) corroborated Brown's findings.

Recent research in second language acquisition is being conducted along the same lines. In a cross-sectional study on children learning English as a second language, Dulay and Burt (1973) have demonstrated an invariant order of eight of the morphemes studied by Brown, although the order was not the same for the second language learners. This difference in order was attributed to the more mature stage in cognitive development of the children in the second language acquisition; these latter children ranged in age from 5 to 8 years. In another study on the acquisition of the same eight morphemes by adults, Bailey, Madden, and Krashen (1974) demonstrated "a highly consistent order of relative difficulty" which agreed with the order established in the Dulay and Burt study.

These findings suggest that second language learning, like first language learning, is systematic, involving a creative construction process on the part of the learner. Research from error analysis supports this view. Second language learners, like first language learners, make errors which show they are dealing with the target language in a creative way (Buteau, 1970; Dulay & Burt, 1973;

Duskova, 1969; Taylor, 1975), instead of completely relying on the native language as previously assumed (Lado, 1957).

The study reported here was undertaken to determine whether adult second language acquisition is systematic to the extent that there is a shared order of difficulty of syntactic structure of a more complex nature than grammatical morphemes. It was hoped that the common order of difficulty, if one were found to exist, would throw more light on the strategies that adult second language learners use in dealing with the target language.

The area investigated was the production of sentential complementation. In traditional grammar, sentential complements, which include gerunds, infinitives, and *that* clause, were viewed as being unrelated grammatically. Generative-transformational grammar, on the other hand, views sentential complementation as a unified syntactic phenomenon whose various surface forms are all derived from the same underlying grammatical structure. The fact that deep structure can be held constant while surface forms are varied makes complementation a potentially revealing area for a syntax acquisition study.

SUBJECTS

The 180 subjects who participated in this study were enrolled in English classes at Catholic University in Ponce, Puerto Rico. They were native speakers of Puerto Rican Spanish ranging in age from 17 to 39 years. Their exposure to English was varied: Some had been taught English by Puerto Rican teachers in the public schools; others had attended private schools where the medium of instruction was English, and others had spent up to 2 years in the continental United States.

One section of each of the six proficiency levels at the Institute of Communicative English was tested, as well as three classes in the English Department: Rhetoric, Introduction to English Literature, and American Literature.

MATERIALS AND TESTING PROCEDURE

The test consisted of 25 multiple choice items and 32 sentences which were to be translated from Spanish into English (see Appendix). A written test was chosen over an oral one primarily because the majority of students were not accustomed to hearing native English pronunciation. This is due to the fact that English is taught in the public schools in Puerto Rico mainly by native Puerto Ricans, many of whom have not mastered English phonology. Further, in many cases, there is a reliance on the written word in English language instruction. For these reasons, a written test seemed to be a better instrument for measuring their knowledge of English.

The test was designed to investigate mastery of the three basic complement types- infinitive, *that* clause, and possessive-*ing*. Other syntactic phenomena related to complementation were investigated as well: sequence of tense rules, the obligatory choice of the possessive-*ing* complement after a preposition. In addition, it was necessary to create new categories after the data were analyzed when it was discovered that there was a difference in difficulty between complements which contained a surface structure subject, and those which had undergone Equi-NP Deletion.[1]

Fourteen of the translation items had two possible correct answers (e.g., *I admitted that I did it/doing it.*) These items were included for two reasons: (1) to test for knowledge of complements which only occur optionally, such as possessive-*ing;* and (2) to gain knowledge of native language transfer and complement preference. If two complement forms were acceptable for a given verb, it was felt that the systematic choice of one form over another would throw light on strategies used in production. However, these 14 items were not used in establishing the order of difficulty because of the problem of quantifying variable responses. The structures included in the test, along with the corresponding test items, are presented in Table 1.

The test was administered during regular class periods and the subjects were allowed one hour in which to complete it. The subjects were not permitted to ask questions after the test began. On the translation section, they were instructed to write sentences in "acceptable" English, rather than to render word-for-word translations.

SCORING PROCEDURE AND DATA ANALYSIS

Multiple choice responses were scored either *right* or *wrong,* but partially correct answers were accepted on the translation section of the test. The translation items were scored according to the following criteria:

3 points: Correct complement choice; perfectly formed response
2 points: Correct complement choice; one error
1 point: Incorrect complement choice; or correct complement choice with two errors
0 points: No reponse, or incomplete response.

The method used in this study to establish the order of difficulty is called the

---

[1]The creation of new categories of structure resulted in an uneven distribution of test items.

Table 1. Structures Included in Test

Structure	Explanation	Example	Test items
1. *that*	*that* complement	*John thinks **that he speaks English well**.*	25, 32, 33, 42, 43, 53
2. Poss-*ing* (Poss)	Poss-*ing* complement	*I remember **your finishing it last week**.*	8, 20
3. Gerund	Poss-*ing* complement that has undergone Equi-NP Deletion	*I finished **studying English**.*	26, 36, 41, 49
4. Prep-Gerund (P-Ger)	Gerund which is preceded by a preposition	*Mary concentrated **on solving the problem**.*	1, 5, 10, 15, 18, 22
5. Inf-NP	Infinitive complement in which the subject of the complement or its post-main-verb coreferent remain in surface structure and take an accusative form if pronominal	*I wanted **you to leave**. My father ordered **me to study**.*	2, 16, 17, 27, 30, 38
6. *to*-deletion (T.D.)	Infinitive complement that has undergone *to* deletion	*My mother doesn't let **me watch TV**.*	3, 12, 13, 23, 29, 40, 45
7. Inf-Equi	Infinitive complement that has undergone Equi-NP Deletion	*I want **to see it**.*	7, 44, 51
8. Tense	Sequence of tenses	*I know that he **left** early.*	21 and all items in the translation section of the test with *that* complements

#	Feature	Description	Example	S.S.S. numbers
9.	Surface structure subject (S.S.S.)	Subject of the complement is obligatorily present in surface structure	*I want you to help them.*	4, 9, 19, 24, and all complements which have an S.S.S. in the translation section of the test
10.	Perfect (Perf.)	Perfect tenses	*She hopes to have read it by next week.*	6, 11, 14
11.	Gerund/that	Either a Gerund or a *that* complement is possible	They denied { *that they did it.* / *doing it.* }	28, 46, 48, 53
12.	Poss-ing/that	Either a Poss-*ing* or a *that* complement is possible	I appreciated { *your doing it.* / *that you did it.* }	31, 39
13.	Inf/that	Either an infinitive or a *that* complement is possible	I decided { *to go.* / *that I would go.* }	35, 37, 47, 54
14.	Inf/Ger	Either an infinitive complement or a gerund is possible	I heard them { *sing.* / *singing.* }	50
15.	Inf-NP Active/Passive	Either an Active or a Passive translation is possible	The shepherd let { *the wolf devour it.* / *it be devoured by the wolf.* }	56, 57

"Ordering-Theoretic Method [Bart & Krus, 1973]." It departs from older methods of analysis in that it does not assume a strict linear ordering of items, and does not use a simple additive model. It is a method that attempts to establish implicational relationships among the items being investigated. Dulay and Burt (1974) introduced this method to second language acquisition research as an alternative to rank ordering in a study on morpheme acquisition in which they were looking for groups of morphemes that were acquired at the same time.

The data were analyzed as follows: Each of the 180 individuals received a binary score of 1 or 0 on each of the structures investigated. A score of 1 indicated acquisition of the structure and a score of 0 indicated "not acquired." The criterion for acquisition was set at 80% correct. The following example should clarify this procedure:

	Individual 062		
Structure	Test items	Percentage score	Binary score
that	25, 32, 33, 42, 43, 52, 55	86% (6 correct)	1
Gerund	26, 36, 41, 49	50% (2 correct)	0
.			
.			
.			
Inf-NP	2, 16, 17, 36, 39, 47	83% (5 correct)	1

Response patterns on all possible pairs of structures for all individuals were then tabulated. The method for tabulating response patterns is illustrated below using only one of the pairs investigated as an example.

	Inf-Equi → Inf-NP	
Individual	Inf-Equi	Inf-NP
001	0	1
002	1	0
.	.	.
.	.	.
180	1	1

The relationship being tested in the above example is: *Inf-Equi is ordered before Inf-NP*. The response pattern 10 for Individual 002 indicates that Inf-Equi was ordered first, and it is called "confirmatory," while the response pattern 01 for

Individual 001 indicates that Inf-NP was ordered first, and it is called "disconfirmatory." The Ordering-Theoretic Method required that only disconfirmatory response patterns be counted. If the disconfirmatory responses exceeded the tolerance level for the sample as a whole, which was set at 5%, the hypothesized order was rejected.

RESULTS AND DISCUSSION

There was a high correlation between the test scores and an independent measure of English proficiency, the EFL section of the Spanish version of the College Entrance Examination Board test used in Puerto Rico. The Pearson product moment correlation coefficient was .80 ($p < .01$).

The results indicated a common order of difficulty. The disconfirmatory response patterns are displayed in the matrix in Table 2. The matrix is to be read in the following manner: The structure designated by the row is ordered before the structure designated by the column if the disconfirmatory response patterns do not exceed 5%.

Upon examining the matrix it can be seen that *Inf-Equi* is ordered before every other structure in that row since all of the figures at the row–column intersections do not exceed 5%. Inf-Equi is followed in difficulty by S.S.S., which is followed by Inf-NP. The categories Tense, Gerund, T.D. (*to*-deletion), and *that* are intermediate, and are exceeded in difficulty by P-Ger, Perf, and Poss.

Three factors were investigated as possible determinants for the order of difficulty: derivational complexity, native language transfer, and the length of the

Table 2. Disconfirmation Matrix

	Inf-Equi	S.S.S.	Inf-NP	Tense	Gerund	T.D.	*that*	P-Ger	Perf	Poss
					Percentages ($N = 180$)					
Inf-Equi	—	**2.0**[a]	**.6**	**1.0**	**.6**	0	**.6**	0	0	0
S.S.S.	11.7	—	**0**	**.6**	0	0	0	0	0	0
Inf-NP	24.4	14.4	—	**3.3**	**3.9**	2.0	1.6	1.0	0	0
Tense	36.7	27.2	14.4	—	**7.9**	7.2	**2.7**	2.0	0	0
Gerund	40.6	31.1	20.0	12.8	—	6.7	**5.0**	2.0	.6	0
T.D.	45.6	36.1	24.4	17.2	11.7	—	8.3	**4.4**	.6	.6
that	48.9	39.4	26.7	16.7	13.3	11.7	—	**6.1**	1.0	1.6
P-Ger	55.0	45.6	32.2	21.7	16.7	13.9	12.2	—	0	1.0
Perf	61.7	56.2	37.8	26.7	21.1	17.2	14.4	7.7	—	1.6
Poss	62.3	53.3	38.9	27.2	22.8	17.8	15.0	7.7	**2.7**	—

Tolerance level: 5%.
[a] Figures in boldface type indicate sequential relationships.

complement, measured by the number of morphemes present in the surface structure.

Derivational complexity is defined in terms of the number of grammatical transformations involved in the derivation of a structure. The more transformations involved in a derivation, the more complex a structure is hypothesized to be. Although the status of the derivational complexity hypothesis in experimental psycholinguistics is at best controversial, based on comprehension studies, it has been more successful as a determinant of difficulty in first language acquisition studies on production. Since the study undertaken here was concerned with production rather than comprehension, it seemed appropriate to consider derivational complexity as a possible metric for determining relative difficulty.

Robin Lakoff's analysis of sentential complementation (1968) was used to describe the structures investigated, and the transformations involved in each structure were counted. The order predicted by the derivational complexity hypothesis is presented below.

1. Three transformations:

   that   *He said **that he would leave**.*
   Poss-*ing*   *He resented **her leaving**.*
   Inf-NP   *She persuaded **him to leave**.*

2. Four transformations:

   T.D.   *She **let him leave**.*

3. Five transformational rules:

   Inf-Equi   *He wanted **to leave**.*
   Gerund   *He regretted **leaving**.*
   P-Ger   *He planned **on leaving**.*

In comparing this order with the actual order of difficulty (Table 2), it can be seen that the hypothesis does not seem to have any empirical validity, at least for the set of structures examined in this study using Lakoff's analysis of sentential complementation. Inf-Equi, which was predicted to be one of the most difficult structures, was actually the easiest to learn, and the *that* complement, which is one of the least derivationally complex structures, was intermediate in difficulty.

The notion of cumulative derivational complexity, introduced by R. Brown (1973) in his studies on first language acquisition, was also investigated. Cumulative derivational complexity predicts that a construction which involves all of the transformations involved in another construction plus one more, will be the more complex and hence will be acquired later.

The only pair of structures in my study which meet this description are the Infinitive and *to*-deletion constructions. *To*-deletion constructions require every rule that Infinitives do, plus one more. They are therefore predicted to be more difficult. This prediction was borne out by the results. Structures like (2) in the following example were more difficult than structures like (1).

1.   *I want **him to go**.*
2.   *I made **him go**.*

The obvious limitation of cumulative derivational complexity in this study is that there was only one pair of structures which met the cumulative complexity requirement. Because of the limited data, the findings should not be regarded as conclusive.

The second factor which was investigated as a possible determinant of order was native language transfer. Transfer was defined in terms of the type of complement in the stimulus sentence, and the corresponding response in English. In Spanish *que* is the equivalent of *that,* so if the stimulus sentence contained a *que* complement for which the correct response in English was a *that* complement, there was potential for positive transfer. If the correct response was an Infinitive, there was potential for negative transfer. The same metric of parallelism was used for defining positive and negative transfer for stimulus sentences in which the complement was an Infinitive.

The results (see Table 3) indicate that the task of producing a *that* complement is less difficult when the stimulus sentence contains a *que* complement. Similarly, when the stimulus sentence contains an Infinitive, the task of producing an Infinitive in English is also less difficult. These facts are evidence that the form of the complement in the stimulus sentence has a definite influence on the facility with which the correct complement in English is produced, which supports the notion of positive transfer.

There was also evidence for negative transfer. An example of this can be found in responses to two items for which the correct response was a *that* complement. In one case, the stimulus sentence contained an infinitive, and in the other case, the stimulus contained a *que* complement. These items are illustrated below.

> Stimulus sentences:
> *Dijo que estaba seguro.*
> *Dijo estar seguro.*
>
> Correct response:
> *He said that he was sure.*

Infinitives composed 18% of the total responses for the stimulus sentence that contained an Infinitive, but only 4% of the responses for the sentence that contained a *que* complement. These results seem to support the notion of negative transfer.

The contrastive analysis hypothesis, which predicts that parallel structures are easier to learn than contrasting forms, seems to have some empirical validity. However, the hypothesis does not predict that the Infinitive is easier to produce

Table 3.   Results (Positive and Negative Transfer)

Stimulus	Correct response	Percentage correct
Infinitive	Infinitive	83.9
que	*that*	61.4
que	Infinitive	57.9
Infinitive	*that*	42.5

than the *that* complement, which turns out to be the case. Since it cannot predict the overall relative difficulty of the various complement forms, its explanatory power is limited.

The third factor investigated as a determinant of order was length. There seems to be some evidence that length, measured by the number of morphemes present in the surface structure, is related to the order of difficulty.

In no case was a complement with a surface structure subject found to be easier than its corresponding Equi-NP form. The Inf-Equi structure was less difficult than the Inf-NP, and the Gerund was less difficult than the Poss-*ing*. These sequential relationships are illustrated below:

I want to go ⟶ *I want him to go.*

I resent going ⟶ *I resent his going.*

Additional support for length as a determinant of difficulty was found in the high rate of functor omission in elementary language learners. (Functors include verb inflections and function words, such as the past tense morpheme, prepositions, and articles.) A comparison among elementary, intermediate, and advanced subjects revealed that there was a much greater tendency on the part of the elementary learner to omit functors. In fact, the corpus of elementary language learners often revealed a "telegraphic" kind of language. Responses like the following were not uncommon:

He said be sure.   (He said that he was sure.)

He quit smoke.   (He quit smoking.)

It may be that the early acquisition of shorter forms and the tendency to omit functors reflect a communication strategy based on an "economy principle." In order to ease the burden of communicating, there may be a tendency on the part of the second language learner to encode information in the fewest possible morphemes.

This same communication strategy may account for an apparent preference for the shorter form when there is a choice between two complement types. There were two test items for which either the that complement or the Infinitive were correct responses. The Spanish stimulus sentences for these items were identical, except in one case the complement was an Infinitive, and in the other case it was a *que* complement. These items are presented below.

Stimulus sentences:
*Decidio **que iria**.*
*Decidio **ir**.*

Correct response:
*He decided **to go**.*
or
*He decided **that he would go**.*

The preferences were overwhelmingly for the Infinitive. When the stimulus sentence contained an Infinitive, 79.4% of the subjects responded with an Infinitive in English. *That* complements made up only 1.7% of the total. Even when the stimulus sentence contained a *que* complement, 46.7% of the subjects responded with the Infinitive.

Additional evidence that shorter forms are preferred was found upon examining overgeneralization errors in complement choice. Overgeneralization errors for the Infinitive were approximately 20 times greater than they were for the *that* complement. For example, when the stimulus sentence contained a *que* complement, and the correct response was *He thought that he would leave,* there was a tendency to use the Infinitive. A typical infinitive overgeneralization error was:

He think to go.

However, when the stimulus sentence contained an Infinitive for which the correct response was an Infinitive in English, *that* complement overgeneralization errors were extremely rare.

The results reported here may be summarized as follows:

1. There was a common order of difficulty of structures intrinsic to sentential complementation.
2. Simple derivational complexity proved to be a poor predictor of the order of difficulty. Cumulative derivational complexity successfully predicted the order of one pair of structures, but there was insufficient data from which to draw any conclusions.
3. There was some evidence for both negative and positive transfer, although the contrastive analysis hypothesis was unable to predict overall relative difficulty.
4. Length, measured by the number of morphemes seemed to account partially for the order of difficulty as well as for complement preference. It has been suggested that in order to ease the burden of communication, the second language learner may adopt the strategy of encoding information in the fewest possible morphemes.

There is need for further research. A longitudinal study should be conducted to determine whether the order of difficulty established in a cross-sectional study, such as this one, corresponds with the order of acquisition across time.

Also, more research should be done to determine the extent to which the native language influences the order of difficulty and the extent to which it is universal. A study should be conducted on a linguistically heterogeneous group of subjects. Learning sequences which are common to the entire group could be assumed to be universal if the structures in the various native languages were not parallel. For example, if it is found that postverbal infinitive complements are learned with the same degree of facility by native speakers of Spanish, in which postverbal infinitives occur, and by native speakers of Persian, in which postverbal infinitive complements never occur, one could safely conclude that the native language does not influence the order of difficulty.

Further research should be done to determine how the findings from a written test such as the one in this study correlate with findings on the same group of subjects based on samples of spontaneous speech. We need to determine whether findings based on a discrete point written test on sentential complementation correlate with findings based on spoken language used in communicative situations.

There are certain pedagogical implications. If the apparent constraint on length found in this study is supported by further research, there are certain implications concerning the strict audiolingual method which insists on correct repetition of structures in the target language. Forcing the correct response may be counter-productive in the early stages of learning if it is natural and inevitable for a learner to go through a stage in which he omits functors and produces a telegraphic kind of speech. A more realistic approach might be for the teacher to call attention to errors, and to model the correct response without insisting on flawless repetition.

APPENDIX   THE TEST

Part I

Instrucciones: Haga un círculo alrededor de la letra que complete correctamente la oración.

Ejemplo:

> *Ford _____ the President of the United States.*
>   a. *are*
>   b. *am*
>   c. *is*
>   d. *be*

1. *The pilot thought of* _____ *to Mexico.*
   a. *to fly*
   b. *flying*
   c. *flied*
   d. *fly*

2. *John wants* _____ .
   a. *my going*
   b. *I go*
   c. *me to go*
   d. *that I go.*

3. *We heard the birds* _____ .
   a. *to singing*
   b. *sing*
   c. *to sing*
   d. *sings*

4. *Mary thought that* _____ *go home.*
   a. *she should*
   b. *should have*
   c. *should had*
   d. *should she*

5. *They prevented him from* _____ *his girlfriends.*
   a. *see*
   b. *to see*
   c. *he saw*
   d. *seeing*

6. *She hopes* _____ *the book by next week.*
   a. *to have read*
   b. *to be read*
   c. *to have reading*
   d. *to have been read*

7. *She offered* _____ *the child's books.*
   a. *carrying*
   b. *to carry*
   c. *carry*
   d. *carried*

8. *I remember* _____ *it last week.*
   a. *you finish*
   b. *you to finishing*
   c. *your finishing*
   d. *you to finish*

9. *John hoped that* _____ *rain.*
   a. *wouldn't*
   b. *wouldn't it*
   c. *wouldn't be*
   d. *it wouldn't*

10. *Mary concentrated on* _____ *the problem.*
    a. *to solve*
    b. *solving*
    c. *be solving*
    d. *solved*

11. *Tom thought that he* _____ *talking too much.*
    a. *may had been*
    b. *may have been*
    c. *may had to be*
    d. *may to have been*

12. *I saw him* _____ *the book.*
    a. *to take*
    b. *took*
    c. *take*
    d. *to taking*

13. *The teacher let the students* _____ *class early.*
    a. *leaving*
    b. *to leave*
    c. *to be leaving*
    d. *leave*

14. *The boy admits* _____ *him last week.*
    a. *have seen*
    b. *having seen*
    c. *have been seeing*
    d. *have been seen*

15. *We plan on* _____ *this today.*
    a. *finish*
    b. *to finish*
    c. *finishing*
    d. *to be finishing*

16. *My father ordered* _____ .
    a. *me to study*
    b. *my studying*
    c. *me studying*
    d. *I study*

17. *Mary wanted* _____ .
    a. *that they play*
    b. *them to play*
    c. *their playing*
    d. *they played*

18. *The man talked about* _____ *in Chicago.*
    a. *live*
    b. *to love*
    c. *lived*
    d. *living*

19. *John was afraid* _____ *an explosion.*
    a. *there would be*
    b. *would to be*
    c. *would be*
    d. *would there be*

20. *We regret* _____ *here.*
    a. *John not to be*
    b. *John's not being*
    c. *John's not to be*
    d. *John not to being*

21. *Bill hopes that Mary* _____ *play tennis tomorrow.*
    a. *will to*
    b. *will*
    c. *would have*
    d. *would*

22. *We are used to* _____ *on week-ends.*
    a. *studying*
    b. *study*
    c. *studied*
    d. *have studied*

23. *My father made me* _____ .
    a. *to work*
    b. *to be working*
    c. *work*
    d. *worked*

24. *I am afraid that* _____ *an accident.*
    a. *there might be*
    b. *might there be*
    c. *might be*
    d. *might to be*

25. *We think* _____ *enough time.*
    a. *to have*
    b. *we have*
    c. *having*
    d. *to be having*

Part II

Instrucciones: Traduzca las siguientes oraciones de español al inglés. Algunas palabras han sido subrayadas, debajo de las cuales está su significado en inglés. Esto es para ayudarles en la traducción de la oración.

26. *Terminé de estudiar inglés.* I finished studying English.

_____

27. *Yo te mando que no te vayas.* I order you not to leave.

_____

28. *El admitió que lo hizo.* He admitted doing it.

29. *Hice llorar el niño.* I made the child cry.

30. *Quiero que los ayude.* I want you to help them.

31. *Resiento que él haga eso.* I resent $\begin{cases} \text{his doing that.} \\ \text{that he does that.} \end{cases}$

32. *El pensaba que saldría el lunes.* He thought that he would leave on Monday.

33. *Juan cree hablar bien el inglés.* John thinks that he speaks English well.

34. *Me prometiste venir.* You promised $\begin{cases} \text{me to come.} \\ \text{you would come.} \end{cases}$

35. *Me persuadió que saliera.* You persuaded $\begin{cases} \text{me to leave.} \\ \text{that I should leave.} \end{cases}$

36. *Ella dejó de fumar.* She stopped smoking.

37. *Decidí irme el sábado.* I decided $\begin{cases} \text{to go on Saturday.} \\ \text{that I would go on Saturday.} \end{cases}$

38. *Yo quería que te fueras.* I wanted you to go.

39. *Yo te agradecé que lo hicieras.* I appreciated $\begin{cases} \text{your doing it.} \\ \text{that you did it.} \end{cases}$

40. *Me madre no me deja ver televisión.* My mother doesn't let me watch T.V.

41. *El terminó de trabajar.* He finished working.

42. *Dijo que estaba seguro de ello.* He said that he was sure of that.

43. *Pienso irme.* I think that I will leave.

44. *Trataré de hacerlo.* I will try to do it.

45. *No me dejaron salir.* They didn't let me leave.

46. *Niego ser comunista.* I deny $\begin{Bmatrix} \text{being a communist.} \\ \text{that I am a communist.} \end{Bmatrix}$

47. *Decidió que iría el lunes.* He decided $\begin{Bmatrix} \text{to go on Monday.} \\ \text{that he would go on Monday.} \end{Bmatrix}$

48. *Admitió haberlo hecho.* He admitted $\begin{Bmatrix} \text{that he did it.} \\ \text{doing it.} \end{Bmatrix}$

49. *Disfruto ir a tu casa.* I enjoy going to your house.

50. *Los oí cantar la canción.* I heard them sing the song.

51. *Quiero verlo.* I want to see it.

52. *Dijo estar seguro de ello.* He said that he was sure of that.

53. *Negaron que lo hicieran.* They denied $\begin{Bmatrix} \text{doing it.} \\ \text{that they did it.} \end{Bmatrix}$

54. *Le creo ser un hombre inteligente.* I believe $\begin{Bmatrix} \text{him to be an intelligent man.} \\ \text{that he is an intelligent man.} \end{Bmatrix}$

55. *Pablo dijo haberlo hecho.* Pablo said that he did it.

56. *Mandé subir las maletas.* I ordered $\begin{Bmatrix} \text{the luggage to be brought up.} \\ \text{someone to bring up the luggage.} \end{Bmatrix}$

57. *El pastor lo dejó devorar por el lobo.* The shepherd let $\begin{Bmatrix} \text{it be eaten by the wolf.} \\ \text{the wolf eat it.} \end{Bmatrix}$

ACKNOWLEDGMENTS

This is a revised version of a paper presented at the Conference on Second Language Learning and Teaching at SUNY/Oswego, July 16–18, 1976. I am indebted to Professor Howard Maclay, Professor Erica McClure, Jeffrey Bright, and Carol Brownscombe for their helpful criticisms and suggestions on this paper. The revisions the paper has undergone since its presentation at the conference in Oswego are due largely to the insightful comments from certain members of the audience at the conference.

REFERENCES

Bailey, N., Madden, C., & Krashen, S. 1974. Is there a "natural sequence" in adult second language learning? *Language Learning, 24,* 235–243.

Bart, W. M., & Krus, J. D. 1973. An ordering-theoretic method to determine hierarchies among items. *Educational and Psychological Measurement, 33,* 291–300.

Brown, R. 1973. *A first language.* Cambridge, Massachusetts: Harvard Univ. Press.

Buteau, M. F. 1970. Students' errors and the learning of French as a second language: A pilot study. *International Review of Applied Linguistics, 8,* 133–145.

de Villiers, J., & de Villiers, P. 1973. A cross-sectional study of the acquisition of grammatical morphemes in child speech. *Journal of Psycholinguistic Research, 2,* 267–278.

Dulay, H. C., & Burt, M. K. 1973. Should we teach children syntax? *Language Learning, 23,* 245–258.

Dulay, H. C., & Burt, M. K. 1974. A new perspective on the creative construction process in child second language acquisition. *Language Learning, 24,* 253–378.

Duskova, L. 1969. On sources of error in foreign language learning. *International Review of Applied Linguistics, 7,* 11–36.

Lado, R. 1957. *Linguistics across cultures: Applied linguistics for language teaching.* Ann Arbor: Univ. of Michigan Press.

Lakoff, R. T. 1968. Abstract syntax and Latin complementation. Cambridge, Massachusetts: M.I.T. Press.

Taylor, P. 1975. The use of overgeneralization and transfer learning strategies by elementary and intermediate students in ESL. *Language Learning, 25,* 73–107.

7 Beyond statistics in second language acquisition research

Carolyn Madden
Nathalie Bailey
Miriam Eisenstein
Lloyd Anderson

The essence of recent second language research is the investigation of patterns of learner behavior, both those which distinguish learners and those which learners have in common. Successful cross-sectional research will show that the same data can be used to locate both individual differences and similarities among learners.

The current research of Bailey, Eisenstein, and Madden (1976) is a cross-sectional study of three groups in an intensive English as a second language program at the English Language Institute, Queens College. The focus of this study was the acquisition of the auxiliaries *is, are, do,* and *does* in Wh-questions by 46 adult ESL learners from Levels 2, 3, and 4 (a total of six levels). There were 14 learners from Level 2, 14 from Level 3, and 18 from Level 4. They represented 12 language backgrounds. Three tasks were administered: cued production, imitation, and intuition. In the first analysis group, statistical results were reported (see Bailey *et al.,* 1976, for results). Concentration was on accuracy and quantity of structures, and omission and noninversion errors. Production was the principle task examined, with supporting data from imitation and intuition results. Other errors, e.g., substitution of one auxiliary for another, were prominent enough to suggest the need for further analysis.

Anderson (1976, 1977a,b) has been developing methods of scaling and graphing data from individual learners, retaining the detailed information which most grouping and statistical summaries lose. The aim is to discover sequences in the learning of grammatical structures—to find which sequences lead to the best mastery of a second language. The method encourages a complete accounting for every response by each learner. When response types are rare, so that the usual statistical approaches are impossible, parallels are sought in other language learning studies.

This chapter presents the results obtained by analyzing individual performance from the Bailey *et al*. study and applying the scaling methods of Anderson to the data. Primarily, we reexamined the imitation data of individuals in addition to group behavior to see what additional insights could be revealed by this approach. We wanted to pursue the question of whether learners were following similar paths of learning as evidenced by their auxiliary substitution errors, or if, in fact, there was more than one prominent structural path. In addition to following our own intuition on what might provide fruitful information about the language learning process—i.e., an examination of individual errors in a group study—we are also attempting to meet the challenge of researchers (Rosansky, 1976a, 1976b) who criticize group analyses because they may obscure individual variability. The results of this second analysis are not meant to be conclusive but are merely an attempt to reduce the amount of data hidden by group analyses.

Imitation was chosen as the primary task to be reexamined because it was a balanced task—16 Wh-questions: 4 *is,* 4 *are,* 4 *do,* and 4 *does*. Unlike production, a balanced imitation task reduces the learner's opportunity to avoid dealing with a structure. As we will show, the learner may try to avoid a structure in imitation by failing to respond, but the imitation task remains more revealing than production since the researcher is aware of those items to which learners do not respond.

TWO TYPES OF LEARNERS

We looked at the imitation task (see Table 1) to examine the relationship between no-response and number correct. It seemed logical that as students' mastery increased, the number of no-responses should decline. Thus, high no-response should be indicative of a low level of mastery, whereas low no-response should indicate greater mastery. The extreme cases would be those in which a student either failed to respond to all of the 16 items in the task (no-response = 16; number correct = 0) **or** responded correctly to each item in the task (no-response = 0; number correct = 16).

Group data for each of the three levels we tested (Figure 1) showed the original prediction to be correct. For Level 2, no-response = 4.9, number correct = 4.2. For Level 3, no-response = 2.4, number correct = 6.4. As number correct rises, no-response declines. Conversely, as number of no-response rises, number cor-

Table 1. Imitation Task

1. *What does your mother always say to your father at dinner?*
2. *Where are Mr. and Mrs. Smith having lunch this afternoon?*
3. *What are you doing about your noisy neighbors down the street?*
4. *How do poor students pay for the university in France?*
5. *Where is Susan going this morning in that big yellow car?*
6. *Where does Secretary Kissinger stay in New York City?*
7. *Where do Americans buy aspirin and other medicine?*
8. *Why are the children crying in class on their first day of school?*
9. *Why do people pay so much for things in pretty boxes?*
10. *What is President Ford saying to the man in his office?*
11. *Why is the pretty girl wearing her brother's blue jeans?*
12. *What do you eat for breakfast every Saturday and Sunday?*
13. *Why does John wear a raincoat even on clear and sunny days?*
14. *How is Mayor Beame getting the money New York City needs?*
15. *How does Elizabeth Taylor feel about Richard Burton?*
16. *How are the scientists testing the drug for curing cancer?*

rect declines. These scores are the means for each group. Median scores yielded consistent results. (Group differences were significant—$p < .05$—between Levels 3 and 4 and between 2 and 4, but did not reach significance between Level 2 and 3 learners.)

There was considerable dispersion in the data. If we look at the graph in Figure 2, the dark line in the middle shows the progression of the average no-response and number correct for each of the three groups tested. The circled areas include students whose behavior was not typical.

For one group of students, there was an unusually high number of no-responses compared to a relatively high number of correct answers. These stu-

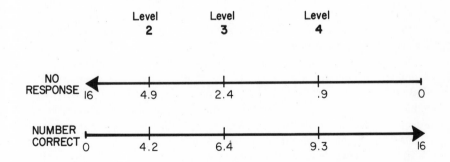

Figure 1. Mean scores for Levels 2–4.

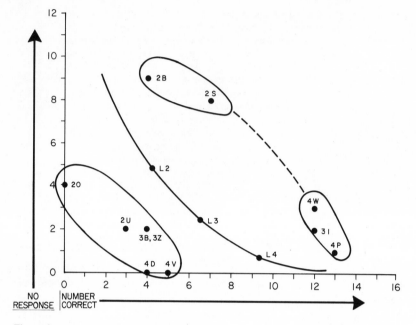

Figure 2. Average and atypical performance on no-response and number correct results.

dents appeared to avoid responding to items they did not know and were willing to imitate a sentence only when they felt the likelihood of making errors was small. For example, Subject 4W[1] had no-response = 3 and number correct = 12. The average student of no-response = 3 should have only about 7 correct.

Another group had relatively low no-response compared to low number correct. These subjects appeared to be guessers. Even when there was little likelihood of being correct, they were willing to try. Subject 20 had no-response = 4, yet number correct = 0! Not a single sentence was correctly imitated, in spite of a relatively low no-response score.

Of course, these are the more extreme cases. Most students exhibited avoidance or guessing strategy to some degree, but not to the same extent as those individuals whose scores are circled on the graph in Figure 2. This interpretation, that guessing or avoidance are "strategies," is possible if we assume that a learner's position in Figure 2 is reliable (that the dispersion is not a random result of the test administration, not a statistical artifact).

There is independent justification to suggest that some learners use avoidance as a learning strategy (Kleinmann, 1976; Schachter, 1974). Teacher's experience

---

[1]The first number in the learner "code" indicates the level of the learner tested, i.e., 2, 3, or 4.

(Bailey *et al.*, 1976) has also shown that some students do avoid using certain structures while others use a more "trial and error" approach, i.e., guessing.

Having suggested the existence of these learning strategies, we would need very specific sorts of evidence if we wished to go further. It would be necessary to show that the extreme groups differ in other ways, beyond the distribution of scores on this particular occasion and imitation task. Traditional methods of research and analysis could help us pursue this idea:

1. Would we be likely to find a predictable proportion of avoiders and guessers among other second language learners? Statistics would help us determine this possibility, assuming the groups tested could be clearly defined.
2. Are guessers or avoiders more successful in second language learning? Retesting the same individuals at a later time, using a longitudinal approach, would help answer this question.
3. Do learners in these categories show differential behavior with respect to other factors? Factor analysis would provide useful information.

Our approach so far having concentrated on language learning strategies of a general nature, we next looked into individual behavior with respect to specific structures.

FOCUS ON SUBSTITUTIONS

We investigated auxiliary substitutions made by 18 students in Level 4. Four students had no auxiliary substitution. One student had only one *do* substitution for the auxiliary *does*. The remaining students divided into two main groups: Group A and Group B. Group A substituted *did* for forms of *be* and *do;* Group B substituted *does* for *be* and *do*. For example, *How is Mayor Beame getting the money New York City needs?* (question no. 14 on the imitation task, see Table 1) would typically be repeated as follows by a Group A learner:

   *How **did** Mayor Beame **get** the money New York City needs?*

and by a Group B learner:

   *How **does** Mayor Beame **getting** the money New York City needs?*

Table 2A provides the percentages of *did* and *does* substitutions for each of the four original auxiliaries tested. For example, Learner 4R in Group A had a total of five substitutions: 100% were with *did*. Learner 4B in Group A had a total of six substitutions: 67% (i.e., four) were with *did,* 0% were with *does,* and the remaining 33% (i.e., two) were with *do*.

Further investigation revealed that there was another structural phenomenon which also supports the division of learners into two groups: *Did* substituters also

**Table 2. Substitutions in Auxiliary Development of Adult Second
Language Learners**[a]

| | | | A. Substitutions | | |
| | | | Percentage | | |
Learner		Total number of substitutions	did	does	Other
Group A	4H	8	13	0	87
(*did*)	4B	6	67	0	33
	4R	5	100	0	0
	4A[b]	3	67	33[b]	0
	4K[c]	3	33[c]	33	33
Group B	4O	4	25	75	0
(*does*)	4D	11	9	73	18
	4E	3	0	100	0
	4F	4	0	75	25
	4V	5	0	60	40
	4P	2	0	50	50
	4S	3	0	33	67
	4Q	3	0	33	67

B. Number of substitutions with and without *-ing*[d]

Substitution	With *-ing*	Without *-ing*
did	0	6[e]
does	13	6[f]

[a] Level 4 (18 learners) Imitation task: 16 *Wh*-questions—4 *is* V-*ing*; 4 *are*
V-*ing*; 4 *does* V; 4 *do* V.

[b] The single *does* from 4A is abnormal in that *-ing* is not preserved.

[c] The single *did* produced by 4K was in an incomplete imitation ("Why
did?"). If it is not counted, then 4K would belong in group B.

[d] Group B learners also added *-ing* five times in the simple present imitations,
while Group A learners never added *-ing*.

[e] Includes learner 4K (incomplete imitation "Why did?").

[f] Includes learner 4A from Group A: 1 *does* but without *-ing*.

deleted *-ing* in the progressive utterance and *does* substituters kept *-ing*. Group B
seemed to be maintaining the integrity of the progressive morphemes, while
Group A made their form consistently simple. For every relevant *did* substitution
(i.e., substitutions in progressive utterances) *-ing* is deleted, and for 13 out of 19
relevant *does* substitutions *-ing* is maintained. (See Table 2B for the pertinent

information.) There were 25 *does* substitutions and 15 *did* substitutions, representing over two-thirds of the total substitutions for Level 4. A possible explanation of such a division is that Group B learners focused on the syntax and consequently overgeneralized a syntactic structure they were learning (i.e., *does* as an auxiliary in questions), while Group A learners focused on the meaning and consequently substituted an auxiliary that maintained the semantic integrity of the utterance. Only one *did* substitution failed to maintain a meaningful utterance.[2]

This evidence suggests that learners differ in the structural paths they follow while proceeding through interlanguage. The strategies are similar, i.e., learners are substituting one auxiliary for another, but the particular structure varies between the two groups and perhaps the focus on syntax or meaning varies. Whether the structural paths are systematic across learners remains to be investigated.

Another researcher (Hatch, 1974) suggests that second language learners differ in their cognitive approach to second language learning. Our evidence supports the claim that while learners vary in their pathways of learning, the variation is systematic. It would be fruitful to investigate whether the structural divisions in any way relate to the other learner differences such as Hatch's data gatherers and rule formers.

We attempted to show a correlation between the two groups of Level 4 and the two learning strategies, avoidance and guessing, discussed earlier. But the evidence did not support this correlation.

There is another very interesting pattern in which two auxiliaries are used, one in the proper position for a question, and a second in the proper position for a statement. The six examples from Level 4 learners are in Table 3. In statistically rather than structurally oriented studies these are usually not considered because they are sporadic, "not frequent enough to consider a persistent type of structure [Bellugi-Klima, 1968]." But they show up in many studies, and Major (1974) has determined substages in the developments. See Table 4. In Major's first substage (1974, pp. 72–74), a or a*, a nonmodal auxiliary such as *do, have,* or *are* is used in the position proper for auxiliaries in questions; in the second substage, b or b*, a modal auxiliary is used which is otherwise frequent and not especially close to the modal in the modeled statement (*You ought to fix your lunch*); in the third substage, c or c*, a modal is used which is closely related to the model in meaning, thus *should* matching *ought*. The stages with two aux-

---

[2]While we support the interpretation of syntax-focused (*does* overgeneralizing) versus meaning-focused (*did* substituting) learners, this may not be a difference in type of learner. It could be that meaning-focused learners are more advanced. These learners are primarily those with low nonresponse rates (Figure 2); 5 of the 12 learners, in fact, had no responses at all.

Table 3. Double Auxiliaries from Level 4 Learners: Type WH Aux NP Aux Verb ...

Modeled sentence (Table 1)	Learner ID No.	Responses
2	4D	*Where **does** Mrs. Smith and Mr. Smith **are** going to lunch this afternoon?*
16	4O	*How **does** a scientist **are** searching for a new medicine?*
8	4N	*Why **are** the children **are** crying in the class in the first day of school?*
8	4A	*Why **are** children **are** crying in class on the first day of school?*
14	4J	*How **is** Beame **can** get the money for city?*
2	4E	*Where **does** Mrs. and Mr. lunch **does**?*[a]
3	4B	*What **do** I do about your noisy neighbor down the street?*

[a] The last two examples resemble double-auxiliary productions, but in 4B's sentence 3, the second *do* is a correct imitation of the main verb (not the auxiliary) in the model. The second *does* in 4E's sentence 2 is also to be counted an auxiliary if from "does have lunch," but is a main verb instead if "to do lunch" replaces "to have lunch."

Table 4. Similar Double Auxiliaries from Other Studies

Study	Context				Examples
Bellugi-Klima (1968)	Child first language	*What*	**shall**	*we*	**shall** *have?*
		Why	**was**	*I*	**did** *break it?*
			Do	*she*	**don't** *need that one?*
			Did	*I*	**didn't** *mean to?*
			Can	*they*	**should** *go down that Mass. Ave.?*
			Is	*it*	**was** *a snake?*
Major (1974, pp. 72–74)	Child first language (modals)	(a)	**Do**	*you*	**ought** *to fix your lunch?*
			Do	*you*	**may** *... /got to ...*
		(b)	**Would**	*you*	**ought** *to ...*
			Will/would	*you*	**might/may** *...*
			Can/could	*you*	**may** *...*
		(c)	**Should**	*you*	**ought** *to fix your lunch?* (5 children)
		(a*)	**Have**	*you*	[∅] *fixed ...*
			Are	*you*	*going to fix your lunch?*
		(b*)	**Can/will**	*you*	[∅] *fix your lunch?*
		(c*)	**Should**	*you*	[∅] *fix your lunch?* (9 children)
Ravem (1968)	Child second language	*Why*	**didn't**	*mommy*	**don't** *make dinner?*
Kypriotaki (1974)	Adult native		**Could**	*X*	**can** *have been baked?*
			Couldn't	*X*	**could** *have been hurt?*
			Had	*X*	**had** *being given?*
			Shouldn't	*X*	**should** *have been built?*

116

iliaries (a,b,c) are earlier than the stage with only one auxiliary in the position appropriate for questions (a*,b*,c*).

Reexamining the imitation data from our Level 4 learners, we found that double auxiliaries were closely related to overgeneralization (see Table 3). Learners 4D, 4O, and 4E substituted *does* for *are, do,* and *is* in imitating other sentences. By contrast, *are* is never substituted for other auxiliaries in Level 4 imitations. So the *are + are* of Level 4 is distinctive (4A did substitute *are* for *do* in the cued production task). Thus, only 4N and 4J produced a double auxiliary in imitation when they did not substitute with the first of those auxiliaries elsewhere.

Our evidence suggests that double auxiliaries and substitution or overgeneralization of the first of the auxiliaries are closely related stages for adults. Furthermore, as Anderson (1971, 1974) has argued, the usual rule for forming questions (invert subject and auxiliary) is not easily applied to the language learning situation. Some learners produce two auxiliaries, one in statement position and the other in question position, and then later suppress the auxiliary in statement position.

More on Overgeneralization

In Level 4, learners overgeneralized primarily with *does* or *did,* and we can almost say that any one individual overgeneralized with only one of them.[3] In Level 3, *is* and *did* were overgeneralized, but again, any given individual substituted with one or the other but not both. This would tend to indicate that learners proceed one step at a time, working on one part of the grammar and then another. We shall present more evidence for this later. So far, we know that *is* was overgeneralized by less advanced learners than *does,* and that the largest concentration of the *is* overgeneralizers was in Level 3.

While *is* was being overgeneralized in Level 3, it was also being correctly imitated more often than any other auxiliary. A rank ordering of correctly imitated auxiliaries for Level 3 showed *is* at the top with 45% correct imitation and *does* at the bottom with 20% correct imitation. In Level 4, where *does* was being overgeneralized, exactly the opposite ordering of correct imitations results. *Does led all the other auxiliaries in correct imitation: 78% of the does items were* imitated correctly, but only 46% of the *is* items were. The improvement in the correct imitation of *does* from Level 3 to 4 was statistically significant ($p < .000x$).

We can make some inferences from this interaction of correct imitation of *is* and *does:*

---

[3]If two abnormal examples are excluded (as in the notes to Table 2), then only two occurrences of *did* remain exceptional, one each from Learners 4O and 4D.

1. The sudden improvement in the accuracy of usage of a grammatical structure (such as *does*) may be accompanied by an increase in the overgeneralization of this same structure into other parts of the grammar. This means
that the distribution of this particular structure is still being learned long
after the mechanics of it have been mastered.

2. A plateau in learning a grammatical structure (such as *is* undergoes where it
fails to make any improvement between Levels 3 and 4) may indicate that
overgeneralization is taking place at the same time with another closely
related or easily confused structure. In this case, the usage of *does* overgeneralized into the distribution of *is*.

In the case of *is* and *does*, surface similarities make the choice of auxiliary
difficult. Both *is* and *does* are used for the third person singular, and moreover,
both are marked by final *s*. On the other hand, the usages of *is* and *does* are
dissimilar in that one is part of a construction marking the continuous aspect of
the verb and one is not. They mark nuances of time distinction which are difficult
for a learner of language to master.

We reorganized our data for further examination of overgeneralization by
interscaling all the subjects in all the levels of our experiment. The effects of
arranging the learners along a scale are (*a*) grouping, and (*b*) rank ordering.
Following the procedures of scaling, the learners were grouped according to what
appeared to be learner types as judged by gross differences between individuals
in types of errors made. (In the study, a major division turned out to be overgeneralization with one auxiliary but not another.) Learners were rank ordered
within these groups from less advanced to more advanced by matching as closely
as possible the type and location of all errors made by individuals who were
ordered next to each other. The purpose of scaling is to use group data to
construct the pathway of learning that might be followed by a single individual.

The clearest results we obtained from scaling had to do with the overgeneralization of *is*. Table 5 contains all of the learners in this study who made any
substitutions with *is*. This includes 23 of the 46 learners. (All of the *is* overgeneralizations for these learners are enclosed in heavy black lines.) These learners were ranked by matching errors, and the resulting order, as it turned out,
placed the majority of the Level 2 learners at the bottom of the ranking and most
of the Level 4 learners at the top, thus providing external evidence that the order
we achieved by matching errors was meaningful. The heavy black lines form
steps which show the environments for *is* overgeneralization expanding and
contracting again. The least advanced two learners within this block (2P and 2K)
substitute *is* for *does* only. Beginning with Learner 2L, *is* is overgeneralized for
are as well as *does*. *Is* is not overgeneralized for *do* until we encounter Learner
2O, and a total of only five learners do it. Starting with Learner 4V, *is* is no
longer substituted for *do*. Starting with Learner 3C, *is* is no longer substituted for

does. The most advanced learners who overgeneralize *is* do so for only one auxiliary: *are*.[4]

Scaling has shown us that our hypothetical learner overgeneralizes *is* for *does* first when he or she starts overgeneralizing with *is*. This confirms what we knew from our group statistics. What we did not suspect before and what scaling displays visually is that when the learner stops overgeneralizing with *is*, he or she does so in a gradual systematic fashion, cutting out one environment at a time. The first environment to go is *do*, then *does*, and lastly, *are*. Thus our further investigation has revealed finely detailed steps in the process of overgeneralization.

A number of interpretations could be imposed on the particular order of environments to which *is* overgeneralization was extended and from which it was retracted. These results will be meaningful to the extent to which subsequent studies confirm the fact that the particular order we found is in fact the order that emerges when more extensive experimentation is done on this hypothesis. Scaling has given us an insight that we might not have arrived at otherwise, but we emphasize that the usefulness of scaling as it is presented here is largely as a hypothesis formation tool, one of many techniques for sorting and analyzing data.

METHODS OF DATA ANALYSIS COMPARED

We have seen the contribution that an analysis of individual errors can make through techniques such as scaling. Some proponents of the kind of individual scaling procedures which have been presented here view scaling as an alternative to statistical measures. Scaling is seen as superior, specifically because it forces the researcher to examine the performance of individuals and small groups rather than a single group average. An example is the examination of *is* overgeneralization discussed earlier.

We wish to state that statistics and scaling procedures can and should be complementary in their application—not mutually exclusive in any sense. In fact, some statistics are available which will tell the researcher to what extent data resemble a certain kind of scale.

---

[4]The following may help explain the method of scaling used to construct Table 5. The easiest decision in rank ordering these learners was that 2P and 2K had to be adjacent because of their large number of similar patterns, and low on the scale-because they have so many omissions and nonresponses. At the other extreme, Learner 4S does not share a large number of pattern similarities with any other learner, and is therefore harder to place. It should be noted in this connection that we have not yet analyzed data from the other two tasks (intuition and cued production) in the detail that would permit us to resolve questions of scaling order. Imitation data alone allow for alternative placements which are equally justifiable.

Table 5. Scaling Results Showing Expansion and Contraction of *IS* Overgeneralization Environments

	(Wh *is* NP V-*ing*)					(Wh *are* NP V-*ing*)			(Wh *does* NP V)				(Wh *do* NP V)			
	5	14	11	10	16	8	2	3	1	6	13	15	4	9	7	12
4Q	∅	does	—	does	was		is						—	—	—	
4K	(*did*)	NoInv can	— NoInv	V∅	is	does	is						—	NoMV	—	NoSbj
3C	NoSbj	NoMV		—	NoMV	NoMV	*did*V∅ does		*do*				—	—	—	
4S			NoInv		*does*V∅	∅V∅	is				∅+*ing* is+*ing*	can	—	∅	*does*	
4V		∅V∅	∅V∅	∅V∅	is	*do*V∅	is	is	is	is	is+*ing* ∅the	isV∅	*does*	*∅the* *did*	isV+NP *is*	∅Vs
4H			∅		—	∅	is		is	is	∅the		—	∅the *is*	*is*	—
3K									is	is	is	—		*∅the*	*is*	
3S	V∅			∅the	V∅	is+*are*	Vs		isVs	is	is	is+is +*ing*	—	is+*ing*	*is* *is*	
2H	V∅ NoInv			V∅	—	∅V∅ *does*	isV∅		is	is *is*	∅+*ing* +*ing*	is	∅	*∅the*	NoMV *is*	
2O	NoInv		*does*	—	—	NoInv V∅	NoInv V∅	NoSbj	—	NoMV	NoInv	—	*does*	—	NoMV	
2G		∅	*does*+is	V∅	—	V∅	*are*+is V∅		*are*	is+*ing*	*are*+*ing*	is+*ing*	∅	*does*		*is*
2U	*does*	—		*was*	—	is			*are*	NoMV	+*ing*	—	NoMV	—	*does*	

120

3E	is+has	ØVø	—	NoInv	—	ØVø			NoMV	is (is)	NoMV	—	NoInv	—	Ø
3B	Vø	Vø	NoMV	Vø	NoMV	ØVø	are+are	is	NoMV	is	NoMV	—	NoMV	NoMV	Øthe
3Z		Vø	NoMV	Øthe	NoMV	ØVø	do	is	is	is	is	is	—	+ing	—
3G	is+is		—		—	ØVø	do	is	is–the	did	—	Øthe	are	Øthe	Øthe
2R	NoMV	NoSbj	NoMV	NoMV	—	NoMV	do	NoInv	is	did	is	—	NoMV	Øthe	NoMV did
2A		—	—		—	is	is	Vs	isVd	did	Vs	is	are Ø	Øthe	NoMV
3N	—		—		is	Ø	NoSbj+ is+	—	Øthe is+is	NoMV	—	Øthe	—	—	—
2L		—	NoMV	Ø Øthe	—	Ø	NoSbj	NoMV	did + is	is+is	NoMV did + is	-	—	Ø	is NoMV
2N	NoMV	—	Vø	Vs	—	Vø	—	NoMV	—	—	VØ	NoMV	—	Ø	NoMV
2P	NoInv	—	—	ØVø	—	ØVø	—	NoMV	—	is NoMV is	—	—	—	Ø	ØVs
2K	NoInv	—	—	ØVø	—	ØVø	—	NoMV	Ø	NoMV	Ø	—	—	Ø	—

Notations: NoMV = no main verb; NoSbj = no subject; NoInv = order Wh Np Aux V; NoInv = order Wh Np Aux V; Aux V + NP = order Wh Aux V NP; Vø = omitted *-ing*; Vs, Vd = 3sg., past forms (including irregular *has*, *saw*, etc.); Ø = no auxiliary; Aux + Aux (*is + can*) = Wh Aux NP Aux V; Blank cell = no change from the model sentence form given on top; — = no response; substituted or added auxiliaries are entered; ( ) = incomplete response. See Appendix for explication and example of error types.

121

Let us consider the question of group versus individual data. There are times when group results can be very useful. In our initial investigation, we focused on errors in three groups. These groups made errors in the structures tested to varying degrees. Traditional statistical methods told us to what extent the differences were likely to have occurred by chance. Thus we determined that the groups as a whole were at different stages in the acquisition of the structures we were investigating. So group scores can be useful.

The extent to which statistics obscure the individual performance of subjects depends upon the researcher's use or abuse of statistics. As the economist Kenneth Boulding has said, "Statistics is the fine art of losing information in an orderly manner [oral remarks at a professional conference in 1955]." It is up to the researcher to choose appropriate procedures and to remember that group measures are just that. There is no reason why statistics cannot be used to investigate individual differences or the existence of several trends within a body of data. The standard deviation can as easily be used to identify individuals who differ from the average as those whose behavior is more similar to that of others within the group. Statistics can also be used to identify trends or modes of subgroups.

If we accept that both statistics and scaling are useful tools in language research, how can we use them together to best advantage? An analysis of variance could help a researcher determine which variables frequently co-occur and help the researcher focus on those items that may be most productive for scaling. In fact, the computer has been used successfully by researchers such as Sankoff and Cedergren (1976) as part of a different kind of multidimensional scaling procedure.

We feel that a valid criticism of traditional experimental methods is that they tend to limit the examination of experimental data to whether or not the data confirm or refute a previously formulated hypothesis. They do not specifically encourage further analysis.

Scaling, along with other examinations of individual data, is particularly useful in that it stimulates the researcher to examine data from many new perspectives and challenges him or her to go beyond the limits of the original experiment. The researcher should be flexible and free to examine data from all angles without preconceived hypotheses as limitations, but all data should be taken into account.

When scaling, researchers are constrained by the fact that the arrangement of subjects must form a continuous progression of learning. Furthermore, the intuition of the researchers comes into play in that they may be influenced by the total of their experience with the language learning process. Having arrived at a new hypothesis, they can test it in the traditional way. Or, having discovered a relationship between variables by use of statistics, they can further explore this relationship through an analysis of individual performance.

Appendix. Explication and Samples of Error Types

Notation	Error type	Subject	Sentence	Examples
is	*is* substituted for another auxiliary	(a) 2R	2	*Where is a Mr. and Mrs. Smith always having lunch on this afternoon?*
		(b) 3K	7	*Where is the American buy medicine?*
are	*are* substituted for another auxiliary	(a) 2R	4	*How are poor students like university in France?*
		(b) 3G	4	*Are you a poor student?*
does	*does* substituted for another auxiliary	(a) 4P	5	*Where does the students going this morning a big yellow car?*
		(b) 4S	2	*Where does Mr. and Mrs. lunch does?*
do	*do* substituted for another auxiliary	(a) 3G	1	*What do Mr. and Mrs. Smith going to have lunch today?*
		(b) 3Z	3	*What do you doing about your noisy neighbor at downstairs?*
did	*did* substituted for another auxiliary	(a) 4H	9	*Why did the people pay much for that pretty boxes?*
		(b) 2A	13	*Why did John wear clear coat for sunny and shiny day?*
Ø	Auxiliary omitted	(a) 2K	9	*Where the people play?*
		(b) 4Q	5	*Where Susan going this morning that big yellow car?*
NoMV	Main verb omitted	(a) 3B	4	*How does poor students about the university in France?*
		(b) 3E	1	*What does your mother and father for dinner?*

(Continued)

Appendix. Explication and Samples of Error Types *(Continued)*

Notation	Error type	Subject	Sentence	Examples
NoSbj	Subject omitted	(a) 4K	12	*What do eat breakfast every Saturday and Sunday?*
		(b) 2A	3	*What are doing without your neighbors down the street?*
NoInv	Auxiliary not inverted with noun phrase	(a) 4S	11	*Why the pretty girl is wearing his brother blue jean?*
		(b) 3G	10	*Why President is saying to man?*
V+NP	Auxiliary and verb inverted together with noun phrase	(a) 4H	7	*Where is buy Americas aspirin and other medicine?*
		(b) 4B	14	*How is getting the mayor the money the city needs?*
+*ing*	*ing* added	(a) 3Z	9	*Why do people paying so much for many boxes?*
V∅	*ing* deleted	(a) 2N	8	*Why are the children cry in school?*
		(b) 4B	14	*How is Mayor Beame get a lot of money?*
Vs	Final *s* added	(a) 3S	1	*What is all your mother often says to your father after dinner?*
		(b) 2P	8	*Why the childrens cryings in the class in first?*
Ved	Final *ed* added	(a) 2A	6	*Where is Secretary Kissinger stayed in New York City?*
∅ *the*	Auxiliary omitted, *the* inserted	(a) 3G	9	*Why the people pay so much?*
		(b) 3B	7	*Where the Americans buy aspirin or another medicine?*
Aux+Aux	Reduplication of auxiliary	(a) 4J	14	*How is Beame can get the money for city?*
		(b) 3E	2	*Where are Mr. and Mrs. Smith and Mr. Smith are having for dinner this afternoon?*

REFERENCES

Anderson, L. 1971. Transformations don't exist? *Papers from the Seventh Regional Meeting, Chicago Linguistic Society,* 1-17.

Anderson, L. 1974. How rule structures grow. On auxiliaries in children. Unpublished manuscript.

Anderson, L. 1976. Scaling interlanguages: Detecting learner hypotheses and strategies. Unpublished manuscript, submitted for publication.

Anderson, L. 1977a. Discovering intermediate stages in language learning through scaling analysis, illustrated on English relative clauses. Paper presented at the Fifth Annual Conference on New Ways of Analyzing Variation Etc. (NWAVE-V), October, 1976, Georgetown Univ.

Anderson, L. 1977b. Knots in the creole net. Paper presented at NWAVE-III. Washington, D.C.

Bailey, N., Eisenstein, M., & Madden, C. 1976. The development of Wh-questions in adult second language learners. Paper presented at 1976 TESOL Convention, March, 1976, New York, N.Y.

Bellugi-Klima, U. 1968. Simplification in children's language. In R. Huxley & E. Ingram (Eds.), *Mechanisms of language development.* London: CIBA Foundation Press.

Hatch, E. 1974. Second language learning—universals: *Working Papers on Bilingualism, 3,* 1-17. Toronto, Canada: Ontario Institute for Studies in Education.

Kleinmann, H. 1976. Avoidance behavior in adult second language acquisition. Paper presented at the Second Annual Conference on Bilingual and Second Language Learning, Queens College, New York, November.

Kypriotaki, L. 1974. The acquisition of Aux. *Papers and Reports on Child Language Development, 8,* 87-103. Stanford Univ., Committee on Linguistics.

Major, D. 1974. *The acquisition of modal auxiliaries in the language of children.* The Hague: Mouton.

Ravem, R. 1968. Language acquisition in a second language environment. *IRAL, 6,* 175-185.

Rosansky, E. 1976a. Morpheme studies and second language acquisition studies: A question of methods. Paper presented at the Tenth Annual TESOL Convention, New York, March.

Rosansky, E. 1976b. Natural sequences and the emperor's new clothes. Paper presented at NWAVE-V, Georgetown Univ., October.

Sankoff, D., & Cedergren, H. J. 1976. The dimensionality of grammatical variation. *Language, 52,* 163-178.

Schachter, J. 1974. An error in error analysis. *Language Learning, 24,* 205-214.

8 Evidence of the need for a second language acquisition index of development

Diane E. Larsen-Freeman

This chapter argues for the need to establish a second language acquisition index of development, a term I have borrowed from Hakuta (1975). Such an index would consist of a description of the stages through which second language learners pass on the way to acquiring any second language. Each stage would be defined by certain speech performance characteristics. While I acknowledge the danger inherent in attempting to divide a process such as language learning into discrete units such as stages, I believe the risk a necessary one which will enable researchers to identify explicitly the population of learners with whom they are dealing.

Those of us involved in second language acquisition research usually adopt very subjective measures of target language proficiency. We identify learners as being beginning, intermediate, or advanced with respect to the target language. Such a classification schema is much too vague to convey to others the level of competence of a particular group of learners. Our colleagues in first language acquisition research enjoy an advantage. They can employ a much more precise measure of the linguistic development of their subjects by calculating their mean length of utterance. Such a measure is obviously not applicable in second language acquisition research where the learner is more cognitively sophisticated and, therefore, capable of producing utterances that are more than a few morphemes in length shortly after initial contact with the target language.

While I would be the first to admit that individual learner variability is evident in second language learning, I also am convinced that there exist general developmental progressions or trends to which learners conform. Furthermore, I believe the delineation of stages in this progression would allow us to address questions which we are currently forced to ignore. Hakuta (1975), for example, conducted a longitudinal study of the acquisition of English by Uguisu, a 5-year-old native Japanese speaker. One of the issues he chose to examine was language transfer as a factor in the second language learning process, and he was specifically interested in the structural avoidance phenomenon observed by Schachter (1974). In order to study this, Hakuta decided to compare Uguisu's use of relative clauses with that of Marta, a 5-year-old Spanish speaker learning ESL, who was then a subject of a study by Cancino, Rosansky, and Schumann.[1] He hypothesized that since Spanish like English, and unlike Japanese, places the head noun to the left of the relative clause, Marta would produce more relative clauses than Uguisu. Hakuta was hampered in this analysis, however, since he had no reliable means of determining whether Uguisu and Marta were at a similar stage of development in English. Had he been comparing the number of relative clauses used by two children learning English as their first language, he could have been reasonably safe in assuming that they were at a similar stage of development since they were both 5-year-olds. Unfortunately, we in second language acquisition research cannot even rely upon the independent yardstick of chronological age as a basis for comparing subjects.

I believe the behavior of the learner and influences on the learning process change as the learner's proficiency in target language increases; therefore, when making any claims about the learner, researchers must specify at which stage of development their subjects are functioning. We tend to get embroiled in controversies because we overlook this. We argue about the influence of a certain factor on the language learning process while overlooking the probability that the influence of any given factor might vary depending upon the level of the learner with respect to the target language. For example, to what extent first language transfer occurs in the process of acquiring a second language has been a hotly debated issue in the second language acquisition field for some time. However, if one accepts Newmark's (1966) view of language transfer—that the L_1 is not a source of proactive inhibition, but rather something the learner relies on less and less as he becomes increasingly proficient at expressing himself in the target language—one realizes that conflicting views about the effect of L_1 transfer could result simply because these views were based on the performance of learners at different stages of development.

I conducted a study in which the linguistic performance of 24 "beginning" adult learners of ESL was analyzed with respect to 10 grammatical morphemes.

---

[1] See Cazden, Cancino, Rosansky, and Schuman (1975).

Table 1. Language Group Performance on BSM at Time One

	Arabic			Japanese			Persian			Spanish		
Morphemes	S^a	P^b	$\%^c$	S	P	$\%$	S	P	$\%$	S	P	$\%$
Aux	48	92	52	40	54	74	44	60	73	38	46	83
3rd sing	16	36	44	18	36	50	12	42	28.5	16	48	33
Poss	4	32	12.5	12	26	46	6	30	20	6	30	20
Cop	50	60	83	38	44	86	47	58	81	42	54	77
Short plu	58	88	66	32	64	50	42	84	50	58	80	73
Art	202	228	88.5	106	158	67	138	216	64	177	192	92

[a] Raw score.
[b] Potential score.
[c] Percentage of suppliance in obligatory contexts.

Among the 24 subjects 6 were speakers of Arabic, 6 of Japanese, 6 of Persian, and 6 of Spanish. I performed a cursory contrastive analysis between English and each of these four different native language backgrounds for these 10 grammatical morphemes. On the basis of this limited contrastive analysis, I made a number of predictions about which morphemes would cause the most difficulty for which language groups.

I administered the Bilingual Syntax Measure (BSM) (Burt, Dulay, & Hernández, 1973) to my subjects and scored for whether or not they supplied the 10 morphemes in obligatory contexts. The score for any given morpheme was dependent upon the percentage of times the morpheme was supplied accurately in obligatory contexts. The decision to reject or accept each hypothesis was predicated upon the relative performance of the language group involved in the prediction as compared with the performance of the other language groups on that particular morpheme. Thus, for example, if I predicted that the Japanese subjects would have trouble with morpheme X and the other groups would have no undue difficulty with morpheme X, I decided my hypothesis was confirmed if the Japanese group scored substantially lower on morpheme X than each of the other three groups. This was not a rigorously controlled study by any means, but I feel it gave me a rough idea of the effect of the L_1 on the subjects' performance in English.

I arrived at 13 predictions,[2] and as the reader can see from Tables 1 and 2, I felt that 9 of my predictions were confirmed, 3 were disconfirmed, and the status of 1 had to remain undetermined owing to the insufficient number of obligatory contexts by which to score the particular morpheme.

After 2 months, during which the subjects underwent intensive English in-

[2] See Larsen (1975) for a discussion of their content.

Table 2. Status of Contrastive Analysis Predictions after Examination of Data at Time One

Language group	Morpheme	Confirmed	Disconfirmed
Arabic	Aux	x	
	3rd sing		x
	Poss	x	
	Cop		x
Japanese	Short plu	x	
	3rd sing		x
	Art	x	
Persian	Short plu	x	
	Poss	x	
	Art	x	
Spanish	Poss	x	
	Cop (certain instances)	x	
	Art (certain instances)	?	?

struction, I repeated the entire procedure. As is evident from Tables 3 and 4, this time I was able to confirm only six of my predictions, while five were disconfirmed, and two were undetermined.

While I recognize the effect of language transfer can be measured in many ways, such as the rate of acquisition, structural avoidance, interference errors, etc., I believe this initial analysis does provide some evidence that the effect of the native language on the English performance of ESL students was reduced somewhat over time. Thus, any claim about the influence of native language transfer on the L_2 acquisition process must be specified for the proficiency level of the learners being studied.

Table 3. Language Group Performance on BSM at Time Two

Morphemes	Arabic			Japanese			Persian			Spanish		
	S^a	P^b	$\%^c$	S	P	%	S	P	%	S	P	%
Aux	62	88	70.5	50	58	86	73	74	99	66	74	89
3rd sing	12	40	30	10	36	28	27	48	56	13	40	32.5
Poss	8	24	33	16	22	73	27	44	61	30	44	68
Cop	45	64	70	34	36	94.5	75	80	94	45	52	86.5
Short plu	58	80	72.5	37	66	56	52	68	76	70	84	83
Art	206	244	84	86	158	54	139	228	61	219	226	97

[a] Raw score.

[b] Potential score.

[c] Percentage of suppliance in obligatory contexts.

Table 4. Status of Contrastive Analysis Predictions after an Examination of Data at Time Two

Language group	Morpheme	Confirmed	Disconfirmed
Arabic	Aux	x	
	3rd sing		x
	Poss	x	
	Cop	x	
Japanese	Short plu	x	
	3rd sing		x
	Art	x	
Persian	Short plu		x
	Poss		x
	Art	x	
Spanish	Poss		x
	Cop (certain times)	?	?
	Art (certain times)	?	?

Taylor (1975) too has contributed support for the notion that the character of the learner's linguistic performance changes depending upon the degree to which the target language has been acquired. He administered a translation test to 20 Spanish-speaking subjects of ESL. The subjects were at two levels of proficiency—"beginning" and "intermediate." The test required the subjects to translate 80 Spanish sentences into English. "A taxonomy of twenty error types was designed to analyze the errors in the AUX and the VP of the translations. The error types were categorized into errors of overgeneralization, transfer, translation, indeterminate origin and errors not considered [p. 73]."

In Figure 1 we can see that the errors made by the elementary and intermediate level students were not qualitatively different.

> However, the subject's reliance on the strategies of over-generalization and transfer were found to be quantitatively different. The elementary subjects' reliance on the transfer strategy was found to be significantly higher than that of the intermediate subjects; the intermediate subjects' reliance on the overgeneralization strategy was found to be significantly higher than that of the elementary subjects [p. 73].

In this study, then, the difference between learner proficiency levels was manifested by a shift in the dominant strategy. The more the learner improved in the target language, the more he exhibited intralanguage, as opposed to interlanguage, errors.

We find further evidence of a qualitative difference in the performance of subjects at different levels of proficiency by considering the demands that an elicited imitation task makes on learners.

Fraser, Bellugi, and Brown (1963), first language acquisition researchers,

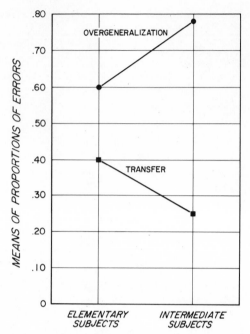

Figure 1.   The means of the proportions of overgeneralization and transfer errors made by the elementary and intermediate subjects. [Reproduced from Taylor ,1975, p. 85.]

found that the children in their study imitated a sentence with greater facility than they could comprehend or produce it. They suggested that this was because imitation was nothing more than the exercise of a motor skill. Naiman (1974), a second language acquisition researcher, challenged this suggestion after he found that his subjects performed better on a comprehension task than on an imitation task. He proposed that imitating demanded much more than the exercise of a simple motor skill, involving instead some sort of cognitive processing of the sentence by the subjects in order for them to be able to reproduce it. Thus, a subject's performance on an elicited imitation task reflected the subject's competence in the target language and was not just a task the subject could perform by rote.

Many other researchers have contributed evidence one way or the other (Fernald, 1972; Keeney, 1969; Keeney & Smith, 1971; Lovell & Dixson, 1967; Nurss & Day, 1971; Slobin & Welsh, 1967; Turner & Rommeveit, 1967.) While I realize that whether or not the learner's language-processing abilities are being tapped in an elicited imitation task might depend on the length of the sentence to be imitated, or other variables, I nevertheless was interested in seeing if imitating task demands on my 24 subjects changed over time.

Sixteen sentences were constructed containing 91 total occurrences of the same 10 morphemes I examined earlier. The sentences were all approximately 15 syllables long, and the position of each morpheme was arranged so that each allomorph appeared at least once in the beginning of a sentence, medially and finally. The experimenter read each sentence once and the subject was asked to repeat each immediately.

Once again the results were scored by determining the percentage of times a subject supplied each morpheme in its obligatory contexts. The scores on each morpheme were summed for all subjects, and the morphemes were ranked according to decreasing percentage. This entire treatment was repeated after the same 2-month interval during which the subjects received intensive instruction in English.

It is very interesting to compare the rank order of morphemes from the first administration of the imitation task with that of the second. From Table 5 we can see that after the first administration of the task, the copula is the only morpheme out of alignment with the natural division which would take place if the other nine morphemes were to be split into two groups—one having perceptual saliency ([+syllable]) and occupying the upper portion of the rank order (prog, art, irreg. past and long plu) and the other group having low perceptual saliency (all bound morphemes; all [−syllable]), sharing phonological forms, and occupying the bottom portion of the rank order (3rd sing, short plu, aux, and poss). The regular past morpheme has both salient (/+d/) and nonsalient (/t/, /d/) allomorphs, and hence should, and does, occupy the medial position in the order.

The rank orders of the morphemes from the second administration of the task

Table 5. Rank Orders of Morphemes on Imitating Task at Two Times

Imitating task—Time one	Imitating task—Time two
1. Prog	1. Cop
2. Art	2. Prog
3. Cop	3. Art
4. Irreg. past	4. Aux
5. Long plu	5. Irreg. past
6. Reg. past	6. Long plu
7. 3rd sing	7. 3rd sing
8. Short plu	8. Short plu
9. Aux	9. Reg. past
10. Poss	10. Poss

no longer conform to this pattern. Instead, the second rank order correlates very highly with the rank order determined from a speaking task using the same morphemes ($r_s = .7455 < .01$). Since we can safely assume that in order to produce these same morphemes in free speech, the subjects had somehow to engage their language processing mechanism, it is possible that an interpretation of the data from the first test would support the notion that imitation is a motor skill and that the subjects were rotely repeating sounds, while the data from the second test would indicate that something more cognitively demanding is being tapped.

Again, we see that the two positions by researchers could both be plausible—the difference in their two views could be accounted for as being due to the difference in proficiency levels of their subjects with respect to the target language.

If I have convinced the reader that we indeed need an independent index of development by which to measure and report the language proficiency of subject populations, what could be the basis for such an index? It seems that we would need to look for something more global than the performance of learners on any given structure or number of structures, since it would be difficult to choose structures which were representative of overall competence in the English language and not biased against any particular language group. Then too, if we really want this to be a second language acquisition index of development, and not simply an ESL index, we would have to look for some way of measuring second language proficiency in a nonlanguage specific way.

Gillis (1975) has suggested using scores on the Peabody Picture Vocabulary Test as a basis for determining stages in second language acquisition. This might work well for ESL, although it probably would not be possible to posit the same stages for both child and adult learners.

In any event, a syntactic measure would probably also be necessary to gauge accurately the level of target language proficiency of any learner or group of learners. Dulay and Burt (1974) offer the Syntax Acquisition Index as a possible discriminating device in this regard.

The length or number of T units (Hunt, 1965) subjects produce might be useful in establishing different stages of development, although Godfrey (1976) did not find a significant difference in their usage among the learners of different proficiencies in his study. Scott and Tucker (1974), however, did note a significant increase in the oral and written production of error-free T units by their subjects over time.

Krashen (1976), in discussing his monitor theory, has recently posited three stages of development on the basis of a survey he conducted of the error analysis literature. The criteria he uses to distinguish among the three stages do indeed deserve serious consideration in our quest for an independent index of development. In Krashen's Stage 1, for example, "utterances are initiated by the L_1

surface order, without any redundant elements such as grammatical morphemes or movement transformations [p. 2].'' This stage is thus characterized by the utilization of L_2 content words using the "kernel" or untransformed word order of the L_1.

While this is very appealing, there are certain limitations to Krashen's analysis. First, by his own admission, the data base for the stages is uncomfortably small. Second, part of the description of each stage is devoted to explicating the influence Krashen's monitor theory has on the learner's performance. The distinction he makes between learning and acquisition is certainly an intriguing one; however, as it has yet to be substantiated by any research project designed expressly for that purpose, I would prefer to see stages constructed without involving the monitor model at this time. Third, Krashen integrates affective variables into each of his stages. For example, he says that the Stage 1 learner's performance results from the speaker's being at a considerable social distance from the target language. I would prefer to see the stages defined in purely linguistic performance terms, relying upon the affective variables for explanations as to why or why not the learner fossilizes at a particular stage or exhibits any aberrations from the normal progression.

Finally, I am hopeful that it is possible to achieve greater discrimination among learner proficiencies than simply by relegating any given learner to one of three stages—particularly since Krashen notes that most second language learners would fall between Stages 2 and 3. The more narrowly we can define a learner's proficiency, the more precisely we can delineate the language learning process and the more discriminately we can convey to the other researchers who the subjects of our studies are.

None of these criticisms is meant to undermine Krashen's contributions. I feel he has given us a good start. From this beginning, we can, it is hoped, go on to test, expand upon, and delete from the stages he has posited till we have indeed constructed an index of second language development to which we can all adhere.

REFERENCES

Burt, M., Dulay, H., & Hernández, E. 1973. *Bilingual syntax measure.* (restricted ed.) New York: Harcourt.

Cazden, C., Cancino, H., Rosansky, E., & Schumann, J. 1975. Second language acquisition sequences in children, adolescents, and adults. U.S. Department of Health, Education, and Welfare. National Institute of Education Office of Research Grants. (Grant no. NE-6-00-3-0014, Project no. 730-744)

Dulay, H., & Burt, M. 1974. Natural sequences in child second language acquisition. *Language Learning, 24*(1), 37–53.

Fernald, C. 1972. Control of grammar in imitation, comprehension and production: Problems of replication. *Journal of Verbal Learning and Verbal Behavior, 11,* 606–613.

Fraser, C., Bellugi, U., & Brown, R. 1963. Control of grammar in imitation, comprehension and production. *Journal of Verbal Learning and Verbal Behavior, 2,* 121–135.

Gillis, M. 1975. The acquisition of the English verbal system by two Japanese children in a natural setting. Master's thesis, McGill Univ.

Godfrey, D. 1976. Cohesion in adult second language learners' extended monologues. Paper presented at Conference on Second Language Learning and Teaching, Oswego, New York.

Hakuta, K. 1975. Becoming bilingual at age five: The story of Uguisu. Unpublished thesis, Harvard College.

Hunt, K. 1965. *Grammatical structures written at three grade levels.* (Research Report No. 3) Champaign, Illinois: National Council of Teachers of English.

Keeney, T. J. 1969. Young children's imitation of nonsense syllable strings, word strings, and grammatical sentences. Paper read to the Society for Research in Child Development, Santa Monica, California.

Keeney, T., & Smith, N. 1971. Young children's imitation and comprehension of sentential singularity and plurality. *Language and Speech, 14,* 373–832.

Krashen, S. 1976. The monitor model of second language performance. Paper presented at the Sixth Annual California Linguistics Association Conference, San Diego, California, May.

Larsen, D. 1975. The acquisition of grammatical morphemes by adult learners of English as a second language. Unpublished Ph.D. dissertation, Univ. of Michigan.

Lovell, K., & Dixson, E. 1967. The growth of the control of grammar in imitation, comprehension, and production. *Journal of Child Psychology and Psychiatry, 8,* 31–39.

Naiman, N. 1974. The uses of elicited imitation in second language acquisition research. *Working Papers in Bilingualism, 2,* 1–37.

Newmark, L. 1966. How not to interfere with language learning. *International Journal of American Linguistics, 32,* 77–83.

Nurss, J., & Day, D. 1971. Imitation, comprehension and production of grammatical structures. *Journal of Verbal Learning and Verbal Behavior, 10,* 68–74.

Schachter, J. 1974. An error in error analysis. *Language Learning, 24,* 205–214.

Scott, M., & Tucker, G. R. 1974. Error analysis and English-language strategies of Arab students. *Language Learning, 24,* 69–97.

Slobin, D., & Welsh, C. 1973 (1967). Elicited imitation as a research tool in developmental psycholinguistics. In C. Ferguson & D. Slobin (Eds.), *Studies of child language development.* New York: Holt.

Taylor, B. 1975. The use of overgeneralization and transfer learning strategies by elementary and intermediate students in ESL. *Language Learning, 25,* 73–107.

Turner, E., & Rommeveit, R. 1967. The acquisition of sentence voice and reversibility. *Child Development, 38,* 649–660.

9

Discourse analysis, speech acts, and second language acquisition

Evelyn Hatch

In this chapter I want to review a very small part of the work we have done on discourse analysis, specifically on conversational analysis of young children learning a second language. Current research appears to center around the order of acquisition of various structures of English (AUX development, negation, question formation, or the *easy/eager* distinction, *promise/tell* patterns, etc.) or on acquisition of English morphology by the second language learner. In an attempt to explain why the child produces the forms that he or she does, whatever their order might be, earlier papers (Wagner-Gough & Hatch, 1975; Larsen-Freeman, in press) have suggested that frequency in the input must be the prime factor influencing the order of acquisition. This has caused us to consider input more seriously, which is impossible to do without turning to conversational analysis.

Our basic premise has long been that the child learns some basic set of syntactic structures, moving from a one-word phase to a two-word phase to more complex structures, and that eventually the child is able to put these structures together in order to carry on conversations with others. The premise, if we use discourse analysis, is the converse. That is, language learning, even at one- and two-word stages, evolves out of learning how to carry on conversations.

The data that I want to discuss are from two different kinds of interviews: first, between child learner and adult investigator and, second, between child language

learner and child native speaker. The data from these two sources are quite
different in nature: in terms of what the child has an opportunity to learn, and in
terms of the kinds of speech acts involved.

What does the child have to do to talk with an adult? Keenan (1974) has
pointed out that the first step the child must make in conversation is to get the
attention of the person with whom he wishes to speak. This can be accomplished
by banging a spoon or by calling a name. This first step is also clear in data of
second language learning children:

[Huang, 1970, Taiwanese, 5 years, Paul]
Paul: (to Kenny) you–you–you–you!
N.S.[1]   Huh?
Paul: I–see–you
            Kenny
Paul: oh–oh!
NS: What?
Paul: this (points to an ant)
NS: It's an ant.
Paul: ant

Attention words (e.g., *oh–oh, hey,* the listener's name, *lookit*) are also very
frequent in child–child interactions. However, this does not mean that every time
the second language learner wants to nominate a discourse topic, he first uses one
of these attention markers. In adult–child conversation, when a child is the object
of the study, the investigator almost always attends to the child (unlike a more
natural situation). In child–child discourse, where it is more difficult to get the
partner's attention, the first step is much more frequent.

Once the learner has secured the attention of his adult conversational partner,
the second task is to get the partner to attend to the topic of discourse. He can do
this by pointing to what he wants to have noticed or he may use other deictics:

Paul: oh–oh!
NS: What?
Paul: that (points at box)

[Young, 1974, Spanish, 5:6, Juan]
(Juan has finished drinking milk)
NS: Allgone?
Juan: (No response. Points at band-aid.)
            this

[1]NS = Native speaker.

NS: Cut.
Juan: cut

While many children appear to favor *that* as a topic nominator, Paul's favorite
was *this:* Paul (pointing toward drum) *this, this, this!*

In a frame, then, the first task for the learner is to get his partner's attention,
the second is to direct that attention to the topic for conversation. In response, the
adult usually identifies the object nominated:

Paul: this (points)
NS: A pencil.
Paul: pencil

One might claim that it is from these conversational exchanges that connected
utterances of more than one word develop:

Juan: that
NS: It's a truck.
Juan: that + + + truck (falling intonation
             on each word) truck

It is possible that such "two-word" utterances (or two one-word utterances
which follow each other) are propositions ("There exists a truck"). It is more
sensible, I think, to simply gloss them as establishing the topic "notice the
truck." In turn (unless the task is one of looking at picture books and naming the
objects seen), the adult does not interpret such utterances as "*this + + + noun*"
as a piece of information. Rather, he accepts it as a topic of conversation. He
does not seem to react as if the child were telling him names of things.

If one can accept that a call for attention (*oh-oh*, etc.), a pointing out of a topic
(*this*, etc.), and the learner's and partner's identifying remarks serve to nominate
a topic for conversation, then we have accounted for the presence of such utterances as "*this + + + NOUN*" in the early data of our learners. That is, we are
saying that this particular structure evolves out of discourse. It evolves not
because of some magic about frequency but because of the conscious desire of
the child to say something, to talk about something.

In some of the data, securing the listener's attention and nominating the topic
make up most of the learner's contribution to the conversation:

[Young, 1974, Spanish, 6 Enrique]
Enrique: lookit. look. look at dat. lookit dat.
                    (continued)

> hey, lookit. ah ha! b (untranscribable)
> (laugh) lookit. /hwa ɪ dæt/? lookit.
> lookit. dat one. lookit. oh, lookit, dat
> one. wow. hey, lookit. hey, /hi bədiflaɪ
> bədiflaɪ/. hey, eek. oooh, lookit /dæ/. lookit
> dat one! eeek, lookit! oooh, lookit dat
> one. oooh/ə tɛssɚ/. oooh, a big one. lookit, etc.

Once the child has secured the listener's attention and has nominated a topic, what happens in the discourse with an adult? Scollon (1974), in his dissertation on a child learning English as a first language, shows how the learner and the partner together build a conversation once the topic is understood. In first language acquisition, of course, there is a good deal of difficulty in getting the topic understood:

[Scollon, 1974, English, 1:8, Brenda]

Brenda:	(A car passes in the street. R does not hear it.) /kʰa/ (repeated four times)	
R:		What?
Brenda:	ɔo/ /gɔo/	
S: (untranscribable)		
Brenda:	/bəiš/ (nine repetitions)	
R:		What? Oh, bicycle? Is that what you said?
Brenda:	/naʔ/	
R:		No?
Brenda:	/naʔ/	
R:		No--I got it wrong. (laugh)

The young second language learner also may have some degree of difficulty in getting his topic nominations recognized, though the problems in control of the vocal apparatus are much less severe. The youngest children do have trouble in getting close enough to the adult model for specific words for the adult to recognize them: For example, Takahiro makes nine attempts at *square* during one exchange. And occasionally, the adult does not attend closely enough to the child to recognize a topic nomination and respond appropriately:

(Adult is reading a story)

Juan:	Lookit
	/də daɪm/
NS:	What?
Juan:	/də daɪm/.
NS:	What?
Juan:	(points to picture) /dæt/
NS:	Oh, the vine.
Juan:	yeh
NS:	(continues reading) There was no room anymore--
Juan:	(frustrated) I know. I know. not you. not you

When the adult does recognize the topic, he responds to it appropriately, and his response is usually a question. The questions require, or at least help, the child to get his one- or two-word utterances into a semantically related series:

[Scollon, 1974, English, 1:8, Brenda]

Brenda:	Kimby
R:	What about Kimby?
Brenda:	close
R:	Closed? What did she close, hmmm?
Brenda:	(looking in picture book at an old woman at a stove) cook say
R:	What'd the cook say?
Brenda:	something

While first language researchers are more interested in describing the child's output in such cases in terms of agent–action–object, entity–attribute, action-locative, and so on, what is especially interesting is that the questions of the adult force the child to put his utterance in this order. Out of these interactions (which Scollon calls vertical structures) develop syntactic structures (which Scollon calls horizontal structures). That is, the words that the child produces one at a time **are** semantically linked. **When the adult asks for more information with questions, he asks for a constituent to fill out the construction.** It appears quite clear that the adult takes the child's first utterance as a topic nomination and then asks for clarification or comment on it. The clarification or comment is semantically related by such questions and the relationship is later made more explicit through syntax. Scollon believes, therefore, that "this interaction with other speakers may well be the means by which Brenda has learned how to construct" syntactic relationships.

The child also begins to produce vertical structures without adult prompting after each word:

Brenda	my turn	this way	bathtub
see that	do it	hold it (three times)	scrub it (two times)
		holding (two times)	paper napkin

But obviously adult questions help her to get all the relationships out:

Brenda:	tape corder	
	use it (two times)	
NS:		Use it for what?
Brenda:	talk	
	corder talk	
	Brenda talk	

From many such examples, Scollon has built a convincing argument that these vertical structures form the prototypes for longer horizontal constructions at a later period. *"This suggests that . . . discourse structure is at the heart of sentence structure from the beginning of its development."*

Our evidence seems to show this same sort of progression in the child–adult discourse of second language learners. However, there is a difference that must be accounted for. The learner in this case has already learned to make syntactic constructions (Scollon's horizontal structures) in his first language. Why doesn't he immediately do so in the second? He has little difficulty physiologically in getting out long streams of speech; therefore, we can't say that the problem is completely in controlling the vocal apparatus. The explanation appears to be that the child is attending to the rules of conversational discourse.

Let's look at the first example:

Paul:	this boat	
NS:		Mmhmm boat.
Paul:	this	
	my boat	

Why doesn't Paul start immediately with *my boat* or *this is my boat?* It would not be beyond his ability to do so. But if we look at conversation function, we know that he must first make sure that the adult has identified the topic for the following discourse (much in the same way that the adult primes the topic *You see that boat?* and gets a response before saying *Well, that's mine*). Following is another example of prior establishment of topic:

Paul:	this	
NS:		Yes?
Paul:	this you?	
NS:		It's Kenny's.

Again, Paul identifies the topic of discourse first before he asks who the ball belongs to.

In the following example, Paul tries to establish a topic but the adult, in turn, nominates another which Paul then must respond to:

Paul:	fish see?	
NS:		Where's the turtle?
Paul:	turtle	
NS:		Mmhmm. Is he in there?
Paul:	no turtle fish	

The next example from Huang's data shows the child establishing a topic and defending his vocabulary choice for that topic:

Paul:	this	
NS:		What?
Paul:	window (looking at fish tank)	
NS:		Where's the window (= challenge?)
Paul:	window this	
NS:		Another window. Show me.
Paul:	another window (echo)	
NS:		Hmmm. Is this a *window* here?
Paul:	yah window fish not window car	

He even responds to requests for imitations as though they were topic nominations on which he should elaborate:

NS:		Paul, can you say "teacher"?
Paul:	teacher	
NS:		Right, teacher.
Paul:	teacher	
	Elsie (name of his nursery school teacher)	
NS:		Very good.

While obeying conversation rules, the learner is still subjected to the same kinds of questions as those found in the Scollon data. And the questions do help to get constituents in order:

Juan:	teacher.	
	lookit (holds up a quarter)	
NS:		Mmhmm. A quarter.
Juan:	quarter	
NS:		For what?
Juan:	for Monday (the day milk money is due)	
NS:		On Monday? For what?
Juan:	for milk	

As the child learns more and more English, the conversation rules of discourse continue to shape much of the data of our second language learners:

Enrique:	hey, lookit / də ka:/ (attention, topic nomination)	
NS:		Mmhmmm.
Enrique:	dat beauty	
	/dæ ka:/	(comment)
	you got /dæ ka:/?	(question)
NS:		No, mine's a different color. It's brown.
Enrique:	I gotta yellow. /dæt/ gotta white. yeh. I gotta yellow. yeh, I got one /hwaɪ/ (= white?) Uh-huh	
Jesus:	I gotta Ford dealer and I gotta Toyota my mother	

A number of people who work in the field of conversational analysis have said that the first rule of conversation must be to "say something relevant." The data that we have looked at so far show that the child does just that. However, what happens when the child knows this rule for conversation from his first language but knows absolutely none of the second language? How does he "say something relevant" when he wants very much to carry on a conversation with a speaker of a language he does not understand?

Itoh's data (Itoh, 1973) show the very first interactions between her subject, Takahiro, and his aunt. The child wanted very much to interact verbally with his aunt but he did not know any English. His strategy was to "say something" even though he did not understand what he said. The only possible way for him to interact verbally was to repeat her utterances after her. However, the intonation of the repetitions made the repetition "relevant." He echoes her statements with rising intonation and her questions with falling intonation:

[Itoh, 1973, Japanese, 2:6, Takahiro]

Aunt:	(parking cars and airplanes)
	Make it one at a time.
Takahiro: one at a time↑	
Aunt:	Park everything.
Takahiro: /evrišin/↑	
Aunt:	Park them.
Takahiro: park them↑	
Aunt:	Does it fly?
Takahiro: fly↓	

As the data collection sessions continued, repetitions became less echolalic:

H:	Do you want to race also?
Takahiro: also racing car↓	
H:	That's all. That's all.
Takahiro: okay, that's all↓	

He then began nominating topics:

Takahiro: /gra:ž/↓	
H:	Garage. OK. I'll make a garage.
Takahiro: ok	

Takahiro: /flo/	
NS:	Flower. Green flower.
Takahiro: green flower	
NS:	Oh, what color is this?

Takahiro: green
              green flower

As in Scollon's data, vertical constructions take place even without adult question prompting:

Takahiro: this
              broken
NS: Broken.
Takahiro: broken
              this /əz/ broken
              broken
NS: Upside down.
Takahiro: upside down
              this broken
              upside down
              broken

Takahiro: garage
NS: It's a garage. Come in garage.
Takahiro: /kəmən/ garage.
              /naɪ/ your (=not yours)
NS: This is yours.
Takahiro: /naɪ/ yours (Note morphology cor-
                   rection.)

While the output data of the learner, then, is shaped by the rules of conversation and by adult input, the adult too is constrained in what he may say by the same rules. He too must "make a relevant reply." There are few directly relevant replies to be made to the kinds of topics the child nominates. For example, if the child nominates *this*, pointing to a fish in a fish tank, the child and adult seem to talk about *this* as a topic in very few, very limited ways: What? Fish. What's this? A fish. Where's the fish? Whose fish is that? Is that yours? How many fish are there? What color is it? What's the fish do*ing*? It's swimm*ing*. Can he swim? *No*, it's not a fish. There are not many etceteras possible. And precisely these questions and responses to the topic can account for the order of acquisition of aux development and in morphology that we talked about elsewhere (e.g., Dulay & Burt, 1974; Hatch, 1974). It gives us a high frequency for equational sentences, plurals, and the *ing* progressive.

The conversation puts the adult under two constraints as to what is a relevant response: (*a*) What information about *this* is shared by adult and child; and (*b*) what are the attributes of *this* that one can talk about? That is, there is nothing immediately obvious about *this* that allows one to ask result/cause questions (unless the fish is floating on top of the water). There is nothing about *this* to allow one to make a **relevant** remark about much of anything beyond *what, where, whose, what color, how many, what doing, can* X Verb, *is* X Verb*ing*. And the first constraint prevents the adult from saying such things as ''you know the price of tuna just went up again'' or ''what's an angel fish doing in a freshwater tank?''

My conclusion, then, is that it is really not so much that the adult knows that the child second language learner cannot answer questions with complex syntactic forms and therefore consciously simplifies the input to the child. Rather, the frequency of *what/where/whose/is* X Verb*ing,* etc., is controlled by the constraints of conversation rules. The rules of conversation, then, put constraints on questions which explain their frequency in the input. That the child then uses (or acquires) these same questions first in the data collected in adult–child discourse should not be surprising.

Turning to child–child discourse, we find a very different picture. The child learner does not receive the same kinds of input in these conversations. In fact, the speech acts required in child–child discourse are not the same, and the rules for conversation are quite different. The major speech act is no longer the giving of information in response to adult questions.

Since space is limited, I shall discuss only one strategy that reveals interesting differences in adult–child and child–child discourse, that of repetition. While repetition is important for child–adult discourse, it is useful in limited ways. As shown earlier in the data of Takahiro, it allows the child to use input in order to participate in conversations even when the child does not understand what he says. Wagner-Gough (Wagner-Gough & Hatch, 1975) has also shown how the child uses the input, incorporating parts of it into his own speech output. For example, Homer, a 5-year-old Persian child learning English, incorporated the speech he heard into his own replies, as in:

[Wagner-Gough, 1975, Persian, 5 years, Homer]

NS:		Come here.
Homer:	no come here (=I won't come)	
NS:		Don't do that.
Homer:	okay, don't do that (=Okay, I won't)	
NS:		Where are you going?
Homer:	where are you going is house	

However, repetition and incorporation are much more extensive and much more appropriate in child–child conversational discourse.

Peck's data, for example, show the child second language learner taking his turns as a conversational partner by repeating or "joining in the chorus" in conversations:

[Peck, in press, Spanish, Angel]
(Child–child conversations during puzzle-working activity)

| | | NS: ... lemme have it. Lemme have it (untranscribable) puzzle. Oops! |

NS: ... lemme have it. Lemme have it (untranscribable) puzzle. Oops!

Angel: (laugh) lemme have! (scream)

NS: Nope. But it goes here.

Angel: here. goes

NS: ... and that's one more like it.

Angel: (laughs to himself) 'smore like it

NS: *Really* more like it.

Angel: I need you–in–the–oooh!

NS: Oooh, darn. Oh darn. Oh. (Sings) doo–doo– (continues)

Angel: (joins in) da–da

NS: Oh *good!* Now there's *one* piece.

Angel: (laughs) there one piece

NS: Lookit how much we've done so far so good.

Angel: lookit all––(sings low:) far so good–good–good. (speaking) good, good, good, good

Such examples have often been dismissed as simply language play. And, in an earlier resume of Huang's work, I pointed out the large number of "language play" routines. Some of them, no doubt, serve no other function than play (not to disparage play), but they all occur within conversations (not just when the child is alone or talking to toys), and they serve several important conversation functions, not the least of which is that of keeping the conversation going. (Would that the adult second language learner could manage this function so easily!) But repetitions also serve a number of other important functions for the learner in terms of the speech acts required in child–child discourse, as shown in the following examples from Young's data.

Repetition is useful for bragging:

NS: I got a real gun.

Enrique: I got a real gun

Adult: A real what?
Enrique   real gun
go like dat (gun noises)

.

.

.

NS: You gotta parachute?
Enrique: hey, yeh. gotta parachute
Adult: What's a parachute?
NS: It have a man go down.
Enrique: yeh (untranscribable). go down,
down, down, down, down (pitch
drops on *down*s) go down, down,
down. I did. my friend got it

Verbal dueling is also a speech act that can be built on repetition with minor changes:

Juan: (drawing picture) I have a /dɪs/ dog
NS: You don't have no dog.
Juan: you no have a nothing dog
NS: Yes I do.
Juan: nuh-uh. lemme see
Enrique: what color /dæ/?
Juan: I have a /dɪs/ dog
Enrique: uh-uh. you /do:/ got *any* dog. I got
          /dæ/ dog
NS: I got this dog.
Enrique: I got, got /dɪs/ dog.
NS: I got Lassie.
Juan: I got bigger Lassie
Enrique: I got Lassie! Blassie! I got Blassie!
NS: Hey, he say ... he say ...
he ... he got Lassie. His
name's not Lassie.

Enrique: no, Blassie
Juan: Blassie
Adult: Did you ever see Lassie on
TV?

It is worth noting that verbal dueling and argument almost always involve the use of comparatives:

NS: Hye, he do more better 'n
                                                       you.

Enrique: he do more better 'n you
NS: I can—
Enrique: I can do more (untranscribable).
            lookit. no more better 'n me.
            lookit. look what is. dumb.
            lookit. (sings: dumb, dumb,
            dumb)

Arguments easily move to threats where, again, repetition is an important part of the speech act:

NS: (at swings) I can beat your
                                                       brother up. I can beat him
                                                       up.

Enrique: you can beat him, huh. I can beat
            him to my party 'n you can beat
            him 'n you can beat my brother.
            he beat you up. you (untranscrib-
            able) it. *I can beat you up*

In this last example, it appears that if there is no gradual buildup of traded insults, the child must sustain what he says over a longer period of time and gradually build up volume so that the final threat is said both at a higher pitch and with greater intensity. In other words, it appears that the speech act itself requires the learner to select length and the plan for increased volume and pitch over the actual syntax of the intermediate material in his threat. Therefore, the material that leads up to his final *I can beat you up* does not make strict sense though it is related to the discourse via repetition of the original boast of the native speaker.

Repetition also appears in speech acts which shift blame:
NS: (to adult regarding Juan) He's
                                                       makin' a stupid boat.
Juan: you makin' a . . . a kaka boat
NS: He said a bad word.
Juan: he say, he say bad word

and for making deals:

NS: I'll trade you one of those for
                                                       one of those rocket things.

Children:	No way.
Enrique:	no way, man. no way
Children:	No way.
Enrique:	dat crazy. boy, you craze. no. him crazy. huh, dat mine. yeh, no way

Repetitions also appear to function well for transfer of orders:

NS:	. . . I'm driving. Take over, E., take over! (shouts)
Enrique:	hey Sean, Kris, look. take over!

.
.
.

NS:	This is your place, E. You have to.
Enrique:	I have to . . . yeh. (car sounds) have to say "take over"
Juan:	E's the driver
Enrique:	he going. ah no! let's take over. I am

Repetitions also occur when the learner is struck by the sounds of particularly delightful words:

Enrique:	fall down!
NS:	Okay–dokey.
Enrique:	what you say?
NS:	What?
Enrique:	you say "okay–dokey"? (untranscribable) "okay–dokey"?
NS:	Okay–dokey. Yeh.
Enrique:	okay–dokey. hey, I did it. okay–dokey (continues saying *okay–dokey* with different stress patterns)
NS:	(disgusted) Oooh, you made a boo-boo.
Enrique:	I made a boo-boo. look what I color.
NS:	. . . boo-boo. lookit

Enrique: so what? all up. boo-boo yep.
             boo-boo. everybody do boo-boo.
             I did wrong (laugh)

And, again, they serve to keep conversation going, as in this exchange from Peck's data:

Angel: this go like *this,* this go
               like *that.*   ┌this goes like that
NS: (mocking)   └goes like tha-it
Angel: ┌go like (giggle) this
NS: └Go like–thiay

                                           (mocking accent) it goes like
                                              ┌this
Angel: └this
NS: ┌It goes like
Angel: └goes like
NS: /ðiš/
Angel: this   ┌goes like
NS: └This goes like this.
Angel: this go
NS: Go–like–
Angel: /rɛkli/ this go *here.*
NS: This goes here.
Angel: be quiet
NS: Sssh! (laughs)

From these few brief examples, it must appear that there are major differences
in adult–child and child–child discourse for the second language learning child.
As we gather more data on conversations of second language learners, I am sure
many more important differences will begin to unfold.

In exchange with adults, the child is continually bombarded with questions,
primarily with questions on identification and elaboration. These are *what* questions, *where* questions, *what-doing* questions. The questions ask the child to
clarify and enlarge on the topics that he or the adult nominates. The questions are
constrained by the rules of adult conversation. The adult does not consciously
simplify his language to the child but rather obeys the rules of conversation that
require shared knowledge as a basis for questions. Further, the questions are
constrained by what is shared on the basis of objects present in the immediate
environment and by ongoing actions. The questions asked the child require him
to give new information in an order specified by the adult. This ordering may
force the child to put constituents into an order which provides the precursor to
more formal syntactic arrangements. Further, the frequency of the question

forms used by the adult is reflected in the order of acquisition that we have found for question formation for the child. This is an important finding because it contrasts with claims that have been made for first language learners in accounting for the order of acquisition of Wh-questions. This does not mean that the cognitive explanation for first language learners is wrong but rather that we might want to consider conversational rules as being important in explaining the order in first language as well as in second.

The profiles that we have drawn on language of second language learners from test data between adult and child or from spontaneous speech between adult and child are, I believe, quite different from those which we might obtain in child–child discourse data. That in itself is of interest to us. But more interesting are the obvious differences in conversation functions, practice possibilities, and the kinds of structures the child has the possibility of learning from each. From the adult he gets notions of how to order extremely controlled sets of question–answer routines based on objects present in the environment and ongoing actions; he gets vocabulary that is visually represented as well; he gets sequenced presentation of structures. From the child he gets, among many other things, an immense amount of practice that allows him to repeat models of the native speaker. The vocabulary is not nearly as tightly controlled, made-up words are frequent. The child learner seems content to join in on repetition of vocabulary even though he cannot know what the vocabulary represents. Word association responses (particularly variations on pronunciation of a word to yield many other words) are wild and frequent. (For example, while working a puzzle, Angel and his native speaker partner went from *pieces* to *pizzas* to *pepsi cola* and the pepsi cola commercial song at a fantastic rate.) Repetition is an important part of one-upmanship in verbal dueling and in many of the other speech acts of child–child discourse. The speech acts in the two kinds of discourse are different: Adults ask for elaboration of information on topics and for permission seeking from the child. Child interactions range over a much wider range—threats, justification, joking, blaming, planning, etc.

It would seem that the child has, indeed, the best of both worlds in terms of language learning opportunity. He gets chances of controlled input with vocabulary made clear from the context in conversations with adults, and he gets a chance to practice 15 repetitions in a row if he wishes when playing with other children.

Since a large portion of this chapter has been on the importance of repetition as a strategy in child–child discourse, and since we have discussed its role in the child's learning from input elsewhere, I would like to stress that repetition alone cannot explain the language learning process:

> It might be assumed, of course, that there is an observable correlation between a child's speech and its environment, and that consequently the process of language acquisition by a child would be considered simply as the mechanical acceptance of external speech forms and meanings through imitation. In contrast, those who emphasized the internal

contributions a child makes to its own speech looked for productions having nothing to do with imitation. . . . We believe that the proper position is a synthesis of these two opinions. In his form of speech a child learning to speak is neither a phonograph reproducing external sounds nor a sovereign creator of language. In terms of the contents of his speech, he is neither a pure associative machine nor a sovereign constructor of concepts. Rather, his speech is based on the continuing interaction of external impressions with internal systems which usually function unconsciously; it is thus the result of a constant "convergence." The detailed investigations pertaining to the development of speech and thought should determine the relative participation of both forces and also show how they accommodate each other [Stern & Stern, 1970, pp. 86–87].

There is little that can be said about the automatic and unconscious part of language learning at this point but there is much that can be said about the structure of conversation and of speech acts. Surely, conversational analysis is important for it looks at the input with which the child has to work in forming the abstract network of his new language.

It is time that we paid closer attention to the rules of conversation and to speech acts. They can explain the makeup of the input and the frequency of forms which determine to a major extent the reported "order of acquisition" in second language learning. There are many areas to be investigated: what kinds of sequencing of input does the child receive; which structures are frequent in various speech acts and therefore receive constant use; and how are the rules and the input different for the adult learner as compared to the child second language learner?

ACKNOWLEDGMENTS

I wish to thank Joseph Huang, Harumi Itoh, Denise Young, and Sabrina Peck for allowing me access to their data transcripts from which I have taken examples for this paper.

REFERENCES

Dulay, H. C., & C. Burt, M. K. 1974. Natural sequences in child second language acquisition. *Language Learning, 24*, 37–53.
Hatch, E. 1974. Second language learning—universals? *Working Papers in Bilingualism, 3*, 1–17.
Huang, J. 1970. A Chinese child's acquisition of English syntax. Unpublished MA-TESL thesis, UCLA.
Itoh, H. T. 1973. A child's acquisition of two languages—Japanese and English. Unpublished MA-TESL thesis, UCLA.
Keenan, E. O. 1974. Conversational competence in children. *Journal of Child Language, 1*, 163–183.
Larsen-Freeman, D. In press. An explanation for the morpheme accuracy order of learners of English as a second language. In E. Hatch (Ed.), *Second language acquisition*. Rowley, Massachusetts: Newberry House.

Peck, S. In press. Child–child discourse in second language acquisition. In E. Hatch (Ed.), *Second language acquisition*. Rowley, Massachusetts: Newberry House.

Scollon, R. 1974. One child's language from one to two: The origins of construction. Unpublished Ph.D. dissertation, Univ. of Hawaii.

Stern, C., & Stern, W. 1907. *Die Kindersprache*. Leipzig: Barth. (Translated by J. Lyon & A. L. Blumenthal.)

Stern, C., & Stern, W., 1970. The language of children. In A. L. Blumenthal (Ed.), *Language and Psychology: Historical aspects of psycholinguistics*. New York: Wiley. Pp. 86–100.

Wagner-Gough, J. 1975. Comparative studies in second language learning. CAL-ERIC, *Series on Languages and Linguistics, 26,* Center for Applied Linguistics.

Wagner-Gough, J., & Hatch, E. 1975. The importance of input data in second language acquisition studies. *Language Learning, 25*(2), 297–308.

Young, D. I. 1974. The acquisition of English syntax by three Spanish-speaking children. Unpublished MA-TESL Thesis, UCLA.

10 The strategy of avoidance in adult second language acquisition

Howard H. Kleinmann

The phenomenon of avoidance behavior has traditionally been studied by psychologists in the context of animal learning, but recently several studies have suggested that second language learners resort to an avoidance strategy when performing in the target language (TL). Schachter (1974) found that Chinese and Japanese subjects (Ss) committed significantly fewer errors in using English relative clauses than did Persian and Arab Ss, leading one to believe that this structure was less difficult for the Chinese and Japanese group. But Schachter also observed that the number of relative clauses produced was much lower for this group and attributed this finding to the fact that the placement of relative clauses in Chinese and Japanese differs so much from their placement in English that the Ss generally avoided their use and consequently produced fewer errors. Schachter argued that contrastive analysis (CA) predicts this difficulty because it is "neutral between comprehension and production [p. 213]," but error analysis (EA), which requires a corpus of actually observed errors, completely overlooks potential cases of avoidance.

Swain (1975) reported that children learning French as a second language in an immersion program omitted relatively many indirect object pronouns when faced with a repetition task, and suggested that the high percentage of omission perhaps reflected an avoidance strategy. Perkins and Larsen-Freeman (1975), in an attempt to elicit certain morphemes, asked Ss to summarize a nondialogue film and found them avoiding the very morphemes that they were trying to elicit.

157

Tarone, Frauenfelder, and Selinker (1975), working with children learning French as a second language, presented Ss with several pictures composing a story which they were supposed to communicate in French. The authors found that some Ss avoided talking about concepts for which their vocabulary was lacking, and concluded that a **semantic avoidance** strategy was operating. Ickenroth (1975) and a study by Varadi (cited in Gorbet, 1974, and Cohen, 1975) reported a similar compensation for a lack of vocabulary knowledge and cited various "escape routes [Ickenroth, 1975, p. 10]" which learners resort to, such as choosing a synonym or superordinate term, paraphrasing, and others.

Another type of avoidance mentioned in the literature on second language learning is **topic avoidance.** This refers to learners' totally avoiding talking about topics for which they lack the vocabulary (Tarone *et al.,* 1975). A similar phenomenon has been labeled by Varadi (Cohen, 1975) "message abandonment."

The observed relative nonuse of a given syntactical structure, morpheme, or lexical item discussed in the above studies, however, is inconclusive in demonstrating an avoidance strategy. An individual cannot be said to be avoiding some linguistic feature of which he has no knowledge any more than he can be said to be avoiding doing anything which he is unable to do. Avoidance presupposes choice. Thus, to be able to avoid some linguistic feature, one must be able to choose not to avoid it, i.e., to use it. It is this notion of avoidance which is the focus of the following study.

METHOD

Subjects

Thirty-nine students enrolled in the intermediate ESL course offered by the English Language Institute of the University of Pittsburgh were divided into two groups: Group I, consisting of 24 native speakers of Arabic, and Group II, consisting of 13 native speakers of Spanish and 2 native speakers of Portuguese. A third group of Ss, consisting of 15 native speakers of English enrolled in an introductory linguistics course, was used as a control for the indirect preference assessment task, which will be described shortly.

Design

Four English structures were investigated: (*a*) the passive voice (e.g., *The car was hit by the bus*); (*b*) infinitive complements (e.g., *I told Mary to leave*); (*c*) direct object pronouns in sentences containing infinitive complements (e.g., *I told her to leave*); and (*d*) the present progressive (e.g., *The man is running*). A CA between English and Arabic, English and Spanish, and English and Portuguese was performed for these structures, based on which predictions were

Table 1.   Difficulty Predictions Based on Contrastive Analysis

English structure	Group I Arabic	Group II Spanish & Portuguese
Passive	Difficulty	No difficulty
Pre Prog	Difficulty	No difficulty
Inf Comp	No difficulty	Difficulty
DO Pron	No difficulty	Difficulty

made as to the relative difficulty Ss in Groups I and II would have with them. The predictions, summarized in Table 1, are that Spanish and Portuguese Ss, relative to Arabic Ss, would experience difficulty with infinitive complements and direct object pronouns, and that Arabic Ss, relative to Spanish Ss, would experience difficulty with passive and present progressive structures. It was hypothesized that when presented with an indirect preference assessment task, the difficulty these Ss would have with those structures would manifest itself in avoidance behavior.

Materials and Procedures

COMPREHENSION TESTING

A multiple choice comprehension test on passive, infinitive complement, and present progressive structures was administered to Groups I and II. This was done to ensure that the Ss in fact comprehended the structures so that their nonuse could not be attributed to a lack of knowledge but, instead, to avoidance. No comprehension test was given on direct object pronouns since it was assumed that intermediate ESL students knew their meaning.

The comprehension test, which appears in Appendix A, consisted of 20 items, two of which were deleted in the data analysis. The fifth item in Part I (*The teacher wanted Bob to help Tom*) was deleted because the underlying structure of the sentence is different from the other six test sentences containing surface infinitive complements. The derivation of this sentence requires a rule of raising to object position, in contrast to the other sentences, which undergo Equi Noun Phrase Deletion. The sixth item in Part II was deleted from the analysis since the only purpose of this item was to interrupt the monotonous succession of items dealing with the present and present progressive tenses.

INDIRECT PREFERENCE ASSESSMENT TASK

Groups I and II were presented with seven pictures, four of which were designed to elicit a passive sentence given the cue, "What happened to the (woman, car, ball, man)?'' The other three pictures were designed to elicit a present progressive sentence given the cue, "Describe the picture in a sentence." All seven pictures were presented to the control group, native speakers of English, to confirm their appropriateness for eliciting the structures just mentioned.

In order to elicit infinitive complements and direct object pronouns, the following situation was devised: Each S was seated in front of the experimenter (E) and next to another person he knew or had been introduced to. The E was talking casually with the S and at some point turned to the third person, announced his or her name, and then said either "Leave!", "Stop!", or "Go!" The E then asked the S, "What did I just $\left\{\begin{array}{l}\text{tell}\\\text{order}\\\text{ask}\end{array}\right\}$ _____?" (the blank represents the third person's name), to which the S was expected to respond. Each S participated in a total of three such vignettes, designed to elicit sentences like *You told him to leave.* The vignettes and picture presentations were extended over two 5-minute sessions.

COMPREHENSION TESTING AND CONFIDENCE ASSESSMENT

It was mentioned above that Ss were given a multiple choice comprehension test on passive, infinitive complement, and present progressive structures. On that test (Appendix A), Ss also rated their confidence in each of their answers on a 5-point scale ranging from "completely unsure" (0) to "completely sure" (4). Three different scores were obtained from this test for each subject. One score was a straightforward measure of the number of items correct for each structure without any consideration of the S's confidence ratings.

Another score was a comprehension score for each structure which took into account the S's confidence ratings by weighting the score on each answer depending on the degree of reported confidence. Specifically, if an item was answered correctly and the S reported that he was completely sure, his score on the item was +4. On the other hand, if in the same situation the S reported that he was completely unsure, his score was 0. Confidence ratings of mostly unsure, half sure–half unsure, and mostly sure resulted in a positive score of +1, +2, and +3 respectively when the item was answered correctly. When the item was answered incorrectly, the S received a score ranging from 0, if he reported that he was completely unsure, to −4, if he reported he was completely sure. Thus, the S was penalized for his incorrect answer, the severity of the penalty being positively related to the degree of reported confidence.

A third score obtained was a straightforward measure of the S's confidence ratings in his comprehension of the various structures. This was obtained by simply summing all the confidence ratings for each of the structures tested. The results on the three measures discussed above—raw comprehension, weighted comprehension, and comprehension confidence—were correlated with the frequency of production of the particular structures elicited through the indirect preference assessment task.

An adapted version of the Achievement Anxiety Test (Alpert & Haber, 1960), consisting of 18 statements, one-half of which were designed to measure the facilitating effects of anxiety on performance, while the other half were designed to measure the debilitating effects of anxiety, was administered to Groups I and II. The statements were adapted to take into account the contexts in which the second language learner finds himself expected to perform and the kinds of performance for which he knows he will be evaluated. Example statements used to measure the degree of facilitating and debilitating anxiety respectively are:

Nervousness while using English helps me do better.

Nervousness while using English in class prevents me from doing well.

Each statement was followed by five choices, ranging from "Always" to "Never," and the Ss were instructed to circle the choice which best described the degree to which the statement applied to them. The Ss were administered translated versions of the test, which were designed to offset any confounding influence the English version might have exerted. The results on this test were correlated with the frequency of production of the various structures on the indirect preference assessment task.

SUCCESS-ACHIEVEMENT AND FAILURE-AVOIDANCE ORIENTATION

A translated version of the Success–Failure Inventory (McReynolds & Guevara, 1967) was administered to the two experimental groups. The test consists of 22 statements, each of which is to be answered as either "true" or "false," and is designed to measure the strength of one's motives to attain success and avoid failure. Example statements used to measure success–achievement and failure–avoidance orientation respectively are:

I have a strong desire to be a success in the world.

I like to follow routines and avoid risks.

The results on this test were also correlated with the frequency of use of the various structures elicited.

RESULTS AND DISCUSSION

The results on the indirect preference assessment task are summarized in Table 2. The American group, in general, confirmed the appropriateness of the techniques used to elicit the various structures. Out of a total of four passive, three infinitive complement, and three present progressive trials, the American group

Table 2. Responses to Indirect Preference Assessment Task

		Passive		Inf Comp		DO Pron		Pres Prog	
N	Group	$\bar{X}$	SD	$\bar{X}$	SD	$\bar{X}$	SD	$\bar{X}$	SD
24	Arabic	1.58	1.35	2.88	.34	1.88	1.33	2.54	.59
15	Spanish & Portuguese	3.20	1.01	1.53	1.19	1.13	1.36	2.20	1.01
15	American	3.40	.74	3.00	0	2.00	1.25	3.00	0

averaged 3.4 (85%), 3.0 (100%), and 3.0 (100%) responses, respectively. That the American group averaged 2.0 (67%) direct object pronoun responses on three trials was somewhat less convincing. Nevertheless, this average was still higher than that of either of the other two groups, which one would expect in view of these Americans' status as native speakers of English.

The prediction that Arabic Ss would experience difficulty with the passive was confirmed by the finding that they produced significantly fewer of them than did native Spanish and Portuguese Ss. Similarly, the Spanish–Portuguese group produced significantly fewer infinitive complement sentences and direct object pronouns compared to the Arabic group, as was predicted. These findings, which are summarized in Table 3, suggest that on a group level an avoidance strategy is operating in accordance with CA predictions. The findings cannot be attributed

Table 3. Significance of Difference between Mean Responses on Indirect Preference Assessment Task: Arabic versus Spanish and Portuguese[a]

Structure	Group	N	$\bar{X}$	SD	t	df
Passive	Arabic	24	1.58	1.35	−3.98**	37
	Spanish & Portuguese	15	3.20	1.01		
Inf Comp	Arabic	24	2.88	.34	5.24**	37
	Spanish & Portuguese	15	1.53	1.19		
DO Pron	Arabic	24	1.88	1.33	1.68*	37
	Spanish & Portuguese	15	1.13	1.36		
Pres Prog	Arabic	24	2.54	.59	1.34	37
	Spanish & Portuguese	15	2.20	1.01		

**p < .01.
*p ≤ .05.
[a] 1 tail.

Table 4. Differences between Comprehension Scores on Three Structures

Structure	Group	N	$\bar{X}$	SD	Percentage correct	t	df
Passive	Arabic	24	4.50	.78	90.00		
						.61	37
	Spanish & Portuguese	15	4.33	.90	86.60		
Inf Comp	Arabic	24	4.12	1.68	68.75		
						.23	37
	Spanish & Portuguese	15	4.00	1.60	66.67		
Pres Prog	Arabic	24	5.83	1.09	83.29		
						−.30	37
	Spanish & Portuguese	15	5.93	.88	84.71		

*p < .05 (t > 2.02).

to differences between the groups' comprehension of the structures, as these differences are not significant (Table 4). Furthermore, Table 4 shows relatively high comprehension scores in terms of percentage correct on the structures, indicating that Ss in both groups knew the structures and that lack of knowledge could not explain their nonuse.

The nonsignificant differences between the groups' use of the present progressive (Table 3) might be attributable to a canceling effect of difficulty due to form as opposed to function. In Arabic there is no present progressive tense as such but, rather, an imperfective form which can also be used to express continuous action. In Spanish there is a present progressive form similar to that of English, but its function is different.

An alternative explanation is also possible. The present progressive is a structure which has a high frequency in English and is therefore emphasized in ESL classes for both comprehension and production, unlike a structure such as the passive, which is frequently taught primarily for comprehension. The present progressive is also a structure which is sequenced relatively early in an ESL syllabus, which gives it maximal review opportunity. This is certainly true of the program in which the Ss in this study were enrolled. Consequently, it is not unlikely that the Ss in the present study learned the present progressive to such a degree that they felt comfortable using it.

Table 5 summarizes the combined-group correlations of the various predictor variables—comprehension, comprehension confidence, weighted comprehension, facilitating and debilitating anxiety, and success-achievement and failure-avoidance orientation—with the four structures elicited through the indirect preference assessment task. The results suggest that, at least in the present data, these variables are not very good predictors of performance. None of the predictor variables correlated consistently with use of the structures in a significant way, although there were scattered significant results. In particular, there was a posi-

Table 5. Correlations between Predictor Variables and Frequency of Use of Structures for Arabic and Spanish–Portuguese Groups Combined

Predictor variables	Passive	Inf Comp	Pres Prog	DO Pron
Comprehension	.03	.00	.40**	
Confidence	.28*	.00	−.07	
Weighted comprehension	.01	−.02	.41**	
Facilitating anxiety	.12	.38*	.14	.26
Debilitating anxiety	−.11	−.19	−.06	−.30*
Success–achievement	.12	.06	−.29	−.03
Failure–avoidance	−.25	.19	.13	.14

**p < .01.
*p < .05.

tive significant correlation between confidence in comprehending the passive and its use, between comprehension and use of the present progressive, and between facilitating anxiety and use of infinitive complements. There was also a significant negative correlation between debilitating anxiety and use of object pronouns. However, no identifiable pattern emerges from these significant correlations.

The within-group correlations are more revealing. Within the Arabic group, a positive significant correlation was obtained between comprehension and use of the present progressive, and between both confidence and facilitating anxiety level and use of the passive (Table 6). Keeping in mind that the passive is the structure the Arabic group avoided on the indirect preference assessment task, when the correlation coefficients relating facilitating anxiety and use of the structures are examined within the Spanish–Portuguese group, one finds signifi-

Table 6. Correlations between Predictor Variables and Frequency of Use of Structures within Arabic Group

Predictor variables	Passive	Inf Comp	Pres Prog	DO Pron
Comprehension	.00	.18	.49**	
Confidence	.47**	.11	−.02	
Weighted comprehension	.12	.12	.45*	
Facilitating anxiety	.47*	−.39	−.01	−.06
Debilitating anxiety	−.13	−.19	.27	−.16
Success achievement	.10	.35	.28	.06
Failure avoidance	−.01	−.14	−.28	.13

**p < .01.
*p < .05.

Table 7. Correlations between Predictor Variables and Frequency of Use of Structures within Spanish–Portuguese Group

Predictor variables	Passive	Inf Comp	Pres Prog	DO Pron
Comprehension	.08	−.15	.41	
Confidence	.38	−.06	−.08	
Weighted comprehension	.21	−.15	.43	
Facilitating anxiety	.07	.64**	.17	.66**
Debilitating anxiety	−.14	−.33	−.44	−.58
Success–achievement	−.41	.47*	−.67	.01
Failure–avoidance	.27	−.48*	.47	−.17

**$p < .01$.
*$p < .05$.

cant results for infinitive complement and direct object pronoun, the very structures that were found to be avoided by this group. Furthermore, **all** the significant correlations within this group involve structures that were avoided by the group (Table 7). In short, the within-group correlations reveal significant relationships between various affective variables and the Ss' use of the structures that are avoided by the group as a whole. This suggests that avoidance operates as a group phenomenon. However, within a particular group use of the generally avoided structure is a function of various affective variables. This finding is consistent with Chastain (1975), who implied a facilitating influence of anxiety based on the result that it was a significant predictor of success in learning Spanish as a foreign language. It may also be a reflection on the syntactic level of the permeability of ego boundaries (Guiora, Beit Hallahmi, Brannon, Dull, & Scovel, 1972) or the ability of learners "to overcome the empathetic barriers set up by ego-boundaries [Taylor, 1974, p. 34]."

This study has attempted to show that second language learners resort to an avoidance strategy that cannot be attributed to a lack of knowledge of the avoided structure. Furthermore, it has suggested that CA is a fairly good predictor of potential cases of avoidance, although admittedly, it cannot predict when a given structure will be avoided as opposed to when it will be produced with the likelihood of error. To do this, psycholinguistic studies need to be undertaken examining in detail variables such as anxiety, confidence, and risk taking in order to give a better profile of potential avoiders and nonavoiders.

At least, however, we must realize that actual errors the second language learner commits are only one clue, but by no means the only clue, to the difficulty he is experiencing with the TL. The recent emphasis, and perhaps overemphasis, on EA studies, as evidenced by the numerous studies adopting this approach, can then be put into proper perspective as a useful, but definitely limited, technique for discovering problem areas in the TL.

In addition, we must reevaluate the generally unquestioned assumption that low frequency of errors implies relatively minor learner difficulty. It may be the case that errors that do not make a quantitative impression are just as or even more symptomatic of difficulty than those which do, if an avoidance strategy is operating.

Sometimes, what a student does not say and write is as indicative of his progress in the TL as what he does say and write. If the avoidance strategy goes unnoticed, we may be fooled into believing that the student has mastered a given teaching point when in fact he has not. Our effectiveness in teaching a second language, consequently, depends partly on our recognizing and dealing with the phenomenon of avoidance.

APPENDIX A   COMPREHENSION TEST AND SELF-CONFIDENCE RATINGS ON ENGLISH PASSIVE, INFINITIVE COMPLEMENT, AND PRESENT PROGRESSIVE STRUCTURES

Part I

In this part of the test, there are 12 sentences. After each sentence, there are five choices: A, B, C, D, and E. Circle the choice which you think best reflects the correct meaning of the sentence. After you circle one of the choices, indicate how sure you are of your answer by circling one of the numbers on the scale. For example, if you are positive that your answer is correct, circle number "4" to show that you are "Completely Sure" of your answer. If you are "Mostly Sure" that your answer is correct, circle number "3." If you are "Half Sure–Half Unsure" that your answer is correct, circle number "2." If you are "Mostly Unsure" of your answer, circle number "1." And if you are "Completely Unsure" of your answer, circle "0." It is very important for you to be honest on this part of the test because if you say you are sure of your answer and it is wrong, you will be penalized and your test score will be lower.

Let's do the following **example:**

John and Mary speak French, but only John reads it.

    A. Mary reads French.
    B. John and Mary read French.
    C. John reads French.
    D. A, B, and C are correct.
    E. None of the above is correct.

0	1	2	3	4
Completely unsure	Mostly unsure	Half-sure/ half-unsure	Mostly sure	Completely sure

1. *John asked Bill to go home.*

    A. John asked Bill something.
    B. John should go home.
    C. Bill should go home.
    D. A and B are correct.
    E. A and C are correct.

0	1	2	3	4
Completely unsure	Mostly unsure	Half-sure/ half-unsure	Mostly sure	Completely sure

2. *The dog was bitten by the cat.*

    A. The cat bit the dog.
    B. The dog bit the cat.
    C. The dog is biting the cat.
    D. A and B are correct.
    E. None of the above is correct.

0	1	2	3	4
Completely unsure	Mostly unsure	Half-sure/ half-unsure	Mostly sure	Completely sure

3. *My brother ordered me to come home.*

    A. My brother should come home.
    B. I should come home.
    C. I ordered my brother.
    D. A and B are correct.
    E. None of the above is correct.

0	1	2	3	4
Completely unsure	Mostly unsure	Half-sure/ half-unsure	Mostly sure	Completely sure

4. *The teacher was believed by the student.*

    A. The student was believed by the teacher.
    B. The teacher believed the student.
    C. A and B are correct.
    D. The student didn't believe the teacher.
    E. None of the above is correct.

0	1	2	3	4
Completely unsure	Mostly unsure	Half-sure/ half-unsure	Mostly sure	Completely sure

5. *The teacher wanted Bob to help Tom.* (This item deleted in the analysis.)

    A. Bob should help Tom.
    B. The teacher should help Tom.
    C. The teacher should help Bob.

168 HOWARD H. KLEINMANN

D. A, B, and C are correct.
E. None of the above is correct.

0	1	2	3	4
Completely unsure	Mostly unsure	Half-sure/ half-unsure	Mostly sure	Completely sure

6. *The policeman was hurt by the thief.*

    A. The policeman hurt the thief.
    B. The thief was hurt by the policeman.
    C. A and B are correct.
    D. The thief hurt the policeman.
    E. None of the above is correct.

0	1	2	3	4
Completely unsure	Mostly unsure	Half-sure/ half-unsure	Mostly sure	Completely sure

7. *They told him to be quiet.*

    A. They should be quiet.
    B. He should be quiet.
    C. They told him something.
    D. A and C are correct.
    E. B and C are correct.

0	1	2	3	4
Completely unsure	Mostly unsure	Half-sure/ half-unsure	Mostly sure	Completely sure

8. *The man was killed by the woman.*

    A. The man killed the woman.
    B. The woman died.
    C. The man died.
    D. The woman was killed.
    E. A and B are correct.

0	1	2	3	4
Completely unsure	Mostly unsure	Half-sure/ half-unsure	Mostly sure	Completely sure

9. *John begged his wife to write a letter.*

    A. John begged his wife.
    B. John's wife should write a letter.
    C. John should write a letter.
    D. A and B are correct.
    E. A and C are correct.

0	1	2	3	4
Completely unsure	Mostly unsure	Half-sure/ half-unsure	Mostly sure	Completely sure

10. *The train was pushed by the man.*

    A. The train pushed the man.
    B. The man pushed the train.
    C. The man was pushed by the train.
    D. A and C are correct.
    E. None of the above is correct.

0	1	2	3	4
Completely unsure	Mostly unsure	Half-sure/ half-unsure	Mostly sure	Completely sure

11. *We asked them to read the book.*

    A. We asked them something.
    B. We should read the book.
    C. They ahould read the book.
    D. A and B are correct.
    E. A and C are correct.

0	1	2	3	4
Completely unsure	Mostly unsure	Half-sure/ half-unsure	Mostly sure	Completely sure

12. *The woman commanded the man to stop.*

    A. The man commanded the woman.
    B. The woman commanded the man.
    C. The woman should stop.
    D. A and C are correct.
    E. B and C are correct.

0	1	2	3	4
Completely unsure	Mostly unsure	Half-sure/ half-unsure	Mostly sure	Completely sure

Part II

In this part of the test, there are eight sentences which contain a blank. For each sentence choose an answer (A, B, C, D, or E) which correctly fills in the blank and circle it. After you circle one of the choices, indicate how sure you are of your answer by circling one of the numbers on the scale.

EXAMPLE:

I _____ 26 years old.

    A. *am*
    B. *is*
    C. *are*
    D. *be*
    E. *have*

0	1	2	3	4
Completely unsure	Mostly unsure	Half-sure/ half-unsure	Mostly sure	Completely sure

1.*The boy* _____ *to school every day.*

    A. *is walk*
    B. *is walking*
    C. *walks*
    D. *is been walking*
    E. *walking*

0	1	2	3	4
Completely unsure	Mostly unsure	Half-sure/ half-unsure	Mostly sure	Completely sure

2. *John and Mary* _____ *television now.*

    A. *are watching*
    B. *is watching*
    C. *watch*
    D. *watches*
    E. *is watch*

0	1	2	3	4
Completely unsure	Mostly unsure	Half-sure/ half-unsure	Mostly sure	Completely sure

3. *At this moment my mother* _____ *for a bus.*

    A. *waits*
    B. *wait*
    C. *is waiting*
    D. *are waiting*
    E. *waiting*

0	1	2	3	4
Completely unsure	Mostly unsure	Half-sure/ half-unsure	Mostly sure	Completely sure

4. *My father* _____ *the newspaper every day at 7 o'clock.*

    A. *is reading*
    B. *reads*
    C. *reading*
    D. *read*
    E. *is read*

0	1	2	3	4
Completely unsure	Mostly unsure	Half-sure/ half-unsure	Mostly sure	Completely sure

5. *John can't speak to you now because he* _____.

    A. *sleep*
    B. *sleeps*
    C. *sleeping*

D. *is sleeping*
E. *is sleep*

0	1	2	3	4
Completely unsure	Mostly unsure	Half-sure/ half-unsure	Mostly sure	Completely sure

6. *The chocolate cake* _____ *by the little boy.* (This item deleted in the analysis.)

A. *was eaten*
B. *eats*
C. *eating*
D. *ate*
E. *eat*

0	1	2	3	4
Completely unsure	Mostly unsure	Half-sure/ half-unsure	Mostly sure	Completely sure

7. *I have a photograph in my wallet. In my photograph, my wife* _____ *on the grass in front of our house.*

A. *sit*
B. *is sitting*
C. *sits*
D. *sitting*
E. *is sit*

0	1	2	3	4
Completely unsure	Mostly unsure	Half-sure/ half-unsure	Mostly sure	Completely sure

8. *The students here* _____ *a test right now.*

A. *taking*
B. *take*
C. *is taking*
D. *takes*
E. *are taking*

0	1	2	3	4
Completely unsure	Mostly unsure	Half-sure/ half-unsure	Mostly sure	Completely sure

Appendix B Individual Scores on Variables

Group	Subject ID	Indirect preference assessment task				Raw comprehension			Confidence			Weighted comprehension			Motivational orientation		Anxiety	
		Passive	Inf Comp	DO Pron	Pres Prog	Passive	Inf Comp	Pres Prog	Passive	Inf Comp	Pres Prog	Passive	Inf Comp	Pres Prog	Success achievement	Failure avoidance	Facilitating	Debilitating
I	1	0	2	0	3	2	1	5	15	15	22	1	−7	10	11	4	18	23
I	2	3	2	0	2	5	4	7	20	24	28	20	8	28	7	9	34	9
I	3	2	3	3	2	4	5	6	18	20	20	12	12	16	11	7	18	15
I	4	0	3	2	2	5	2	7	20	19	27	20	−5	27	13	3	10	2
I	5	0	3	0	2	4	3	6	12	20	26	12	2	20	9	9	9	20
I	6	4	3	2	3	5	6	6	20	23	26	20	23	20	10	6	19	7
I	7	0	3	3	2	4	5	6	12	16	23	6	10	19	8	10	24	19
I	8	1	3	0	3	5	5	6	20	22	25	20	16	19	15	3	24	15
I	9	2	3	3	2	4	2	3	15	17	25	9	−3	−1	12	7	20	9
I	10	0	3	3	3	5	6	6	20	22	25	20	22	21	13	5	18	10
I	11	2	3	0	3	5	2	5	20	24	27	20	−8	11	12	2	17	8
I	12	3	3	0	3	3	5	7	20	15	28	4	15	28	16	6	26	8
I	13	4	3	3	0	4	6	5	19	22	27	13	22	11	12	3	23	11
I	14	0	3	3	1	5	5	6	16	22	26	16	18	−2	11	4	20	5
I	15	3	3	3	3	5	5	7	20	19	25	20	15	21	14	7	19	22
I	16	0	3	1	3	5	1	6	12	18	19	12	−12	19	14	4	20	15
I	17	2	3	0	3	5	6	6	18	20	24	18	23	20	18	3	21	19
I	18	2	3	2	3	5	5	6	20	23	24	20	14	20	12	0	21	18
I	19	2	3	2	2	5	3	5	20	20	23	20	−1	21	12	5	24	15
I	20	2	3	3	3	4	5	6	20	23	27	12	11	21	13	7	21	10
I	21	3	3	3	2	5	6	6	17	17	25	13	24	21	13	4	24	15
I	22	0	3	3	3	5	2	7	20	24	28	20	−7	20				
I	23	1	3	3	3	5	4	7	20	23	27	20	4	27				
I	24	2	3	3	3	5	5	7	20	24	24	20	17	24				
II	1	3	3	3	3	5	5	7	20	23	27	20	17	27	13	1	25	9
II	2	4	3	3	3	5	6	6	19	22	28	19	22	20	16	2	25	6

Group	No.	1	2	3	4	5	6	7	8	9	10	11	12	13	14	15	16	17
II	3	3	2	0	3	5	3	5	20	22	27	20	2	13	12	3	13	12
II	4	4	3	2	1	5	1	7	15	21	27	15	-13	27	16	0	22	16
II	5	4	0	0	3	4	5	6	16	23	27	10	15	21	8	6	10	13
II	6	2	3	0	2	4	4	6	15	22	26	7	8	20	18	2	14	17
II	7	2	1	0	0	4	2	4	20	17	28	12	-1	4	18	1	14	17
II	8	4	0	2	3	4	4	6	20	20	27	12	8	19	10	4	12	10
II	9	1	1	1	2	5	6	5	13	21	25	13	21	9	15	1	16	16
II	10	3	2	3	1	2	5	5	13	16	22	-3	12	10	15	2	19	13
II	11	4	0	0	1	3	3	6	19	23	28	3	-1	20	16	2	13	18
II	12	4	1	0	3	5	6	6	19	18	27	19	18	21	13	1	23	22
II	13	2	2	3	3	4	2	6	15	19	19	9	-7	15	14	3	20	9
II	14	4	2	0	2	5	3	7	15	18	22	15	2	22	14	3	14	8
II	15	4	0	0	3	5	5	7	19	23	25	19	17	25				
III	1	4	3	3	3													
III	2	4	3	3	3													
III	3	4	3	3	3													
III	4	2	3	2	3													
III	5	3	3	1	3													
III	6	4	3	3	3													
III	7	3	3	3	3													
III	8	3	3	0	3													
III	9	4	3	3	3													
III	10	4	3	2	3													
III	11	2	3	3	3													
III	12	3	3	3	3													
III	13	3	3	0	3													
III	14	4	3	0	3													
III	15	4	3	1	3													

Note:

Group I   = Arabic
Group II = Spanish–Portuguese
Group III = American

ACKNOWLEDGMENTS

I am grateful to Thomas Scovel for his comments in the final revision of this chapter.

REFERENCES

Alpert, R., & Haber, R. N. 1960. Anxiety in academic achievement situations. *Journal of Abnormal and Social Psychology, 61,* 207–215.

Chastain, K. 1975. Affective and ability factors in second-language acquisition. *Language Learning, 25,* 153–161.

Cohen, A. D. 1975. Error correction and the training of language teachers. *Modern Language Journal, 58,* 414–420.

Gorbet, Frances. 1974. "Error analysis: What the teacher can do." In *Errors: A new perspective.* Ottawa, Canada: Public Service Commission of Canada, Research Division, 30–78.

Guiora, A. Z., Beit Hallahmi, B., Brannon, R. C. L., Dull, C. Y., & Scovel, T. 1972. The effects of experimentally induced changes in ego states on pronunciation ability in a second language: An exploratory study. *Comprehensive Psychiatry, 13,* 421–428.

Ickenroth, J. 1975. On the elusiveness of interlanguage. Progress report, Utrecht.

McReynolds, P., & Guevara, C. 1967. Attitudes of schizophrenics and normals toward success and failure. *Journal of Abnormal and Social Psychology, 72,* 303–310.

Perkins, K., & Larsen-Freeman, D. 1975. The effect of formal language instruction on the order of morpheme acquisition. *Language Learning, 25,* 237–243.

Schachter, J. 1974. An error in error analysis. *Language Learning, 24,* 205–214.

Swain, M. 1975. Changes in errors: Random or systematic? Paper presented at the Fourth International Congress of Applied Linguistics, Stuttgart.

Tarone, E., Frauenfelder, U., & Selinker, L. 1975. Systematicity/variability and stability/instability in interlanguage systems. Paper presented at the Sixth Annual Conference on Applied Linguistics, Ann Arbor.

Taylor, B. P. 1974. Toward a theory of language acquisition. *Language Learning, 24,* 23–35.

11 Individual variation in the use of the monitor[1]

Stephen D. Krashen

In this chapter I will attempt to sketch a general model for adult second language performance, and what contributions this model makes in characterizing individual variation in second language use.

In previous reports (Krashen, 1975, 1976), the Monitor Model was represented as in Figure 1. Here, the initiation of utterances in adult second language performance occurs according to what the performer has **acquired** through natural language use, that is, by rules internalized in ways similar to the way children acquire language: subconsciously, and without overt teaching on the part of native speakers. Acquisition, then, is a technical term that refers to the "creative construction" process found in both child first and second language acquisition (Dulay & Burt, 1972) and the model presented here claims that adults have access to this process as well.

When conditions permit, and when performers are concerned with the form of their utterances, the output of the acquired system may be inspected and altered by a **learned** system, often before the utterance is actually spoken. Learned language consists of conscious mental representations of linguistic rules and is the result of either a formal language learning situation or some kind of self-study program. Krashen and Seliger (1975) have suggested that formal learning situa-

[1]Reprinted by permission from *A Survey of Linguistic Science,* ed. by William Orr Dingwall. Revised and expanded edition. Greylock Publishers (Stamford, Conn.), 1977.

Figure 1.   The Monitor Model for adult second language performance.

tions are characterized by the presence of feedback, or error correction, absent in acquisition environments, and "rule isolation," the presentation of artificial linguistic environments that introduce just one new aspect of grammar at a time.[2]

"Primary linguistic data" are utilized differently by language acquisition and language learning: Learners may use language data as a way of practicing or testing consciously learned rules (deductive) or as a data source for inducing the forms of rules, while for language acquisition, or the creative construction process, input is thought to activate the operation of a "language acquisition device [Chomsky, 1965]."

Most second language teaching methods designed by adults presume that language learning is at least the central if not the only means available to adults for internalizing linguistic rules. There is, however, suggestive evidence that adults can and do acquire (for details, see Krashen, 1975, 1977). An important part of this data that also reveals the operation of the Monitor Model deals with adult performance on "grammatical morphemes," or functors, a line of research begun by Brown (1973) for first language acquisition. It has been found that in certain situations (usually on oral tests), adult subjects show the same "accuracy order" for grammatical morphemes as do children acquiring English as a second language (child data from Dulay & Burt, 1973, 1974, 1975; adult data from Bailey, Madden, & Krashen, 1974, and Larsen-Freeman, 1975). Also, groups of adult ESL acquirers with different first languages agree with each other with respect to accuracy order. When pencil and paper tasks are given, however— tests that encourage a focus on form and that require more processing time—this agreement breaks down, and overall accuracy rises (Krashen, Sferlazza, Feldman, & Fathman, 1976; Larsen-Freeman, 1975). This result can be explained quite easily in terms of the Monitor Model: Tests that involve editing one's output bring in language learning as well as language acquisition. In tests such as the Bilingual Syntax Measure (Burt, Dulay, & Hernández, 1975), however, used in the Dulay and Burt child studies and the Bailey *et al.* and Larsen-Freeman adult studies (oral part), where the focus is on communication and where processing time is limited, subjects are not able to access their conscious grammatical knowledge and are thus dependent on what has been ac-

---

[2]Optimal acquisition environments may also contain rule isolation, or simplified input. See Cazden (1972); Snow (1972); Wagner-Gough and Hatch (1975).

quired. Their error patterns therefore resemble what is seen in younger acquirers, children acquiring English as a second language. These younger acquirers, for the most part, utilize just language acquisition in production.[3] The similarity seen among performers reflects the uniformity of the language acquisition process in everyone (Brown, 1973; Ervin-Tripp, 1973; Slobin, 1973). When more processing time is available, the more idiosyncratic learned grammar shows through.

INDIVIDUAL VARIATION IN THE USE OF THE MONITOR

Given the model just described, one might suppose that individual second language performers would vary with respect to the extent to which they utilize the Monitor in second language production. At one extreme end of the continuum, some performers might utilize conscious knowledge of the target language whenever possible. Extreme Monitor users might, in fact, be so concerned with editing their output to make it conform to their conscious rules that fluency would be seriously hampered. At the other end of the continuum, we may find those who almost never monitor their output.

These sorts of individuals do exist, and their case histories are revealing, both as to the theoretical question regarding the operation of the Monitor Model, and with respect to the practical question of what role instruction should play in helping second language performers improve.

GENERAL CHARACTERISTICS OF MONITOR USERS

Before describing the extreme cases, we shall first turn to some typical instances of Monitor utilization in adult second language performance. Several informal case studies will be presented to illustrate some general characteristics of Monitor users, namely:

1. Successful Monitor users edit their second language output when it does not interfere with communication.
2. This editing results in variable performance, that is, we see different types and amounts of errors under different conditions. Monitoring generally improves accuracy levels, and as we have noted above, under edited conditions, where attention is on form, we no longer see the child's "natural" difficulty order.
3. Monitor users show an overt concern with "correct" language, and regard their unmonitored speech and writing as "careless."

[3]Older children may also be able to self-correct by rule (Cazden, 1975; Hatch, 1976). Their conscious grammar may, however, be less extensive than that used in performance by the adult Monitor user.

CASE STUDIES OF MONITOR USERS

An interesting case study, illustrating some of the points mentioned above, is P, a fairly typical successful Monitor user studied by Krashen and Pon (1975). P was a native speaker of Chinese in her 40s, who had begun to learn English sometime in her 20s when she came to the United States. About 5 years before she was studied by Krashen and Pon, she had enrolled in college, and had graduated with an "A" average.

Krashen and Pon studied P's casual, everyday language production. Observers, native speakers of English (usually P's son), simply recorded her errors from utterances she produced in normal family living or in friendly conversational situations. Immediately after an utterance containing an error was recorded, it was presented to the subject. The data were gathered over a 3-week period and about 80 errors were tabulated.

Upon considering P's self-correction behavior, the investigators came to what was then an unexpected conclusion:

> We were quite surprised to note . . . that our subject was able to correct nearly every error in the corpus (about 95%) when the errors were presented to her after after their commission. In addition, in nearly every case she was able to describe the grammatical principle involved and violated. Another interesting finding was that for the most part the rules involved were simple, "first level" rules (e.g. omission of the third person singular ending, incorrect irregular past tense form, failure to make the verb agree with the subject in number (is/are), use of 'much' with countable nouns, etc.) [p. 126].

The fact that the vast majority of P's errors were self-correctable suggested that "she had a conscious knowledge of the rules" but did not choose to apply this knowledge. Further evidence that this is the case "is our observation that the subject is able to write a virtually error-free English. . . . In writing, and in careful speech, she utilizes her conscious linguistic knowledge of English, while in casual speech she may be too rushed or preoccupied with the message to adjust her output [p. 126]."

P thus illustrates the general characteristics of the successful Monitor user noted above. She is able to communicate well in both Monitor free and edited situations, applying the Monitor when it is appropriate to focus on form. Her performance is variable, in that she makes some errors in unmonitored speech, while her written output is quite close to the native speaker's norm. In a sense, she is able to achieve the illusion of the native speaker's syntactic level of performance by efficient, accurate monitoring.

Cohen and Robbins (1976) describe two more cases like this in their in-depth study of learner characteristics. Ue-lin, like P, can self-correct successfully, and describes her errors as "careless." She reports that she likes to be corrected and has the practice of going over teacher's corrections on her written work. Her background includes formal training in English.

Eva, also described by Cohen and Robbins, is also a Monitor user. Eva made the following statement, which appears to indicate a conscious awareness of Monitor use: "Sometimes I would write something the way I speak. We say a word more or less in a careless way. But if I take my time, sometimes go over it, that would be much easier. . . . Whenever I go over something or take my time, then the rules come to my mind [p. 58]." This statement is easily translated into the vocabulary of the Monitor Model. "Sometimes I would write something the way I speak" reflects the use of the acquired system in language production when monitoring is not involved.[4] Eva's comments about the "carelessness" of her spoken language, which are similar to Ue-lin's statement, simply reflect the fact that ordinary casual speech is usually unmonitored. "The rules come to [her] mind" when she focuses on the form of her utterance ("whenever I go over something"), rather than just on its function as communication.

Until the creative construction process has completed its mission in the adult second language performer, the use of monitoring in edited language can certainly be an aid. The world often demands accurate language, even from second language users, in just those domains where Monitor use is most possible—in the written language—and a clear idea of linguistic rules can be a real asset for the performer. An overconcern with correctness, however, can be a problem. The overuser may be so concerned with form that he or she is unable to speak with any fluency at all.

THE OVERUSER

Stafford and Covitt (in press) present an instructive case of a Monitor overuser: S, a Finnish speaker who, like P, knows many of the rules of English, but who is often unable to communicate in speech. While her written English is quite accurate, Stafford and Covitt remark that "she speaks very little, because she tries to remember and use grammar rules before speaking." S's self-correction behavior reveals her lack of faith in her acquired knowledge of English. Stafford and Covitt report that she generally does not trust her intuitions about English syntax but relies on conscious rules. S describes her own situation

---

[4]We would expect that when second language performers actually do "write the way they speak" they would show a "natural order" (= child's difficulty order) for grammatical morpheme performance. Krashen, Butler, and Birnbaum (1977) have recently found just this. Adult ESL students were asked to write compositions and were instructed in such a way that their focus was on communication and not on form. Analysis of the eight grammatical morphemes studied by other experimenters showed a difficulty order that was quite similar to that found by Bailey *et al.*, Larsen-Freeman, and Dulay and Burt. Also, in agreement with previous studies, there was no first language influence on the difficulty order. This demonstrates that it is not the modality or particular elicitation instrument that determines difficulty order: What is crucial is whether or not natural communication is emphasized.

as follows: "I feel bad . . . when I put words together and I don't know nothing about the grammar ."

Birnbaum (1976) characterizes the speech of Hector, another adult second language performer and ESL student who shows signs of overuse, as follows: "In a segment of conversation that lasted slightly less than fifteen minutes, there is not a single lengthly utterance that is not filled with pauses, false starts, repetitions, and other speech repairs. . . . There are over 69 . . . instances of repair (not counting pauses)." We are not surprised to learn that Hector's written English, his class compositions "produced in a situation where extreme monitoring is possible—are among the best in his section ."

Why are some people overusers? Does the overconcern with correctness revealed in second language performance extend to other nonlinguistic domains? Birnbaum provides a clue, noting that "Hector's personality is an accurate predictor of his reliance on the monitor. He tends to be a quiet, intellectual, and somewhat introverted person . . . ."

Let us look at certain personality changes that take place at the close of the "critical period for language acquisition" as a clue to the overuser. I have suggested elsewhere (Krashen, 1975) that the Monitor may owe its source to Piaget's Formal Operations stage (Inhelder & Piaget, 1958). At around 12 years, the adolescent is able to think in purely abstract terms for the first time, that is, he is able to relate abstract concepts to other abstractions, dealing with them as if they were concrete objects. This new ability may allow the adolescent to become more conscious of abstract grammatical rules.

Elkind (1970) has suggested that profound psychological changes that occur at this time may be related to this cognitive change. He suggests that formal operations permits the adolescent "to conceptualize the thought of other people." This may lead the adolescent to the false conclusion that other people are not only thinking about him but are focusing on just what he considers to be his inadequacies. He assumes that "others are as admiring or as critical of him as he is himself." This leads to the feeling of self-consciousness and vulnerability that one often sees in adolescents. In the case of the overuser, this fear of making what one perceives to be an error may extend into the linguistic domain and may remain in the individual long after adolescence.

THE UNDERUSER

At the other extreme are adult second language performers who do not seem to use a monitor to any extent, even when conditions encourage it. Such performers, like first language acquirers, appear to be uninfluenced by most error correction and do not usually utilize conscious linguistic knowledge in second language performance.

In previous reports (Krashen, 1975; see also Krashen, 1977), the case of Hung was discussed in this regard. Hung, described by Cohen and Robbins (1976), is, for the most part, unable to self-correct his own errors in written English and does not have a conscious knowledge of the rules he breaks. When he does attempt to self-correct, he reports that he does so "by feel" ("It sounds just right"), reflecting reliance on his acquired competence. Hung reports that his English background is nearly entirely "submersion." He came to the United States at 10 and did not receive formal training in ESL. He also reports that he does not like "grammar."

Stafford and Covitt describe several cases of Monitor underusers, and make the interesting point that underusers may pay lip service to the importance of linguistic rules but in reality may hardly use them at all. First consider the case of V, an ESL student whom they depict as "verbal and energetic." V values the study of grammar very highly. On a questionnaire administered by Stafford and Covitt, he wrote, "Grammar is the key to every language." V thinks he uses conscious rules in performance—"When I know a grammar rule, I try to apply it"—but careful questioning reveal that V actually knows few rules and self-corrects "by feel." The following exchanges, taken from a conversation between V and one of the investigators, illustrate this:

Int.: [When you write a composition] . . . do you think of grammar rules? Do you think "Should I have used the present tense here or would the present continuous be better or. . . .

V: I don't refer that to the books and all that, you know. I just refer it to this uh, my judgment and . . . sensing it if I'm writing it right or wrong. Because I really don't know . . . what where exactly how . . . the grammatical rules work out.

Int.: Do you correct yourself when you talk?
V: Yeah, I watch out for that very good.
Int.: How do you know you made a mistake?
V: . . . it doesn't sound right . . . sometimes what I said I feel it that it doesn't register the way I want it.

Int.: Do you think grammar rules are useful?
V: Useful? Yeah. When you want to write they are very very useful.
Int.: But you don't use them when you write.
V: Yeah, I know. I don't use them . . . I don't know how to use them!

Another case described by Stafford and Covitt is I, an Israeli woman who has studied English formally and who also values conscious rules highly but utilizes them very little in performance. She is described as being "very friendly . . . loves to talk to people, and is not embarrassed to make mistakes." This outgoing, uninhibited personality type seems to be shared by V, discussed above, and is in contrast to the self-conscious, introverted personality of the overuser. I remarks that even in written performance "first of all I listen to myself as it sounds. I mean I write it and then I see if it sounds correct." Also, "I listen to things, I don't know the rules. Really, I don't know them." On the other hand, she feels that conscious rules are necessary to speak "correctly." Interestingly, however, she advises a nonrule approach to second language study: "I think when you are a foreigner in a country and you need the language just to speak it daily, you need an audio-visual course, and not, not grammar ."

While students like I and V may not directly profit from a rule-type approach to second language, they think they will, and this fact may be a factor in lesson planning.

CONCLUSION AND SUMMARY

Table 1 summarizes the sorts of individual variation discussed here. While this certainly is not an exhaustive listing of every kind of variation seen in adult second language classrooms, it may cover some common types.

Table 1. Individual Variation in Monitor Use

Monitor user	Spoken style	Uses conscious rules?	Personality type
Optimal	−Hesitant	Yes	
Overuser	+Hesitant	Yes	Self-conscious
Underuser	−Hesitant	No[a]	Outgoing

[a] May pay lip service to value of rules (see text).

ACKNOWLEDGMENTS

I thank Marina Burt and Heidi Dulay for their help and comments.

REFERENCES

Bailey, N., Madden, C., & Krashen, S. 1974. Is there a "natural sequence in adult second language learning?" *Language Learning, 24,* 235–243.
Birnbaum, R. 1976. Transcription and analysis of the speech of an adult second language learner. Term paper, Linguistics 525, Univ. of Southern California.
Brown, R. 1973. *A first language.* Cambridge, Massachusetts: Harvard Univ. Press.
Burt, M., Dulay, H., & Hernandez, Ch. E. 1975. *Bilingual syntax measure.* New York: Harcourt.
Cazden, C. 1972. *Child language and education.* New York: Holt.

Cazden, C. 1975. Hypercorrection in test responses: An example of test-induced distortions in children's speech. *Theory into Practice, 14,* 343–345.

Chomsky, N. 1965. *Aspects of the theory of syntax.* Cambridge, Massachusetts: MIT Press.

Cohen, A., & Robbins, M. 1976. Toward assessing interlanguage performance: The relationship between selected errors, learner's characteristics, and learner's explanations. *Language Learning, 26,* 45–66.

Dulay, H., & Burt, M. 1972. Goofing: An indicator of children's second language learning strategies. *Language Learning, 22,* 235–252.

Dulay, H., & Burt, M. 1973. Should we teach children syntax? *Language Learning, 23,* 245–258.

Dulay, H., & Burt, M. 1974. Natural sequences in child second language acquisition. *Language Learning, 24,* 37–53.

Dulay, H., & Burt, M. 1975. A new approach to discovering universal strategies of child second language acquisition. In D. Dato (Ed.), *Development psycholinguistics: Theory and applications.* Georgetown Univ. Round Table on Languages and Linguistics 1975. Washington, D.C.: Georgetown Univ. Press. Pp. 209–233.

Elkind, D. 1970. *Children and adolescents: Interpretive essays on Jean Piaget.* New York: Oxford Univ. Press.

Ervin-Tripp, S. 1973. Some strategies for the first two years. In A. Dil (Ed.), *Language acquisition and communicative choice.* Stanford, California: Stanford Univ. Press. Pp. 204–238.

Hatch, E. 1976. Comments on Monitor theory. Presentation at the USC-UCLA Second Language Acquisition Forum, May 25, UCLA.

Inhelder, B., & Piaget, J. 1958. *The growth of logical thinking from childhood to adolescence.* New York: Basic Books.

Krashen, S. 1975. A model of second language performance. Paper presented at the Linguistic Society of America, San Francisco, December.

Krashen, S. 1976. Formal and informal linguistic environments in language acquisition and language learning. *TESOL Quarterly, 10,* 157–168.

Krashen, S. 1977. The monitor model for adult second language performance. In M. Burt, H. Dulay, & M. Finocchairo (Eds.), *Personal viewpoints on aspects of ESL.* New York: Regents.

Krashen, S., & Pon, P. 1975. An error analysis of an advanced ESL learner: The importance of the Monitor. *Working Papers on Bilingualism, 7,* 125–129.

Krashen, S., & Seliger, H. 1975. The essential contributions of formal instruction in adult second language learning. *TESOL Quarterly, 9,* 173–183.

Krashen, S., Butler, J., & Birnbaum, R. 1977. The use of the Monitor in free and edited compositions in English as a second language. Paper presented at the Los Angeles Second Language Research Forum, UCLA.

Krashen, S., Sferlazza, V., Feldman, L., & Fathman, A. 1976. Adult performance on the SLOPE test: More evidence for a natural sequence in adult second language acquisition. *Language Learning.*

Larsen-Freeman, D. 1975. The acquisition of grammatical morphemes by adult ESL students. *TESOL Quarterly, 9,* 409–420.

Slobin, D. 1975. Cognitive prerequisites for the development of grammar. In C. Ferguson & D. Slobin (Eds.), *Studies of child language development.* New York: Holt. Pp. 175–208.

Snow, C. 1972. Mother's speech to children learning language. *Child Development, 43,* 549–565.

Stafford, C., & Covitt, G. In press. Monitor use in adult second language production. *ITL Review of applied linguistics.*

Wagner-Gough, J., & Hatch, E. 1975. The importance of input data in second language acquisition studies. *Language Learning, 25,* 297–308.

12 Why speak if you don't need to? The case for a listening approach to beginning foreign language learning

Judith Olmsted Gary

INTRODUCTION

Why speak if you don't need to? In this chapter I will describe the rationale and strategies of a language teaching approach found to be extremely effective with both adult and child learners which does not require the language learner to speak until he feels comfortable doing so. I will survey both past and current applications of this delayed oral practice approach to language learning.

Research has shown that language learners **not required** to speak immediately—though they **are allowed** to if they wish—make more significant gains in reading, writing, and speaking, as well as in listening comprehension, than students required to speak right away in a typical audiolingual approach. The period of delayed oral practice may last up to 3 months or longer, depending on the intensity of classes and the students' readiness. It is taken as a given that many variables come into play in achieving effective language learning—including personality, attitude and motivation, language aptitude, and cognitive style. Thus the language learning strategy to be described in this chapter should be looked upon as one alternative approach to second language teaching which may be particularly appropriate for certain students under certain conditions, as determined by assessment of individual needs and experimental research. The purpose of this chapter is to encourage experimentation with a delayed oral practice

185

approach to language teaching and to suggest alternative strategies for implementation of this approach.

RATIONALE AND STRATEGIES FOR DELAYED
ORAL PRACTICE

Active Listening

You may be asking yourself how this could be possible. How can listening training transfer to speaking, reading, and writing skills? First of all, it is important to clarify what I mean by listening. I am not speaking of listening as the process of passively hearing meaningless sounds; I am referring to **active listening,** a process whereby the student is actively attempting to understand and respond effectively to oral communication carefully presented in a meaningful context. Listening can thus be described as an active learning process in which the student's listening competence can be expanded by orally giving him or her nonverbal tasks to carry out. The student can respond nonverbally in a number of ways. For example, he or she can respond by pointing, nodding, or checking appropriate items on a worksheet.

The following sketches illustrate several possible approaches to teaching and assessing listening comprehension using nonverbal responses. One or all of these approaches could be utilized for purposes of instruction.

In the first approach, students are required to make a **pictorial–audio** match. For example, students can be asked to demonstrate comprehension of commands. Students hear novel combinations of lexical items previously learned (through this approach). For each command heard, they circle the letter of a picture which illustrates the action in the command. Thus, suppose they hear the command *John, walk to the chair*. In front of them they have a worksheet with pictures (a)–(d), as in Figure 1. The students circle a letter and are given immediate feedback that (b) was the appropriate answer.

Figure 1.   Example Worksheet I for pictorial–audio match approach.

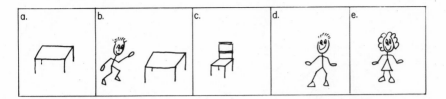

Figure 2.   Example Worksheet II for pictorial–audio match approach.

A second example of students making a pictorial–audio match is students demonstrating comprehension of information questions. For example, upon hearing the tape-recorded command *John, walk to the table,* the students can be asked questions such as the following, which again can be novel combinations of familiar lexical items:

1.   *What's John going to walk to?*

2.   *What's John going to do?*

3.   *Who's going to walk to the table?*

The students respond by checking the appropriate picture among (a)–(e) in Figure 2. They are then given immediate feedback as to the correctness of their response. Of course, alternative questions such as *Is John going to walk to the chair or the table?* could also be asked.

In the second approach, students are required to make a **physical response–audio** match. In this approach, students can also be required to demonstrate comprehension of both commands and questions. For example, upon hearing questions 1, 2, and 3 above, students called upon demonstrate their comprehension by: (*a*) pointing to the table, or (*b*) walking to the table, or (*c*) pointing to or touching John. Or if a command such as *Walk to the chair* is given, the student, having previously seen the teacher or puppet model this command along with other commands, walks to the chair (and not, for example, to the table) if he has correctly understood the command. The teacher immediately remodels the appropriate response if he makes an error.

In the third approach, students are required to make a **graphic–audio** match. In this approach, students match a written response with a sentence they hear. As in the other approaches, the written responses would be familiar lexical items previously introduced through graphic–pictorial–audio matching. For example, the students may hear the sentence *The man's giving a block to the boy.* Visual reinforcement would be given by including a picture of the action being talked about, as in Figure 3. The students are then asked to circle one of four written responses to the questions they will hear. So, for example, they could be asked

Figure 3. Example worksheet for graphic–audio match approach.

the question *Who's the man giving the block to?* and be given these choices of answers:

(a) the girl
(b) in the circle
(c) yes
(d) the boy

After they have responded, they receive feedback in the form of the correct answer, (d). If (c) had been chosen, it would mean the student had mistakenly heard the *who* question as a yes–no question. If (a) or (b) had been chosen, it would mean the student had either misunderstood the information question or the preceding sentence.

We have now looked at three approaches to active listening: **pictorial–audio matching, physical response–audio matching,** and **graphic–audio matching.** One or more of these approaches can be utilized in teaching and assessing listening comprehension.

The Perception–Production Process

As well as clarifying what is meant in this chapter by active listening, I would also like to discuss the nature of listening and speaking skills. As listening and speaking skills require the same kind of language knowledge, not two different kinds of knowledge, transfer from receptive skills such as listening to productive skills such as speaking is not too surprising. Judging from current language teaching methodologies, language teaching theorists have often failed to grasp fully that exactly the same set of rules (or perhaps a subset) is used in language

THE PERCEPTION - PRODUCTION PROCESS

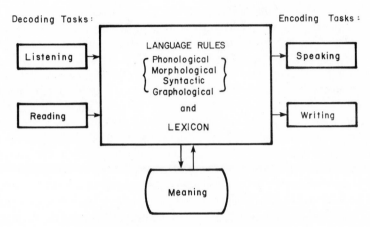

Figure 4. The perception–production process.

comprehension as in language production. I have tried to illustrate this graphically in Figure 4. This simplified model claims that when we comprehend something—decoding spoken or written symbols into meaning—we arrive at the meaning by the rules of the grammar which in normal human language relate meaning and sound sequences. Similarly, when we produce or encode a meaning, as in speaking or writing, we do so by utilizing the same phonological, syntactic, and semantic rules that we used in decoding. The only substantial difference between encoding and decoding is the motor skills required for the encoding process, be it writing, speech, or sign language. The rules are the same. Any instructional methodology which teaches these rules will of necessity have effects on the total language competence. The question then is which methodology teaches these rules most efficiently.

Arguments for Delaying Speaking

If the same rules underlie speaking and listening, why not work on speaking first and listening later? The obvious answer is that one cannot say what he does not know. That is, one has to understand how a language works—what its rules are—before he can create a sentence in it.

We then come to the crucial question. Why not teach listening comprehension and speaking together, as in the typical audiolingual approach? Why teach listening comprehension first and worry about speaking later? There are several strong arguments for teaching listening first for an extended period of time. These arguments are related to both the affective and cognitive dimensions of language acquisition.

From an affective point of view, perceptual and psychological readiness for speaking are extremely important for effective speech behavior. Both first and second language students—adults **and** children—generally prefer not to speak a language whose rules and meaning they have only imperfectly perceived, let alone internalized (see, e.g., Ervin-Tripp, 1974; Sorenson, 1967). How can students most efficiently internalize knowledge of the language? One thing we know with respect to the cognitive dimension of language learning is that oral mimicry and memorization of sentences others say to us do not play a major role in language learning. Miller, Galanter, and Pribram (1960, p. 146) have pointed out that language learning by stimulus–response (S–R) conditioning would require an uninterrupted childhood 100 years long with perfect retention for every 20-word string heard only once! The fact that the child can in principle both construct and understand an infinite number of sentences which are new to him, yet are grammatically acceptable in his language, cannot be accounted for by an S–R view of language learning, as argued by Slobin (1971), Bellugi (1970), Slobin and Welsh (1968), Ervin (1964), Chomsky (1959, 1964, 1965, 1966, 1972), Carroll (1963), and others. There is no reason to assume that first and second language learning are not alike in this respect.

Note that a normal child learning his first language appears to demonstrate comprehension of sentences at least 6 months prior to his demonstrating readiness for speaking (Lenneberg, 1967). That is, the child does not start speaking the moment he starts comprehending. In fact, one doesn't ever have to speak in order to acquire language competence—i.e., in order to utilize for communicative purposes the rule system of the language—as seen in Lenneberg "Understanding Language without Ability to Speak: A Case Report [1962]." Furthermore, second language learning research has shown that having to practice speaking immediately while trying to develop listening comprehension interferes with the student's learning, disrupting the association process necessary for integration and recall of the language (see, e.g., Asher, 1969; Gary, 1974, 1975; Postovsky, 1970, 1974, 1975). It also provides learners with incorrect models of speech.

How then might we summarize the main advantages of a delayed oral practice to language learning? I would summarize them as follows: (1) the cognitive advantage, (2) the affective advantage, (3) the efficiency advantage, and (4) the utility advantage.

With respect to (1), the **cognitive advantage,** there is strong empirical evidence that having to focus simultaneously on speaking performance and on listening comprehension distracts the learner from his main objective of understanding the language system underlying what he is hearing. Postovsky (1975) argues convincingly that requiring learners to produce material they have not yet stored in their memory will lead to language interference and overload of short-term memory. Experimental studies support his position, showing a high degree of transfer between a listening-only focus and other language skills—with lower scores in the four language skills reported when students were required to develop speaking and listening skills simultaneously (see, e.g., Asher, 1969; Postovsky, 1970, 1974).

With respect to (2), the **affective advantage,** for many learners, particularly older children and adults, an attempt immediately to produce sentences in front of others is very stressful and embarrassing and reduces the learner's concentration and effectiveness in language learning (see, e.g., Gary, 1974; Asher, 1969). Even an apparently "simple" production task such as mere mimicry requires considerable effort in addition to that necessitated by decoding (see, e.g., Ervin-Tripp, 1970).

With respect to (3), the **efficiency advantage,** clearly the case is that in second language learning, as in first language learning, there is a considerable lag between the development of one's receptive competence and one's productive competence (see, e.g., Ervin-Tripp, 1974). One can learn a language much more efficiently if one does not have to worry about producing all the language data to which one is exposed. In other words, the learner can be exposed to much more of the target language in much less time if he is not required to verbally retrieve it. Ingram, Nord, and Dragt (1974) have found "that the range of foreign language aptitude is not nearly so divergent in listening comprehension as in oral responses [p. 7]." That is, when required to perform nonverbally, the lower aptitude students overperform. They apparently absorb language much faster and more efficiently when not required to speak.

With respect to (4), the **utility advantage,** it is often the case that the receptive skills—listening comprehension and reading—are more needed by the foreign language learner than the productive skills. Ingram *et al.* (1974) have pointed out that even in conversation the need for listening skills far exceeds the need for speaking skills. One can speak using a very restricted subset of familiar language structures, but he cannot force the other speaker to use only language which he knows. Furthermore, language learners who have been taught to capitalize on the advantages of a receptive approach to language learning can easily and skillfully continue their language study alone, independently of a particular language program. This can be carried out, for example, by listening to the radio, watching films and television, and reading.

We have now discussed the four main advantages of a delayed oral practice approach to language learning: They are the cognitive advantage, the effective advantage, the efficiency advantage, and the utility advantage.

Assumptions Underlying Delaying Speaking

What are the assumptions underlying a delayed speaking approach to language learning? These assumptions include at least the following:

1. Language is not speech. It is a set of principles establishing correlations between meaning and sound sequences or other overt forms of communicative language such as sign language.
2. Learning a first or second language does not occur through habit formation. Rather it occurs by an inductive–deductive process whereby the learner starts with a general theory of grammar and, given the linguistic data of a particular language, constructs a grammar for the language based on this theory.
3. The development of receptive skills is necessary for the development of productive skills. That is, speaking is a **result, not a cause** of language learning, and therefore should be postponed, at least in the early stages of language learning.
4. Effective listening comprehension training must be meaningful, challenging, require overt learner response, and provide immediate feedback to the learner as to the correctness of his response.

PAST AND PRESENT APPLICATIONS OF DELAYED ORAL PRACTICE

Having discussed some assumptions and advantages of delayed oral practice, let us now look at empirical evidence supporting such an approach. We will discuss some past and ongoing research concerned with the effect of delayed oral practice on language learning. Much of this research has been concerned with adult second language learning—though some of it is concerned with children. Some of the experiments have been extremely carefully controlled; in other looser classroom studies, this was not possible. In some cases, the mode of response during listening training was gross motor movements such as pointing or running; in other cases, it was writing or simply checking off appropriate picture or writing responses on a worksheet. In some cases, students had intensive practice; in other cases, it was not intensive but was distributed over a fairly long period of time. Such variables must be considered when determining the implications of particular experimental results. Let us begin by looking at some adult studies.

Adult Language Learning

In two extensive and extremely well-controlled 12-week studies of adults learning Russian at the Defense Language Institute, Presidio of Monterey, Postovsky (1970) compared a delayed oral practice approach to second language learning with an audiolingual approach where students were required to mimic what they heard from the first day on. The nonverbal response mode for the experimental subjects was writing.

Postovsky argues that in an intensive 6-hour a day program, listening training that requires writing responses is more efficient than listening training that requires gross motor movements. Introducing the writing system also provides a vehicle for assigning 2 to 3 hours of homework a night. No significant problem of graphic interference is created by introducing the Cyrillic alphabet, apparently because of the fairly regular correspondences between Russian orthography and phonology. Postovsky's experiment was designed to test the effect of delayed oral practice on the productive skills of speaking and writing as well as on the receptive skills of listening and reading. The experimental subjects made a transition to speaking after 4 weeks, 120 hours of instruction. Test measures of all four language skills favored the experimental group over the control group, both at the end of 6 and at the end of 12 weeks. At 6 weeks the most significant differences favoring the experimental group were in speaking, reading, and writing, and at 12 weeks differences significantly favoring the experimental group were in listening comprehension.

In a recent unpublished evaluation of another ongoing intensive program for teaching Russian at the Defense Language Institute, Postovsky (1976) reports that Experimental Subjects had oral practice delayed for 7 weeks—240 hours— while Control Subjects started speaking from the beginning in an audiolingual approach. The nonverbal or training responses are writing or selecting the appropriate choice of several written or pictorial responses. The experimental group's language training has included classroom exercises, a language lab component, and an audiovisual television component based on Winitz and Reeds' (1973) language teaching model in which language material and pictorial events are represented simultaneously. Up to four pictures can be projected on the television screen, forcing the student to select among several alternatives in making a direct sound–symbol association. A large variety of grammatical structures can be introduced in this approach.

After 14 weeks the experimental group showed significantly superior performance on the Russian Level I Proficiency Test in both comprehension and speaking. While his test results favor a delayed oral practice approach to language learning, Postovsky concludes that the test results must only be interpreted as indicative of a general trend favoring delayed oral practice, owing to the looseness of certain experimental controls.

Another adult program emphasizing the use of listening comprehension for teaching language skills has recently been conducted at Michigan State University; this program also taught Russian. The experimenters, Ingram *et al.* (1974), indicate that oral practice was delayed throughout the entire program. The program consisted of 9 contact hours per week over three terms (30 weeks). The 20 students utilized Asher's Total Physical Response Technique—responding nonverbally with physical movements—the first 3 weeks of instruction. The classes following emphasized language lab work that tested comprehension of every utterance through worksheets and gave immediate feedback as to correctness.

One of the major conclusions of this project was that "a continuing focus on listening for comprehension of newly introduced materials is readily transferred to other language skills, especially speaking." It was also concluded that "when task overload is minimized, a much higher degree of student motivation is manifested in the form of reduced attrition and extended student perseverance [p. 13]."

Asher, the San Jose State University proponent of the Total Physical Response Technique (TPRT), has also experimented with delaying oral practice in both adult and child language learning. However, in Asher's approach, delayed oral practice and a physical response mode are two inextricable—i.e., obligatory— parts. In the TPRT as described by Asher, students listen to a command in a foreign language, such as *Run to the table,* and then respond immediately, together with the instructor, with the appropriate physical action. Asher's work has demonstrated that listening comprehension of both adults and children can be accelerated through delayed oral practice and physical response training, and that there can be positive transfer from this approach to other language skills. Some of his major findings are as follows.

In a brief lab experiment, Asher (1969) reported that adults learning Russian through the TPRT had acquired significantly greater skill in listening comprehension than adults who simultaneously repeated and acted out the commands. Other brief lab experiments by Asher (1969) have shown that adult students learning samples of Russian or Japanese who acted or observed during training and acted individually in retention tests had significantly better retention than students who acted or observed during training but were required to translate into English the target language commands during the retention test.

In a less rigorous 32-hour classroom study of adults learning German through the TPRT, with speaking delayed about 16 hours, Asher (1972) reports that college students learning through the TPRT achieved significantly better listening comprehension results compared with students who had either 75 or 150 hours of regular college instruction in German. However, these results may not seem too surprising when we are told that the Control Groups' courses focused on reading and writing training. That is, we would expect that a program focusing on listening training would result in better listening comprehension than a program that did not. What is interesting, however, is that Asher's students' reading performance did not significantly differ from those students in the reading-oriented class who had more than twice as many hours of training.

Transfer from the TPRT to reading can also be seen in the results of application of the Flemming Reading Test, developed by a San Jose State University graduate student (Flemming, 1973) and given at the end of 1 year of training to adult ESL students who had been placed in one of four levels by a routine placement test at the San Jose Metropolitan Adult Education Center. Beginning students used the TPRT, delaying speaking until after about 12 hours of classes. After 120 hours of training, they performed as well in reading proficiency as audiolingually trained higher level students who had received as many as 240 hours of study. Asher's approach thus cut needed classroom time in half.

Asher, Kusudo, and de la Torre (1974), in a 90-hour classroom study of adults learning Spanish through the TPRT, have also found a high level of listening comprehension and transfer from listening to other skills. It was reported that after 45 hours of training, the experimental subjects had significantly higher listening comprehension and reading scores than college students who had about 75 hours of conventional instruction. Compared with students who had 150 hours of conventional training in Spanish, the experimental subjects had significantly higher listening comprehension scores, and there was no significant difference in reading skills between the groups. Unfortunately, writing and speaking tests appear not to have been made. However, the time saved by learning listening comprehension and reading through Asher's approach was phenomenal in this study.

The TPRT has also been found effective for teaching adults sign language. Students respond to questions and commands made in sign language but are not required to produce them in early stages of sign language learning. This is yet another interesting example of receptive language being shown to have priority over productive language in language teaching.

Child Language Learning

What about experimental studies of **children** learning a foreign language through an extended period of delayed oral practice? As described above, there have been a number of long-term research studies of adults learning through delayed oral practice and some form of nonverbal response. However, the fact that no such experimentation had been done with children and that even most of the adult studies had not tested the effects of delayed oral practice on **speaking** ability prompted my 1972 study (Gary 1974, 1975).

The main purpose of this investigation, conducted over a 5-month period, was to determine in an elementary school setting the effects on children's listening comprehension **and** speaking skills of delayed oral practice and a physical response mode in beginning stages of learning Spanish as a foreign language. The subjects consisted of 50 lower elementary school children randomly distributed between experimental and control groups. To control the content and teacher variables, the students were taught the same language structures by the same teacher 25 minutes a day. However, the experimental group participated in a 14-week period of totally delayed oral practice, which—after a brief transition period—was followed by a 7-week phase of partially delayed oral practice. Speaking during this latter period was not required until the second half of each daily lesson. A typical audiolingual format required the control group to speak from the first day of the experiment.

Statistically significant test results in listening comprehension were found to favor the experimental group over the control group. While this was not the case in speaking ability, results of individual tests given at the completion of the experiment were shown to favor the experimental group. A further interesting fact was that while the control subjects' test scores had decreased between experiment Mid and Final individual tests, experimental subjects' test scores had increased. This suggests that had the language program been longer than 5 months, the experimental group's test scores might have more dramatically exceeded that of the control groups.

I am aware of no other studies which have been done of the effect on children's **speaking** ability of a delayed oral practice approach to second language teaching. Carroll (1973) has suggested that a delayed oral practice or extended listening approach to foreign language learning may have promising possibilities at the intermediate or plateau stage of language learning as well as at beginning stages.

Have any other studies been done recently of the effects of delayed oral practice on children's language skills other than speaking?

In a recent, unpublished paper, Asher (1976) has described a series of informal, loosely controlled classroom studies of children in first, second, and fifth through ninth grades learning Spanish with a delayed oral practice and physical response approach in three 20-minute classes a week for a year. Some general conclusions were that listening comprehension was substantially accelerated by a delayed oral practice and physical response approach, and there was a high degree of transfer of learning to reading and writing. Speaking was not tested.

QUESTIONS YET TO EXPLORE

What are the implications for the classroom teacher and second language researcher of the promising possibilities of a delayed oral practice approach to language teaching? As we have observed, there remains an infinite variety of interesting possibilities to be explored with respect to this approach. There are many questions yet unresolved regarding its optimal effectiveness. Some of the interesting questions remaining to be explored are:

1. In a delayed oral practice approach, **what mode of nonverbal response is most appropriate for what age group?** Several possible modes of response have been discussed and illustrated in this paper. They include gross motor physical responses and writing responses. Perhaps a combination of these response modes would be more effective than simply utilizing one of them.

2. For particular age groups and learning styles, **what is the most appropriate amount of extended listening practice before requiring speaking?** Language teaching projects have differed greatly to date with respect to this

variable. In the Michigan State Russian program described in this chapter, speaking was never required. At the Defense Language Institute at Monterey, California, students currently learning Russian are not required to speak for the first 7 weeks or 240 hours. In the following 180 hours (6 weeks) of their program, students are required to speak only 1 out of 6 daily class hours; in the final 24 weeks, they are required to speak 2 out of 6 daily class hours. Asher's subjects, on the other hand, generally start speaking after 12 to 16 hours of instruction. As Postovsky has reported a high degree of transfer to speaking, reading, and writing skills when oral practice is delayed for a much more extended period of time, one might consider experimenting with fairly long periods of delayed oral practice.

That such a long period of delayed oral practice can be effectively utilized by elementary school children as well as by adults can be seen, for example, in Navajo and Spanish-speaking children's English kindergarten curriculum—developed by Consultants in Total Education of Los Angeles—where children are not required to speak English during the entire school day for 3 months. Unfortunately, no test results are available with respect to the specific effects of delayed oral practice as isolated from the other variables affecting these children's learning. However, the fact that numerous lower elementary school children utilizing these materials for a number of years in Arizona, New Mexico, and California have functioned happily and successfully within the demands of their total school setting seems to support the efficacy of delaying oral practice in child language learning. We have already noted my experiment (Gary, 1974, 1975) in which lower elementary school children not required to speak Spanish for 7 weeks functioned happily and effectively. At first not even aware they were not speaking, the children inquired how they differed from the other (speaking) group.

3. **How can this approach be optimally used to individualize instruction?**
A delayed oral practice approach lends itself to infinite possibilities for individualization of instruction, utilizing tape recordings, filmstrips, movies, video cassettes, radio, television, computer-assisted instruction, and other valuable teacher supplements. It offers a new lease on life to the language lab. Slower learners, given worksheets to fill out in the language lab, can replay the appropriate selections as many times as is necessary for developing adequate immediate feedback about their responses. One imaginative method used by Ingram et al. is called a latent image response. The correctness of student responses—either in the form of choices or writing responses—is immediately confirmed by the student's applying a special chemical with a felt-tipped pen which causes the correct response to appear on the paper.

4. Finally, more experimentation is needed on the transfer of learning hypothesis, again with different age groups and learning styles. **What combinations of delayed oral practice and types of response modes can most effec-**

tively lead to transfer of learning from listening comprehension to speaking, reading, and writing, and hence to enormous savings in classroom time and energy?

I conclude with these questions and hope that this chapter will encourage further research into the numerous possibilities of a delayed oral practice approach to language learning.

ACKNOWLEDGMENT

I would like to dedicate this paper to Dr. Valerian A. Postovsky of the Defense Language Institute, Monterey, California, who died February 10, 1977. Of all the research in language teaching with which I am familiar, his has been among the most thorough, the most progressive, and in my opinion, the most meaningful with respect to achieving effective and efficient language instruction. He was an outstanding scholar and educator, a supportive friend, and a warm human being.

REFERENCES

Asher, J. J. 1969. The total physical response approach to second language learning. *Modern Language Journal, 53*(1), 3–17.

Asher, J. J. 1972. Children's first language as a model for second language learning. *Modern Language Journal, 56,* 133–139.

Asher, J. J. 1976. Learning a second language through play: Some age differences. Unpublished manuscript, San Jose State Univ.

Asher, J. J., Kusudo, J. A., & de la Torre, R. 1974. Learning a second language through commands: The second field test. *Modern Language Journal, 58*(1–2), 24–32.

Bellugi, U. 1970. Learning the language. *Psychology Today, 4*(7), 32–35.

Bellugi, U., & Brown, R. W. (Eds.). 1964. The acquisition of language. *Monographs of the Society for Research in Child Development, 29*(1).

Carroll, J. B. 1963. Research on teaching foreign languages. In N. Gage (Ed.), *Handbook of research on teaching.* Pp. 1060–1100.

Carroll, J. B. 1973. Some suggestions from a psychologist. *TESOL Quarterly, 8*(2), 355–367.

Chomsky, N. 1959. A review of B. F. Skinner's verbal behavior, *Language, 35,* 26–58.

Chomsky, N. 1964. Formal discussion of "The development of grammar in child language" by Wick Miller and Susan Ervin. In U. Bellugi & R. Brown (Eds.), The acquisition of language. *Monographs of the Society for Research in Child Development, 29*(1), 35–39.

Chomsky, N. 1965. *Aspects of syntax,* Cambridge, Massachusetts: MIT Press.

Chomsky, N. 1966. Linguistic theory. In G. G. Mead, Jr. (Ed.), *Language teaching: Broader contexts.* Northeast Conference on Teaching of Foreign Languages: Reports of the working committees. New York: MLA Materials Center. Pp. 43–49.

Chomsky, N. 1972. *Language and mind.* (2nd ed.) New York: Harcourt.

Ervin, S. M. 1964. Imitation and structural change in children's language. In E. H. Lenneberg (Ed.), *New directions in the study of language.* Cambridge, Massachusetts: MIT Press. Pp. 163–190.

Ervin-Tripp, S. M. 1970. Structure and process in language acquisition. *Round Table Monograph No. 21.* Washington, D.C.: Georgetown Univ. School of Languages and Linguistics.

Ervin-Tripp, S. M. 1974. Is second language learning like the first? *TESOL Quarterly, 8*(2), 111–128.

Flemming, J. 1973. The development of an ESL placement test. Advanced Student Project in Linguistics, San Jose State Univ.

Gary, J. O. 1974. *Effects on children of delayed oral practice in initial stages of second language learning.* (Ph.D. dissertation, UCLA) Ann Arbor, Michigan: University Microfilms. Order No. 74-22946.

Gary, J. O. 1975. Delayed oral practice in initial stages of second language learning. In M. K. Burt & H. C. Dulay (Eds.), *New directions in second language teaching, learning and bilingual education.* Washington, D.C.: TESOL.

Ingram, F. , Nord, J., & Dragt, D. 1974. Developing a programmed workbook for listening comprehension in Russian. Paper delivered at the Soviet–American Conference on the Russian Language, Amherst, October.

Lenneberg, E. H. 1962. Understanding language without ability to speak: A case report. *Journal of Abnormal and Social Psychology, 65,* 419–425.

Lenneberg, H. H. 1967. *The biological foundations of language.* New York: Wiley.

Miller, G. A., Galanter, E., & Pribram, K. H. 1960. *Plans and the structure of behavior.* New York: Holt.

Postovsky, V. A. 1970. The effects of delay in oral practice at the beginning of second language teaching. Unpublished Ph.D. dissertation, Univ. of California, Berkeley.

Postovsky, V. A. 1974. Effects of delay in oral practice at the beginning of second language learning. *Modern Language Journal, 58*(5–6), 229–239.

Postovsky, V. A. 1975. The priority of aural comprehension in the language acquisition process. Paper presented at the Fourth AILA World Congress, Stuttgart, August 25–30.

Postovsky, V. A. 1976. Interim field test report (Defense Language Institute Work Unit 0141, the RACC Project). M.S. DLI, Monterey, California.

Slobin, D. I. 1971. *Psycholinguistics.* Glenview, Illinois: Scott, Foresman.

Slobin, D. I., & Welsh, C. A. 1968. Elicited imitation as a research tool in developmental psycholinguistics. Working Paper No. 10 of the Language Behavior Research Laboratory, Univ. of California, Berkeley.

Sorenson, A. 1967. Multilingualism in the Northwest Amazon. *American Anthropologist, 69*(6), 674–684.

Winitz, H., & Reeds, J. A. 1973. Rapid acquisition of a foreign language (German) by the avoidance of speaking. *IRAL, 11*(4), 295–317.

13 Language learning and language teaching—any relationship?

Wilga M. Rivers

There is an old saying: "The French have a word for it." This is very true in the context of my title. In French one word fulfills the functions of "to learn" and "to teach": *apprendre.* We may consider the two sentences: *il/elle apprend l'anglais* and *je lui apprends l'anglais* as representing a mutual enterprise of cooperative learning (Rivers, 1976, p. 251). Of course, one can say *j'enseigne l'anglais à mes élèves,* thus placing the emphasis on the subject matter and the teacher's role in inculcating it. In that case, whether the student learns or not is not the particular concern of the speaker. *Apprendre,* on the other hand, is like the piece of paper in the Saussurian metaphor: If one cuts into one side, one cuts into the other. It is this concept of interwoven learning and teaching that the reader should keep in mind in the following discussion, which addresses specifically the problems of the second language learning of late adolescents and adults in formal situations. These are acute problems the world over. They will not be solved by applying uncritically what we know about first language, or even second language, learning by children, and they will not go away. We need serious research in this area.

Recent findings clearly indicate differences between adult second language learning and both first and second language learning by children. The real problem in discussions of these processes is always at what level of generality does one declare there to be a similarity or a difference. We would expect to observe

201

more similarities between the process of acquiring a language at 2 and acquiring a language at 20 than between learning a language and learning to balance a book on one's head. In the following discussion, we will take into account both basic similarities of all language learning and specific differences in situation, which include differences deriving from age of acquisition.

There seems to be general agreement at present that it is at about puberty that one loses the ability to acquire a language in a "natural" (childlike) way through much exposure to it, without actual formal instruction (Krashen, 1975, pp. 211–224). This is the so-called "critical period." Rosansky and Krashen consider this change to be related not so much to neurological development—the lack of plasticity of the brain tissue as reported by Penfield and Lenneberg—but to the stages of cognitive development described by Piaget (Krashen, 1975, p. 220; Rosansky, 1975).

According to Piaget's studies, it is at about 11 or 12 that the individual enters into the stage of formal operations. At this age, students are able to use hypothetical reasoning. They begin to think in the abstract with propositions. They are able to isolate variables and deduce potential relationships. At first, they are satisfied with the search for a single constant factor in correspondences. They can perform the formal operation of implication by which they assume that a determinate factor produces the observed consequences in all cases. By the age of 14 or 15, students are capable of hypothetico-deductive reasoning performed as a mental operation divorced from actual material objects. They are able to isolate and combine variables which depend on a number of factors, performing all the 16 binary operations of logical thought.[1] They do not have to limit their considerations to one relationship at a time, but consider the possible effect of several variables, testing the effect of each by holding other factors constant. They feel the need to find the reason for the relations they observe and perform the operations of implication and equivalence, disjunction, and simple and reciprocal exclusion (Inhelder & Piaget, 1958). They are ready, then, to think about and comprehend the many complexities of syntax.

Whether these changes are due to maturation or to educational factors in our society, as some have suggested, will not concern us here. These are our adolescent/adult students. It should not surprise us that at this age students feel uneasy with what they do not understand about a new language and, if deprived of explanation and systematization of the way the language works, will seek out such explanations in old books, discovered in the attic, or bombard instructors with questions in and out of class.

---

[1]It can be shown that a concept such as the agreement of the past participle in French in all its ramifications involves nearly all of these logical operations. This explains why some aspects of grammar are difficult for a young child to grasp through explanation. Even French children have to be taught meticulously and thoroughly drilled in the complete series of these agreements, many of which are written language phenomena.

Carroll also considers the learning of a second language after the "critical period" to be a very different process from the acquisition of the first language (Carroll, 1973), while recognizing certain broad similarities. Both, for instance, require the capacity to remember and reproduce sounds and to acquire and apply grammatical rules, by whatever process. He proposes a

> somewhat modified theory of language acquisition that would apply to both native and second languages, namely that, while there may be a 'critical period' in the early years of life, during which the individual has a heightened capacity to learn ANY language (be it native or foreign), there are individual differences in the degree to which this capacity declines, and that these individual differences are, in effect, differences in foreign-language aptitude [Carroll, 1973, p. 6].

The major components of this aptitude seem to Carroll to be phonetic coding ability (identification and storage of sounds), grammatical sensitivity, and inductive ability. "Persons with high foreign-language aptitude at puberty and beyond," he says, "are those who have for some reason lost little of the language acquisition ability with which they are natively endowed [Carroll, 1973, pp. 6–7]." Carroll recognizes that this position is speculative and calls for more longitudinal studies to confirm it. Such speculation is, however, foundational to the design of empirical studies.

Thus, more and more researchers are recognizing the distinct character of adolescent/adult second language learning. No longer is there that carefree attribution to pedagogical ineptitude of the very real problems posed by the acquiring of a second language at this age. It may certainly seem easier to send them all as young children to an area where the language is spoken and thus ease their language learning problems. This may indeed be "a consummation devoutly to be wished," preserving us from:

> The heartache and the thousand natural shocks
> That flesh is heir to.[2]

It is also manifestly an impossible dream in 99% of the cases (bilingual situations aside). When we have faced the fact that for most adolescent/adult learners a native-sounding accent and full nativelike competence in syntax and semantics may never be achieved (cf. Krashen, 1975, pp. 217–218), we may be willing to settle for less: ability to operate comprehensibly and acceptably in the language without inhibitions, conveying and receiving messages through the oral or graphic medium.

We come, then, to our fundamental question: How can our teaching stimulate the language learning of the student who has reached the stage of formal operations, passed the "critical period" of natural language acquisition, and whose

[2]Shakespeare, *Hamlet*, III, i.

natural language learning ability has declined (that is, our normal adolescent/ adult student)? Here we can, I believe, look seriously at research into the teaching and learning of language and language-dependent activities in the native language, especially with subjects of a similar age, and see what kinds of problems they highlight for our second language learner in the formal classroom. The native language students who have been the subjects of this research do not possess a mature and rounded competence in their first language; in fact, many are impoverished in this regard. They are still language learners. The problems for the second language learner are compounded, to be sure, by the need to acquire and use with flexibility another symbol system. Nevertheless, many of the skills and processes involved in language use are so poorly understood in the first place by second language teachers that they are liable to identify as distinctively second language learners' problems many that are essentially problems of language use wherever the knowledge of the language is incomplete. Thus they have little solid foundation on which to base their analyses and explanations of the difficulties they observe and their proposals for better teaching. The solutions they develop tend to be ad hoc where they might be given firmer underpinnings if the observer possessed more knowledge of language using processes. For exemplification, I shall concentrate on processes associated with reading (and, to some extent, listening) and show how radically different our approach might be, if we were aware of certain recent research findings.

According to much recent thinking, speech perception and speech production are different processes independently represented in behavior.[3] Perception is primarily dependent on semantic apprehension, moving from sense percept to idea, with recourse to syntactic knowledge where the meaning is not clear or an ambiguity or misdirected interpretation is detected. In a second language situation, where the listener does not have full control of the syntactic system, even this stage may be bypassed by recourse to processes of inference. The major planning unit, according to Bever (1975), is "something close to the 'deep structure sentoid'." Speech production, on the other hand, expresses the intention (or idea) through the operation of the syntactic system which gives structure to the semantic intention of the message. Here the planning unit is "something close to the 'surface structure clause' [Bever, 1975, p. 66]."

With this distinction between independent systems in mind, the second language teacher would expose the student to much authentic material for listening and reading,[4] without worrying whether all the structures and vocabulary were

---

[3]Belasco (1971) observed this fact at the 1960–1961 Pennsylvania State Academic-Year French Institute. "I was rudely jolted," he says, "by the realization that it is possible to develop so-called 'speaking ability' and yet be virtually incompetent in understanding the spoken language [p. 3]."

[4]For a discussion of the use of authentic listening materials, see Rivers and Temperley (1978), Chapter 3.

familiar, while encouraging students, when expressing themselves in speech or writing, to keep as much as feasible within the framework of what they have been learning. This does not mean resorting only to learned phrases, but using their limited knowledge of the syntax to the fullest by paraphrasing, simplifying, avoiding, circumlocuting, and even extrapolating from rules they know in the second language when caught in a bind, so as to make the most of what they control without being forced to borrow surface structure realizations from their first language system to meet their needs.

This approach parallels Carroll's two-stream proposal. Carroll (1974) points to the "two somewhat conflicting demands" which "arise from a consideration of language-learning processes" (and we may relate these comments to what was said earlier about the stage of cognitive development the adolescent/adult language learner has reached). Carroll suggests that:

> Second-language learners appear to be helped by guidance and explanations with respect to particular aspects of instructional content. Some learners, at least, seem to need to have the instructional content develop "logically" so that new learnings can build on prior learnings. . . . However, normal speech contains an unpredictably large variety of content (vocabulary, grammatical constructions), and selection and sequencing of instructional content may never capture this full richness and variety.

Carroll proposes, then, that:

> A program of instruction should contain two parallel streams, one devoted to exposing the learner to materials containing a relatively uncontrolled variety of linguistic elements (for example, vocabulary and grammatical constructions) and the other devoted to a rather carefully developed sequence of instructional content. The two streams would presumably have interactive effects, in the sense that the second stream would give the learner the specific guidance that would help him in his efforts to master the materials of the first stream [pp. 140–141].

If Bever's psychogrammar, whose function has been to equilibrate the capacities of the two distinct systems of speech perception and speech production during their development, has not withered away, as Bever (1975) postulates, its usefulness can presumably be revived at this adolescent/adult stage, so that much of what is learned through the perceptual system by listening to and reading authentic materials can be sorted out and provide an experiential basis for learning how to express the equivalent semantic intentions through the production system. The psychogrammar, having served as a mediator between the autonomous perception and production systems of the first language, can furnish useful inductions about the functioning of the new language, by identifying universal features of language and highlighting differences between the old and the new grammar at a basic conceptual level. In this way, it can serve as an inductive filter which will help second language learners establish mentally a schematic overview of structural relations which will make more comprehensible to them the place within the system of what is being presented in the structured program. Clearly the aim is to reach the stage in the second language where the systems of speech perception and production operate independently of the psychogrammar as in native language use, except at points of difficulty when we reflect and cogitate on what was said to unravel its complexities or when we deliberate on how best to express a complicated idea. This supports the view that much of language behavior must become automatic, in the sense that most of its operations are carried through below the level of conscious awareness. Such a supremely confident operation can be developed at the adolescent/adult level only through a clear understanding of interrelationships within the language system.

Moving to another area of research, we need to look rather more carefully than we have been wont to do at the reading process. In second language teaching, we have been prone to lean far more heavily than is warranted on the fact that our adolescent/adult students already "know how to read." Unless there is a new script to be learned (and learning a new script is not usually a lengthy process), we pay scant attention to how our students read, frequently putting reading material into their hands and sending them off to "read" it for the next day. Just what they do with it does not seem to concern us, so long as on their return they can tell us something about the content. We are particularly interested usually in the factual details. If our consciences smite us and we feel we should be "doing something about reading," we stand them up and make them read aloud, preferably from previously unseen texts, to demonstrate "how well they read." Then, to cap our ineptitude, we ask them questions on what they have just been reading aloud. Each of these common procedures could hardly be better designed to thwart the student who really wishes to learn to read the second language effectively, in the sense of drawing coherent meaning from the test.

For the adolescent/adult second language learner in a formal setting who is already literate in one language (that is, the majority of such learners, at least in this country), the decoding of letters and words is not the major problem in reading. The need to learn to decipher a new alphabet is not of itself even a prolonged disability. Students may learn to associate a new sound system with an old graphic symbol system with minimum effort and still find the extraction of meaning to be a problem. The more the second language reader becomes bogged down in individual words, the harder the task becomes. Goodman (1967) calls fluent reading "a psycholinguistic guessing game" which requires "skill in selecting the fewest, most productive cues necessary to produce guesses which are right the first time." Robeck and Wilson (1974, p. 33) call this performance "that of a reader with basic recognition skills confronted by material that is beyond his independent reading level." What a vivid picture we have here of the average second language reader—a picture which makes Goodman's approach seem all the more appropriate for our students.

Here the "three radical insights" which Frank Smith (1973) highlights in his discussion of the thinking and research of linguists and cognitive psychologists with regard to reading are worth serious consideration. Just stating these three insights, without examining further the research on which they are based,[5] will give pause to our conventional teacher addicted to such procedures as those I have described.

1. Only a small part of the information necessary for reading comprehension comes from the printed page.
2. Comprehension must precede the identification of individual words.[6]
3. Reading is not decoding to spoken language [Smith, 1973, p. v].

What are the implications for second language teachers of these insights? In what ways do they suggest changes in our procedures to ensure the nurturing of that efficient reading which is surely a priority in most second language programs? Let us consider some of these implications.

First, only a small part of the information necessary for reading comprehension comes from the printed page, according to a number of reading researchers.

This insight, rather startling when we first encounter it, certainly runs counter to conventional ideas on reading. Taking it seriously can have a most salutary effect on our practice. Readers have expectations about the content of what they are about to read and its development which are further stimulated as they continue to read by what they have already understood. The function of the symbols on the printed page is to reduce the uncertainty of the reader as information (or meaning) is derived from the script. For this reason, an efficient reader needs only schematic indications of the actual visual forms. Here we can think of those children's reading games where only portions of letters are given or where the usual presentation of letters is distorted in some way. It also explains why we often "read" from the page synonyms of the words before us, even when these equivalents have quite different visual shapes from what is actually printed: *friend* for *buddy*, for instance.[7] (We also report "hearing" such substitutes.) This explains why two readers can draw quite different content from the same script (or "hear" different messages from the same signal) even when the input has

---

[5]Smith bases his "insights" on the theoretical and experimental work of G. A. Miller, K. S. Goodman, P. A. Kolers, D. L. Holmes, C. Chomsky, P. Rozin, and J. Torrey.

[6]Models of this type are sometimes referred to as analysis-by-synthesis models. Gibson and Levin (1975, pp. 449–453) discuss the pros and cons of this approach. K. Goodman (1967) calls his model "a psycholinguistic guessing game" which "involves an interaction between thought and language." A. R. Luria (1970) describes normal reading in similar terms.

[7]Kolers (1973) conducted bilingual experiments in reading which demonstrated the natural tendency of the reader to perceive words directly in terms of their meanings (pp. 47–48). Bilingual readers presented with texts which mixed segments of two languages would read out some segments which were in L_1 as their equivalents in L_2.

been carefully composed. This is a normal and common experience in native language reading, yet we often expect a perfect rendering of the details of the script and the one "right" answer or interpretation of the content in second language reading. Here again we should reflect and observe. Redundancies built into language act as a backup when comprehension falters. They are an aid particularly to the second language reader for whom the extraction of meaning is a more laborious and inexpert procedure.

It seems, then, that inefficiency in reading is related to the amount of knowledge a person has, not only of language forms, but also of the conceptual and informational area in which the passage has been written. The less readers know, the more visual information they require. This again is paralleled for listening. As Olson (1972) has observed: "If the listener doesn't 'know' what you are talking about you have limited linguistic resources to make yourself known [p. 143]."

Which brings us to the question of "literal" meaning: The first thing inexperienced second language readers seem to demand is "But what does it *really mean?*" as they rush to a bilingual dictionary to find "the meaning" of isolated words.

This is a state of mind we must change. We have to encourage second language readers to tolerate vagueness, so that they will be open to the unfolding meaning as segment is added to segment and first impressions are corrected by later information. Miller and Johnson-Laird (1976) are emphatic on this point:

> Perhaps we should say that there is no such thing as the literal meaning of a sentence, only the literal meaning that a given listener [or reader] places on a given utterance of it. Or perhaps we should say that the literal meaning of a sentence (divorced from any particular context) consists of procedures that can be called in many different orders, even omitted in certain cases, by higher-order programs responsible for verifying statements, answering questions, obeying commands, storing information in episodic memory.
>
> The moral for the mental lexicon is clear. If the meaning of a word were a fixed set of procedures or structured set of semantic markers, it would be impossible to handle structures of a given sentence with sufficient flexibility [p. 704].

The acceptance of the flexible, changing nature of meaning in context is essential to the development of efficient reading techniques. The willingness to withhold judgment, to resist a tendency to closure, to fill in the gaps by inference—these require a certain courage on the part of the anxious reader. It is important, then, to have much reading for pleasure, for reading's sake, which is not tested at all: reading to develop confidence in reading.

It may be argued that here we are talking about comprehension of the author's intentions in a text, rather than "reading," yet this is what **reading** for adolescent/adult students implies. Carroll (1973) has made clear how difficult it is "to distinguish 'pure' comprehension of language texts from processes of inference, deduction, and problem solving that often accompany the reception of language [p. 3]." Our students are impatient to comprehend the content and the import of what they are reading as they do in their own language, and the new language should be merely a barrier they must learn to hurdle with confidence, not a fence to climb up laboriously. Chall (1973) says that "to read at the highest level of maturity means thinking and reasoning, and to have an advanced command of language, concept, and experience [p. 119]." Our students are at an age when they feel the need to think and reason about what they read and they possess "an advanced command . . . of concept and experience." The only similarity between them and children learning to read the native language is their lack of command of an extensive vocabulary in the new language and their ignorance of some areas of syntax. Here, their wider knowledge of concepts and their many life experiences enable them to bridge this gap with expectations based on the general theme and its development. Apart from further language work in the course which feeds back into reading, it is through much reading that the students' knowledge of vocabulary and syntax increases—for each individually and independent of the teacher. This is the added bonus of encouraging much confident reading in areas of interest to the student.

Clearly, with a second language, some of the conceptual content in reading material is related to the values, institutions, and preoccupations of the cultural group, or even of the subcultural group, from which the writer springs. Just as a passage about the process of nuclear fission can be incomprehensible to a person whose major interest in life is comparative economic systems, so can a passage in English be largely incomprehensible to an Arab who does not understand the American or British way of looking at life's experiences. So once again knowledge of language forms is not enough for efficient reading. In summary, to quote Frank Smith (1973): "There is a trade-off between visual and non-visual information in reading—the more that is already known 'behind the eyeball,' the less visual information is required to identify a letter, a word, or a meaning from the text [p. 7]."

This is also why the reading of specialized material in a technical area in which the second language learner is well informed is a recognition and identification problem which is quite different, and requires quite different approaches, from teaching second language reading to an elementary school child. The reading material provides amplification of what the student already knows and confirms expectations, even in the area of new and surprising details and conclusions, because the student is already familiar with a great deal of what is contained in the text. These same details would not appear surprising, nor the conclusions novel, to one who did not have this prior knowledge and whose expectations were much less precise as a result.

As with all other areas of language use, then, one can "know" the forms of a language (the vocabulary and grammar) without being able to operate within it, because one does not have the necessary links within the conceptual networks to the new forms. In this sense, comprehension must precede the identification of individual words. (This is Smith's second insight.) It is as one pieces together the meaning, receiving confirmation of what one has inferred, so that one may finally make judgments as to relationships, that one is able to identify words in their essential roles in the evolving tapestry of discourse. (In English, it is clear that homonyms like *bear, bow,* and *lie* cannot be identified, or in some cases even pronounced, until the passage in which they are embedded has been comprehended, and there are many ambiguous structures, yet we are able to read texts despite these problems.) If we ignore this fact in our teaching we will penalize students for natural responses and confuse them on what reading is all about.

Similarly, reading in its fullest sense is not decoding to speech, but precedes decoding to speech—Smith's third insight. For this reason, reading aloud from a passage can be a pro forma relating of rules of sound–symbol correspondence to graphic material, accompanied by the activation of appropriate articulators, without indicating a high degree of comprehension. This lack of real comprehension will be evident from misapplication of stress, juncture, and intonation rules in particular, since these indicate proper allocation of words to meaningful segments. If there is sufficient reason for requiring reading aloud as a demonstration of comprehension, the comprehension must come first through a preliminary silent reading before the oral reader can give it full expression. At this point it is the silent activity which may rightfully be termed "reading." The oral activity is not of itself a useful activity, except for a future newscaster or court recorder, and can have the effect of training students to look closely at individual words, or even syllables, rather than words in context where true meaning lies. In this way, it can inculcate reading habits that are ultimately detrimental to efficient extraction of meaning from graphic material.

Experimentation has shown that concentrating on sound–symbol correspondences and hearing oneself read aloud actually hinder students in extracting a message from a text by preventing them from rehearsing adequately the elements of the evolving meaning as they proceed, and from retaining what they have extracted long enough to relate it to later parts of the text. We must remember that the "meaning" at one point in a discourse may be radically modified by later information, even by something we read much later, so that holding elements in immediate memory until the full meaning has been extracted is an important aspect in reading comprehension.

Reading aloud in a second language may be useful as an exercise in pronunciation and in the identification of syntactic segments from surface structure indicators, but must not be confused with reading for meaning. Reading as comprehension of a message and of the writer's intentions may complicate life for the second language teacher, but it is the only valid goal.

The discussion to this point highlights the importance in second language instruction of building reading practice into a matrix of purposeful activity, so that the attention of the reader is on the extraction of information from the text, rather than on the reading process itself. This applies equally to listening activities. In one sense, we cannot **teach** reading or listening, or any other language skill; all we can learn from research is how to assist its development more efficiently and provide for the student many opportunities to perfect its use. Sticht (1972) makes a distinction which the second language teacher may well take to heart between "teaching reading" (or listening) and "teaching learning (comprehending) by reading" (or listening). Here the emphasis is not on decoding and orthography, but on "teaching meanings of words, concepts, reasoning with the information gained by reading [p. 294]." Similarly, testing comprehension by reading can also be through purposeful activity. Comprehension of what has been read can be tested through activity: the performance of some task using information derived from reading, or the completion of some project which requires the reading of material from a number of sources.

Carroll (1972) has pointed out the difficulties of testing "reading comprehension" as opposed to "learning by reading" (or "listening comprehension" as opposed to "learning by listening"). In a lengthy analysis, he shows how difficult it is to separate the extraction of meaning from a text (that is, language comprehension) from processes of inference and memory in any meaningful or useful way.[8] If reading and listening are purposeful activities, these need not be separated out, because they are part of the process of "learning by reading" (or listening). We must continually remind ourselves that reading (and listening) comprehension draw on situational and contextual factors as well as what is conveyed by particular words and phrases. Without an assessment of what is not in fact expressed, what is hinted at, the matrix of language in which a particular group of words is embedded, who the writer (or speaker) is, and the circumstances of the emission of the message, the meaning of a particular group of words may be completely misinterpreted. Bever (1972, p. 101) distinguishes three "different kinds of knowledge that are components of every concept indicated by language": semantic meaning, cultural ideas (of which linguistic ideas are an important subset), and personal ideas. Clearly, then, inferential processes must inevitably be part of any real act of comprehension.

[8]Referring to the work of H. H. Clark reported in "Linguistic Processes in Deductive Reasoning," *Psychological Review*, 1969, 76, 387–404, Carroll (1972) says:

> Clark's data suggests a continuum ranging from comprehension of the simple surface structure in terms of what he calls its 'functional relations' up through inferential processes of considerable complexity. . . . The problem we face is whether it is actually useful to draw a line between what I have called 'simple comprehension,' on the one hand, and 'inferential processes,' on the other, and if so, where on the continuum the line should be drawn [p. 8].

In the early stages of second language reading (or listening), it may be useful to pinpoint, through quizzing or testing, the student's ability to draw specific information from particular linguistic items or structures. This type of testing must, however, wither away, as soon as its limited usefulness has been exhausted, to be replaced by the testing of the results of reading (or listening). This has its implications for standardized testing programs, as well as for local situations, and is demonstrably more useful and interesting.

I shall not pretend that I have considered all the specific problems of reading in a second language. Others I have discussed in some detail elsewhere (Rivers & Temperley, 1978). If I have set a few ideas coursing through the reader's mind, that is all I can hope for in this complicated and little researched area. Let us recognize the validity of the slogan, "the right to read in any language," and do our part to encourage reading and more reading as a satisfying and useful activity which will remain with our students, and which they will be able to perfect without our help, long after they have ceased to be "official" language learners.

REFERENCES

Belasco, S. 1971. The feasibility of learning a second language in an artificial unicultural situation. In P. Pimsleur & T. Quinn (Eds.), *The psychology of second language learning.* New York: Cambridge Univ. Press. Pp. 1–10.

Bever, T. G. 1972. Perceptions, thought, and language. In J. B. Carroll & R. O. Freedle (Eds.), *Language comprehension and the acquisition of knowledge.* New York: Wiley. Pp. 99–112.

Bever, T. G. 1975. Psychologically real grammar emerges because of its role in language acquisition. In D. P. Dato (Ed.), *Developmental psycholinguistics: Theory and applications.* Washington D.C.: Georgetown Univ. Press. Pp. 63–75.

Carroll, J. B. 1972. Defining language comprehension: Some speculations. In J. B. Carroll & R. O. Freedle (Eds.), *Language comprehension and the acquisition of knowledge.* New York: Wiley. Pp. 1–29.

Carroll, J. B. 1973. Implications of aptitude test research and psycholinguistic theory for foreign-language teaching. *International Journal of Psycholinguistics, 2,* 5–14.

Carroll, J. B. 1974. Learning theory for the classroom teacher. In G. A. Jarvis (Ed.), *The challenge of communication.* ACTFL Review of Foreign Language Education, Vol. 6. Skokie, Illinois: National Textbook. Pp. 113–149.

Chall, J. 1973. Learning to read. In G. A. Miller (Ed.), *Communication, language, and meaning.* New York: Basic Books. Pp. 117–127.

Gibson, E. J., & Levin, H. 1975. *The psychology of reading.* Cambridge, Massachusetts: MIT Press.

Goodman, K. S. 1967. Reading: A psycholinguistic guessing game. *Journal of the Reading Specialist, 6,* 126–135.

Inhelder, B., & Piaget, J. 1958. *The growth of logical thinking from childhood to adolescence.* New York: Basic Books.

Kolers, P. A. 1973. Three stages of reading. In F. Smith (Ed.), *Psycholinguistics and reading.* New York: Holt. Pp. 28–49.

Krashen, S. D. 1975. The critical period for language acquisition and its possible bases. In D. Aaronson & R. W. Rieber (Eds.), *Developmental psycholinguistics and communication disorders.* New York: New York Academy of Sciences. Pp. 211–224.

Luria, A. R. 1970. *Traumatic aphasia*. The Hague: Mouton.

Miller, G. A., & Johnson-Laird, P. N. 1976. *Language and perception*. Cambridge, Massachusetts: Harvard Univ. Press.

Olson, D. R. 1972. Language use for communicating, instructing, and thinking. In J. B. Carroll & R. O. Freedle (Eds.), *Language comprehension and the acquisition of knowledge*. New York: Wiley. Pp. 139–167.

Rivers, W. M. 1976. *Speaking in many tongues*. (2nd ed.) Rowley, Massachusetts: Newbury House.

Rivers, W. M., & Temperley, M. S. 1978. *A practical guide to the teaching of English as a second or foreign language*. New York: Oxford Univ. Press.

Robeck, M. C., & Wilson, J. A. 1974. *Psychology of reading: Foundations of instruction*. New York: Wiley.

Rosansky, E. J. 1975. The critical period for the acquisition of language: Some cognitive developmental considerations. In M. Swain (Ed.), *Working papers in bilingualism, 6*, 93–100. Toronto: Ontario Institute for Studies in Education.

Smith, F. (Ed.) 1973. *Psycholinguistics and reading*. New York: Holt.

Sticht, T. G. 1972. Learning by listening. In J. B. Carroll & R. O. Freedle (Eds.), *Language comprehension and the acquisition of knowledge*. New York: Wiley. Pp. 285–314.

Index